T0214698

Lecture Notes of the Institute for Computer Sciences, Social Informatics and Telecommunications Engineering   445

More information about this series at https://link.springer.com/bookseries/8197

Dragan Perakovic · Lucia Knapcikova (Eds.)

Future Access Enablers for Ubiquitous and Intelligent Infrastructures

6th EAI International Conference, FABULOUS 2022
Virtual Event, May 4, 2022
Proceedings

 Springer

Editors
Dragan Perakovic ⓘD
Faculty of Transport and Traffic Science
University of Zagreb
Zagreb, Croatia

Lucia Knapcikova ⓘD
Faculty of Manufacturing Technologies
Technical University of Košice
Prešov, Slovakia

ISSN 1867-8211   ISSN 1867-822X (electronic)
Lecture Notes of the Institute for Computer Sciences, Social Informatics
and Telecommunications Engineering
ISBN 978-3-031-15100-2   ISBN 978-3-031-15101-9 (eBook)
https://doi.org/10.1007/978-3-031-15101-9

This Springer imprint is published by the registered company Springer Nature Switzerland AG
The registered company address is: Gewerbestrasse 11, 6330 Cham, Switzerland

Preface

We are delighted to introduce the proceedings of FABULOUS 2022 – the 6th EAI International Conference on Future Access Enablers of Ubiquitous and Intelligent Infrastructures, which is the result of fruitful cooperation between the European Alliance for Innovation, the Faculty of Transport and Traffic Sciences of the University of Zagreb, and the Faculty of Manufacturing Technologies with a seat in Prešov of the Technical University of Košice.

Our ambition is to establish channels of communication and disseminate knowledge among professionals working in manufacturing and related institutions. Therefore, we cordially invited experts, researchers, academicians, and practitioners in relevant fields to share their knowledge on the management of manufacturing systems at the conference. The themes of FABULOUS 2022 were Teletraffic and Intelligent Networks, the Internet of Things, Cyber Security, Artificial Intelligence, Machine Learning, Smart Environment Applications/Scenarios, and Multimedia.

The technical program of FABULOUS 2022 consisted of 18 full papers in video presentation sessions, all in full online conference format. The papers were selected from 70 submissions based on a blind review process, with a minimum of 3 reviews per paper. We are grateful to all the authors of accepted, who prepared scientific presentations of their research work. We sincerely appreciate their constant support.

It was also a great pleasure to work with such an excellent organizing committee team. Heartfelt thanks are due for their hard work in organizing and supporting the conference. In particular, we are grateful to the Technical Program Committee, who helped to put together a high-quality scientific program, and Goran Marković (general co-chair) and Alexandru Vulpe (web chair) for all their support. We are also grateful to the Conference Manager, Karina Ogandjanian, for her support and all the reviewers for their excellent work.

The 6th EAI FABULOUS conference provided a good platform for all researchers, developers, and practitioners to network and discuss all science and technology aspects that are relevant to ubiquitous and intelligent infrastructures. We strongly believe that FABULOUS 2023, which will take place in Zagreb, Croatia, will be as successful and stimulating as this year's conference.

May, 2022

Dragan Peraković
Lucia Knapčíková

Organization

Steering Committee

Chair

Imrich Chlamtac · University of Trento, Italy

Co-chairs

Dragan Peraković · University of Zagreb, Croatia
Lucia Knapcikova · Technical University of Kosice, Slovakia

Organizing Committee

General Chairs

Dragan Peraković · University of Zagreb, Croatia
Goran Marković · University of Belgrade, Serbia
Lucia Knapcikova · Technical University of Kosice, Slovakia

Technical Program Committee Chairs

Marko Periša · University of Zagreb, Croatia
Marko Krstić · RATEL Beograd, Serbia
Anca D. Jurcut · University College Dublin, Ireland
B. B. Gupta · National Institute of Technology Kurukshetra, India
Annamária Behúnová · Technical University of Kosice, Slovakia

Web Chair

Alexandru Vulpe · Politehnica University of Bucharest, Romania

Publicity and Social Media Chair

Petra Zorić · University of Zagreb, Croatia

Workshops Chair

Gordana Jotanović   University of East Sarajevo,
                                                     Bosnia and Herzegovina

Sponsorship and Exhibits Chair

Dragan Peraković   University of Zagreb, Croatia

Publications Chairs

Dragan Peraković   University of Zagreb, Croatia
Lucia Knapcikova   Technical University of Kosice, Slovakia

Posters and PhD Track Chair

Ivan Grgurević   University of Zagreb, Croatia

Local Chair

Ivan Cvitić   University of Zagreb, Croatia

Technical Program Committee

Alberto Huertas Celdran   University of Murcia, Spain
Aleksandar Jevremovic   Singidunum University, Serbia
Alessandro Ruggiero   University of Salerno, Italy
Alexandru Vulpe   Politehnica University of Bucharest, Romania
Anca D. Jurcut   University College Dublin, Ireland
Andrii Shalaginov   Kristiania University College, Norway
Anna Otsetova   University of Telecommunications and Post,
                                                     Bulgaria
Annamária Behúnová   Technical University of Kosice, Slovakia
Arcangelo Castiglione   University of Salerno, Italy
Arianit Maraj   Kosovo Telecom and AAB College, Kosovo
B. B. Gupta   National Institute of Technology Kurukshetra,
                                                     India
Dalibor Dobrilovic   University of Novi Sad, Serbia
Dharma Agrawal   University of Cincinnati, USA
Dražan Kozak   University of Osijek, Croatia
Dušan Šimšík   Technical University of Kosice, Slovakia
Goran Marković   University of Belgrade, Serbia
Goran Jauševac   University of East Sarajevo,
                                                     Bosnia and Herzegovina
Gordana Jotanovic   University of East Sarajevo,
                                                     Bosnia and Herzegovina

Imran Razzak	Deakin University, Australia
Ivan Pavlenko	Sumy State University, Ukraine
Ivan Cvitic	University of Zagreb, Croatia
Ivan Grgurević	University of Zagreb, Croatia
Jakub Kaščak	Technical University of Košice, Slovakia
Jan Pitel	Technical University of Kosice, Slovakia
Janusz Grabara	Czestochowa University of Technology, Poland
Jerzy Winczek	Czestochowa University of Technology, Poland
Jozef Husár	Technical University of Kosice, Slovakia
Katarzyna Huk	University of Zielona Góra, Poland
Marcel Behún	Technical University of Kosice, Slovakia
Marko Krstic	Regulatory Agency for Electronic Communications and Postal Services, Serbia
Marko Matulin	University of Zagreb, Croatia
Marko Periša	University of Zagreb, Croatia
Martin Straka	Technical University of Kosice, Slovakia
Michael Herzog	Technical University of Applied Sciences Wildau, Germany
Milan Čabarkapa	University of Belgrade, Serbia
Mirjana Stojanović	University of Belgrade, Serbia
Miroslav Vujić	University of Zagreb, Croatia
Natalia Horňáková	Slovak University of Technology in Bratislava, Slovakia
Pavel Necas	Matej Bel University, Slovakia
Peter Kolarovszki	University of Žilina, Slovakia
Petr Skrehot	Expert Institute of Health and Safety, Czech Republic
Phuc Do	Vietnam National University - Ho Chi Minh City, Vietnam
Rachit Garg	Lovely Professional University, India
Raffaele Olivieri	University of Messina, Italy
Raymond Choo	University of Texas at San Antonio, Texas
Štefica Mrvelj	University of Zagreb, Croatia
Valentina Radojičić	University of Belgrade, Serbia
Vesna Radonjić Đogatović	University of Belgrade, Serbia
Vitalii Ivanov	Sumy State University, Ukraine
Vladimir Brtka	University of Novi Sad, Serbia
Željko Stojanov	University of Novi Sad, Serbia

Contents

Information and Communications Technology

Sustainable Communications and Computing Infrastructures

Future Access Networks

Evaluation of an Inertial and Optical Sensors Based Mapping and Localization System

Stefan Hensel[1], Marin B. Marinov[2]([✉]) [ID], and Max Schmitt[1]

[1] Department for Electrical Engineering, University of Applied Sciences Offenburg,
Badstraße 24, 77652 Offenburg, Germany
[2] Department of Electronics, Technical University of Sofia,
8, Kliment Ohridski Blvd., 1756 Sofia, Bulgaria
mbm@tu-sofia.bg

Abstract. , The visual-inertial mapping and localization system *maplab* is analyzed by its implementation and subsequent evaluation. The mapping or localization is based on environmental feature detection. In addition to creating maps, there is also the option of fusion of several maps and thus mapping extensive areas and using them for further analysis of data. In this way, various software tools can be used to optimize the existing data sets.

Two sensor components are needed: an inertial measuring unit (IMU) and a monochrome camera, which are combined by a hardware rig and put into operation for the analysis of the visual-inertial system. System calibration is crucial for precision and system functioning and is based on nonlinear dynamic state estimation. This ensures the best possible estimate of the position of the environmental feature and the map. *Maplab* is particularly suitable for mapping rooms or small building complexes as the implementation and evaluation of the results in different application scenarios show. Special emphasis is laid on the evaluation of larger scenarios, in which is shown, that the system is struggling to keep up geometric consistencies and thus provide an accurate map.

Keywords: maplab · Robot Operating System (ROS) · Simultaneous Localization and Mapping (SLAM)

1   Introduction

Robot-assisted system developments and the improved performance of algorithms in the software area made it possible to use unmanned vehicles in almost any sphere of human activities. The process of development leads to a broad spectrum of possible autonomous systems with the ability to operate unassisted. As a result, there is the possibility of applications into areas that cannot be reached by man.

It is important to have an accurate visual idea of the surroundings for navigation in unstudied areas. This requires image processing and interpretation algorithms that create a digital image from the real world. In this way, it is possible to use the available

D. Perakovic and L. Knapcikova (Eds.): FABULOUS 2022, LNICST 445, pp. 3–15, 2022.
https://doi.org/10.1007/978-3-031-15101-9_1

environmental information later. Current developments in the field of robotics allow for the effective design of efficient mapping and localization systems.

This work evaluates the effectiveness of the visual-inertial mapping and localization system maplab. Procedures for improving the system in the processes of mapping and localization are also studied.

ETH Zurich has provided the main frame lab as a basis for further research projects in the area of navigation of mobile robot platforms [1]. A monochrome camera, and an inertial measurement unit (IMU), with the necessary software packages, are available for evaluation. These two components comprise a system and its analysis and the evaluation of the results are used to obtain an assessment as a so-called SLAM (Simultaneous Localization and Mapping) system.

A mobile robot platform is available to test possible maplab applications, which is additionally equipped with a reference mapping system based on 3D laser point clouds.

2   State of the Art and Related Work

Robot mapping and localization have been studied for several years beginning with the seminal papers of [2]. After tackling the problem with tools of dynamic state estimation (see e.g. [3]), a paradigm shift to graph-based SLAM for online and offline processing could be observed [4, 5]. A sub-field of the area is the use of optical systems to solve the SLAM problem, pointing to named visual SLAM [6, 7].

As camera systems and computer vision show bottlenecks due to the amount of processed data, the slower processing is compensated by the incorporation of inertial sensors to improve the accuracy of the orientation estimation. This is basically a sensor fusion process resulting in so-called visual-inertial SLAM approaches [8, 9].

Recent work in the was focusing on the improvement of computational speed [10] and the handling of large-scale maps, e.g. for autonomous driving.

This contribution evaluates the maplab framework described in [11]. The system is a combination of a hardware visual-inertial setup and a given software framework. Emphasis was set on designing a cheap and mobile device, as described in previous work [12] and adopting the maplab system to the sensor system. Another contribution is the comparison and verification of the setup by another state-of-the-art localization framework, that uses expensive sensors in form of 3D LiDARs to localize. A thorough evaluation was done for certain scenarios and setups, assessing usability, precision, and needed resources for the system.

The rest of the paper is structured as follows: Section 3 describes the system setup with a focus on the software parts, to differentiate from previous publications in [13].

In Sect. 4, a description of the researched scenarios is given, explaining choice and setup. Section 5 is the main part of the publication, giving a detailed explanation and insight into the system evaluation before Sect. 6 concludes the paper.

3   System Setup and Components

3.1   The Maplab Framework

The maplab framework is a visual-inertial SLAM system. A variety of tools can be used to solve the SLAM problem. These include [13]:

(i) Creation and localization in maps, (ii) Multi-session map combination, (iii) Loop closure detection, (iv) Deep reconstruction, (v) Visualization of maps.

3.2 Robot Operating System

A robot operating system (ROS) is available to ensure communication and exchange of data between the camera or IMU and the computer. The widespread and frequent use of this system in robot applications formed a huge collection of software tools and libraries [14, 15]. These allow the user to install simply and easily the necessary drivers for various sensors. A so-called *rosbag* is a file format in ROS for data storing [16].

3.3 ROVIO and ROVIOLI

The *maplab* system uses the ROVIO (RObust VIsual Odometry) framework [17]. The extension with a localization module leads to ROVIOLI (RObust VIsual Odometry with Localization Integration). ROVIO is, so to speak, the basic building block for the detection and tracking of environmental features.

All the necessary data for the lower-level Kalman filter must be available within a certain time for ROVIOLI to correctly detect and track environmental features. According to the selected data rates of the electronic components, this "time window" is $t = 50$ ms.

It is possible to operate the camera with automatic exposure time and to map or position it in an environment despite possible strong exposure changes with the help of specific extensions of the camera driver. The schematic structure of the visual-inertial system is shown in Fig. 1. [12] gives details on the hardware implementation and calibration of the Camera-IMU system.

3.4 Mobile Platform Hardware

As sensor carrier is used the Husky mobile robot platform from Clearpath Robotics. It is a mobile base that can be equipped with different sensors, controllers, and batteries for power supply due to its payload of 75 kg. Its compact dimensions, wheelbase, wheel height, and skid-steer drive allow for it to be used both outdoors and indoors and make it possible to evaluate mapping for structured and natural environments. The maximum speed is 1 m/s, and the runtime of one battery charge is about 3 h.

4 Creating Scenarios for Evaluation

To achieve the best possible quality of evaluation this work adheres to the basic structures of the standards for evaluation of Gesellschaft für Evaluation e.V. (DGEval for short) [18]. In these standards, it is particularly emphasized that all available information must be presented, which is essential for a high-quality and correct evaluation. Extensive analyses are performed and evaluated for this process to cover the widest possible spectrum of use cases. This section presents different scenarios and discusses the experience gained with maplab in this work. The investigations and evaluations of the results should answer the following questions:

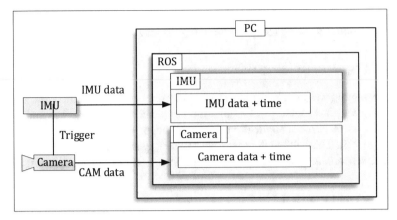

Fig. 1. Construction of the hardware of the visual-inertial system.

- Is maplab suitable as a new SLAM method in addition to existing mapping systems?
- Does maplab have sufficient mapping and localization precision?
- What is the performance of maplab inside and outside of buildings?
- How well does the optimization algorithm work?
- Is the framework suitable to equip mobile robot platforms with it and localize their position?
- What possible applications are there, considering the evaluation results?
- What hardware capabilities are required for the calculations?
- Is there a way to continue the research in the SLAM field with maplab?

4.1 Approach for Creating Evaluation Scenarios

Experience with the visual-inertial system has been gained by creating multiple rosbags that record camera and IMU data. While the use of the IMU is simple and straightforward, the electrical properties of the camera present difficulties.

This should be taken into account when working with this component. A particular problem here is the sensitivity of the camera to the strong light incidence in the lens.

If there are significant contrasts in lighting incidents in a scene, the camera software ensures the best possible representation of the bright surroundings. The resulting increase in exposure time means that environmental characteristics are no longer visible in dimly lit environments. However, these play an essential role in mapping and localization with maplab. The resulting lack of environmental features leads to a loss of information in certain areas. The result is interruptions in the continuity of the map.

For effective loop detection and the merging of several maps, it is also necessary to examine scenarios with identical starting and endpoints.

4.2 Presentation of the Created Scenarios

The following scenarios have been selected for high-quality evaluation, which allows for the use of most of the tools available in maplab.

a) Analysis and evaluation of the loop closure detection in maplab
   The aim is to determine the performance of maplab in terms of mapping and recognition of already known environmental features and of increasing the geometric consistency of the maps.
b) Creation of the so-called multi-session maps
   The aim is to determine the performance of the algorithm for merging multiple maps.
c) Investigation of the localization ability using a mobile robot platform
   The aim here is to determine the precision of the positioning of a mobile robot for solving the SLAM problem.

The choice of scenarios is intended to cover as many application cases as possible and to study the main features of maplab (see [1]). Maplab offers the option of displaying the route covered during mapping. In addition to showing the distance in a single mapping process, it is also possible to show the sum of the distance in the case of a multi-session. Results of the evaluation of the accuracy in measuring distances are given in [19].

5 Evaluation of Mapping Performance

5.1 Analysis and Evaluation of Loop Closure Detection in Maplab

With loop detection, the recognition of already known environmental features should be guaranteed and thus an increase in the geometric consistency of the entire map should be achieved.

To determine the maximum performance of this ability, a distance traversed several times is recorded with the visual-inertial system. As soon as a certain number of loops is reached, the recording of the data at the starting point is stopped. The existing, changing difference between the starting point and the identical endpoint should now be minimized and displayed by carrying out the loop closure detection several times. Based on this analysis, a statement can then be made about the performance of the recognition of already known environmental features in maplab.

A laboratory room at the Offenburg University of Applied Sciences is used as the environment to be mapped. Starting from a starting point, the room is traversed several times in a circle and thus areas that have already been detected are entered several times. This process is finally terminated at the former starting point. The length of the route included during mapping is about 150 m. The starting point has the coordinates

$$s_0 = \begin{bmatrix} x_0 \, y_0 \, z_0 \end{bmatrix}^T = [0\,0\,0]^T. \tag{1}$$

After the area has been mapped with maplab, the coordinates of the last data point can be determined. This has the coordinates:

$$p_0 = \begin{bmatrix} p_{x,0} \, p_{y,0} \, p_{z,0} \end{bmatrix}^T = [-1.0525 \, 1.0042 \, - \, 0.2228]^T. \tag{2}$$

The distance between the start and endpoint can be determined using Eq. (2).

$$d_{3d,n} = \sqrt{(p_{x,n} - x_0)^2 + (p_{y,n} - 0)^2 + (p_{z,n} - z_0)^2}. \tag{3}$$

Here n indicates the number of loop closure detection executions. If you now calculate the distance from the point p_0 to s_0 using (2) before loop closure detection is carried out, this results in a value of $d_{3d,n} = 1.4717$ m.

After applying the algorithm for finding loop closure one gets a new coordinate for the endpoint caused by the loop detection. This endpoint p_1 has the form:

$$p_1 = \left[p_{x,1}\, p_{y,1}\, p_{z,1} \right]^T = [-1.1518\ 0.0991 - 0.0076]^T \tag{4}$$

Here, too, the difference to the origin of the map s_0 can be calculated. The result is a value for $d_{3d,1}$, which is presented in Table 1 for reasons of clarity.

A significant minimization of the distance can already be seen by looking at the coordinates of the point p_1. It is preferable to perform the optimization and loop detection process a second time. This again results in a new endpoint coordinate p_2 with the values:

$$p_2 = \left[p_{x,2}\, p_{y,2}\, p_{z,2} \right]^T = [0.0001 - 0.0014\ 0.0001]^T \tag{5}$$

The final distance between s_0 and p_2 can be seen in Table 1.

Table 1.   Illustration of the effects of loop closure detection.

Number of runs n of an LCD	0	1	2
Distance $d_{3d,n}$, m	1.4717	0.0181	0.0017

In this analysis, the good performance of the loop detection can be seen very well. From a former initial distance between the starting point and the identical endpoint of 1.4717 m, this is reduced significantly to an absolute error of 1.7 mm.

In this way, the algorithms of the loop closure detection and the optimization process can be evaluated. It turns out that a significant improvement or minimization of distance $d_{3d,n}$ can be achieved with an increasing number of loop detections and with the implementation of the optimization process. In addition to the recognition of already known features, this increases geometric consistency, as already stated. However, it should be mentioned that this analysis takes place under ideal conditions.

By repeatedly entering already known scenes, a particularly large collection of descriptors is available, which can then be compared for matches in loop closure detection. As a result, the position of the environmental features and the location related to them can be estimated with considerably greater precision.

5.2 Ecording Multiple Multi-sessions

One of maplab's most distinctive capabilities is map fusion. This option allows for mapping large areas. Changing perspectives or external environmental influences such as weather or exposure changes should not play a role in the alignment of all maps to each other [1].

Mapping of a Laboratory Room
The result of merging maps in a small room is examined by recording four separate

sessions in a laboratory room. In this application, the focus should be on the quality and precision of the merging algorithm. The general presentation of the inventory of the laboratory, i.e., the arrangement of the laboratory tables or the depiction of the measuring devices, is decisive for the evaluation of the resulting map. To ensure that the starting point remains consistent in all individual recordings, a simple template was created on which the entire camera IMU system can be placed and aligned almost identically for all sessions. To detect as many environmental features as possible at the beginning of each session, the starting point is chosen between two laboratory tables, with the visual-inertial system aligned in the middle of the room. At the same time, the starting point will be the beginning of the necessary start and end sequence, which ends after about 6 m.

Each of the four individual recordings includes a different part of the laboratory. The laboratory in which the mapping is performed is shown in Fig. 2. As can be seen in Fig. 2, there is a window in front on the left that floods the room with daylight. Here, as explained, attempts are made to keep the strongest light source behind the visual-inertial system.

Opposite the window front is the corridor of the university building, which is spatially separated by a glass front. To avoid the influence of scattered light, the entire camera IMU system is preferably aligned towards the center of the room.

In contrast to the usual approach of mapping by recording *rosbags*, in this use case mapping is performed using the *rostopics* of the camera and IMU. Thus, instead of evaluating the visual and inertial data afterward, the detected features are immediately mapped. The advantage of this procedure is the immediate display of the extraction of visual-inertial information from the environment because of the detection of environmental features. This also makes it possible to recognize the current exposure in the picture. This enables, on the one hand, focusing on features that are still to be detected and, on the other hand, reacting to strong light sources. This leads to an increase in the information content in the recording.

Fig. 2. Photo of the laboratory room.

However, the only disadvantage of mapping using rostopics is that the recordings are not available as rosbags. For this reason, subsequent reevaluation of these visual and inertial data will no longer be possible.

First, the result is presented, which is obtained when all four maps are loaded into the maplab console. The maps were neither aligned to each other nor were an optimization process carried out.

In Fig. 3, in addition to the individual maps, which are shown in different colors, the course of the mapping process can be seen in a blue line. To illustrate the performance of the fusion algorithm and its accuracy, the dartboard on the left of the image is used as the object. Due to its coloring, this has a high contrast with very low reflection.

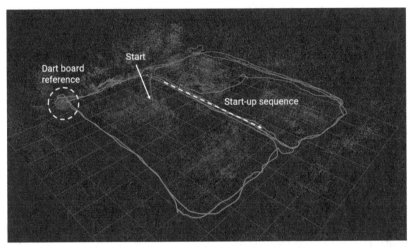

Fig. 3. Result of the mapping of the measurement and sensor technology laboratory in an unoptimized and unaligned condition.

A side view of this dartboard can be seen in Fig. 4.

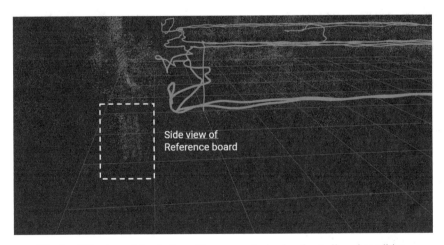

Fig. 4. Side view of the dartboard in an unoptimized and not aligned condition.

If you look at the two preliminary results in Fig. 3 and Fig. 4 of the fusion, there is a slight offset. Since both Fig. 2 and Fig. 3 were taken from a similar perspective, conclusions can be drawn about the general performance of maplab.

For the evaluation of the fusion algorithm, the optimization process is now carried out to optimize the display of the combined map and to obtain only those features that are most meaningful for a possible localization. Special mention should be made of the importance of the keyframing command, which significantly reduces the complexity of the map. The result of the mapping of the laboratory after the fusion is presented in Fig. 5.

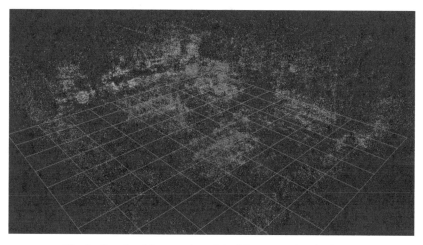

Fig. 5.   Result of the mapping of the laboratory after the fusion.

If the two maps in Fig. 3 and Fig. 5 are compared, a slight improvement in the representation of the individual features can be seen. To clarify this, the dartboard is again used as a reference.

If the two recordings of the dartboard from Fig. 4 and Fig. 6 are compared, a clear minimization of the offset can be seen, which results in a more accurate mapping result. Incidentally, it is even possible to guess the position of the darts (see marking in Fig. 6).

Looking at the results of the map fusion and the effects of the optimization process, maplab potential for mapping environments can be predicted. In addition to mapping closed spaces, there is the possibility of detecting and mapping the inventory and, relatively small objects.

5.3   Evaluation of Maplab Localization Capability

One of the crucial tasks for solving the SLAM problem is the localization of a mobile robot. Positioning relative to a map is to take place using a current or already carried out mapping of the environment. The robot platform "Husky" is used to evaluate the performance of the localization algorithm. A rosbag containing all visual and inertial data is also recorded here for data evaluation. What is special about this route is the

Fig. 6. Side view of the dartboard after the fusion.

high number of features already detected, which has a high information density due to repeated mapping. As a result of this large data collection, a significant increase in localization capability for the robot platform should be expected.

To carry out the localization, a map is created that only contains the ground floor of the building complex of the Offenburg University of Applied Sciences. It turns out that reducing the number of decks increases the fusion precision. This resulting map is used as a reference against which localization is performed. The map is shown in Fig. 7. In addition to the starting point, the associated route of the robot is also entered there.

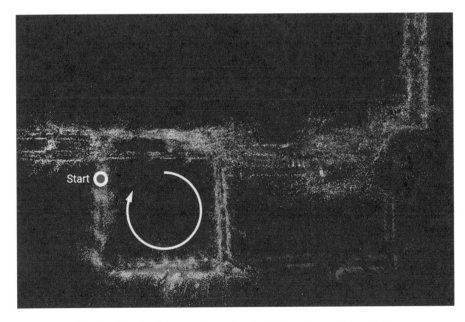

Fig. 7. Result of the mapping using the fusion of ground floor data.

To test the performance of the localization algorithm, the starting point of the recording is changed. It is possible to display positively detected features of the reference map during the extraction of the environmental features from the rosbag with the help of ROVIOLI. The procedure here is identical to that for loop closure detection. If a feature is successfully recognized, the robot is positioned relative to the known map. This is represented by a red dot. To clarify the route of the robot, the colors of the point clouds in Fig. 7 are unified to increase the contrast. In Fig. 8 the predicted route is shown based on the recognized environmental features.

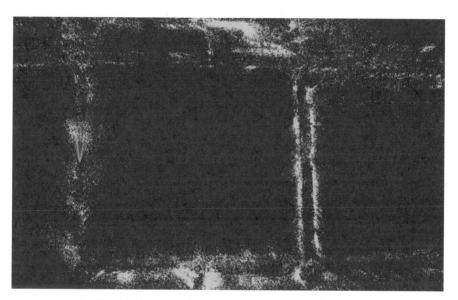

Fig. 8. Positioning of the robot relative to the ground floor map.

It is also possible to display the feature vectors recognized by ROVIOLI at runtime relative to the current position (see Fig. 9).
To perform a preliminary assessment of the possibility of localization using maplab, a surprisingly positive result can be achieved based on the investigations carried out. In addition to the retrieval and exact positioning relative to the ground floor map and the possibility of displaying positively detected features, a good localization capability is guaranteed. This is increased by the possibility of using a "live source", whereby positioning at runtime is conceivable. This contributes significantly to solving the SLAM problem.

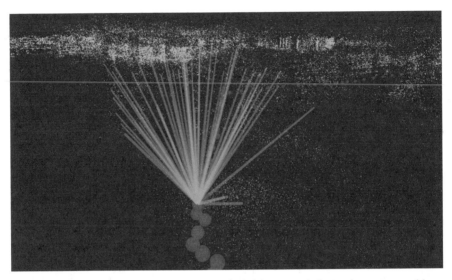

Fig. 9. Representation of the vectors of recognized features relative to the current position.

6 Conclusions and Future Work

To conclude the performance of maplab in terms of mapping and localization, the paper presents several possible uses and the results obtained.

Looking at the results of the individual mapping [19] with the fusion map in Subsect. 5.2 there are significant differences in accuracy and geometric consistency. With an increasing number of maps or area inspections, the density of features within the resulting map can be increased many times over, but at the same time, the risk of producing geometric inconsistencies is increased. However, if you look at the result of the mapping in Subsect. 5.3, this is mapped according to reality with certain errors. A reduction in the number of maps for fusion can lead to an increase in geometric consistency.

Based on the surprisingly positive outdoor mapping the statement can be made that maplab is not only suitable for use in building complexes but also for mapping areas outside such premises.

With further research projects and extensions of the current maplab software, it would be conceivable to equip mobile robot platforms or even unmanned aerial vehicles (UAV) with this SLAM system.

As a result, and based on the experience gained in dealing with maplab, there are a variety of application scenarios. One conceivable possibility would be the automated following of pre-programmed trajectories in buildings.

Acknowledgments. This research is supported by the Bulgarian National Science Fund in the scope of the project "Exploration the application of statistics and machine learning in electronics" under contract number КП-06-Н42/1.

References

1. Schneider, T., et al: Maplab: an open framework for research in visual-inertial mapping and localization, CoRR, vol. abs/1711.10250, 2017
2. Durrant-Whyte, H., Bailey, T.: Simultaneous localisation and mapping (SLAM): Part I the essential algorithms. IEEE Robot. Autom. Mag. 1–9 (2006)
3. Dissanayake, G., Durrant-Whyte, H., Scheding, S.: An experiment in autonomous navigation of an underground mining vehicle. IEEE Trans. Robot. Autom. **15**, 85–95 (2000)
4. Grisetti, G., Kümmerle, R., Stachniss, C., Burgard, W.: A tutorial on graph-based SLAM. IEEE Intell. Transp. Syst. Mag. **2**, 31–43 (2010)
5. Hess, W., Kohler, D., Rapp, H., Andor, D.; Real-time loop closure in 2D LIDAR SLAM. In: IEEE International Conference on Robotics and Automation (ICRA) (2016)
6. Nüchter, A.: 3D Robotic Mapping - The SLAM Problem with Six Degrees of Freedom, Springer, Heidelberg (2009)
7. Cadena, C., et al.: Past, Present, and future of simultaneous localization and mapping: towards the robust-perception age. IEEE Trans. Robot. **32**(6), 1309–1332 (2016)
8. Weiss, C., Achtelik, W.M., Siegwart, R.: Real-time onboard visual-inertial state estimation and self-calibration of MAVs in unknown environments. In: IEEE International Conference on Robotics and Automation (ICRA) (2012)
9. Bloesch, M., Omari, S., Hutter, M., Siegwart, R.: Robust visual inertial odometry using a direct EKF-based approach. In IEEE/RSJ International Conference on Intelligent Robots and Systems (IROS) (2015)
10. Zhang, J., Singh, S.: LOAM: lidar odometry and mapping in real-time. In: Robotics: Science and Systems Conference, Berkeley (2014)
11. Schneider, T., Dymczyk, M., Fehr, M., Egger, K., Siegwart, R.: Maplab: an open framework for research in visual-inertial mapping and localization. IEEE Robot. Autom. Lett. **3**, 1418–1425 (2018)
12. Hensel, S., Marinov, M.B., Schmitt, M.: System setup for synchronized visual-inertial localization and mapping. In: 2020 XXIX International Scientific Conference Electronics (ET), Sozopol, Bulgaria (2020)
13. Corke, P.: Robotics, Vision and Control. Springer, Berlin (2011)
14. Blasdel et al.: About ROS.Version (2020). https://www.ros.org/about-ros/
15. Quigley, M., et al.: ROS: an open-source robot operating system. In: ICRA Workshop on Open Source Software (2009)
16. Bjelonic, M.: YOLO ROS: real-time object detection for ROS, 2016–2020. https://github.com/leggedrobotics/darknet_ros
17. Bloesch, M., Omari, S., Hutter, M., Siegwart, R.: Robust visual-inertial odometry using a direct EKF-based approach. In: Proceedings of the 2015 IEEE/RSJ International Conference on Intelligent Robots and Systems (IROS), Hamburg, Germany, 28 September–3 October 2015
18. Deutsche Gesellschaft für Evaluation e.V., Standards für Evaluationen, Köln: Redaktion: Dr. Wolfgang Beywl, Zimmermann-Medien (2002)
19. Hensel, S., Marinov, M.B., Schmitt, M.: Experimental setup for investigation and evaluation of a mapping and localization system. In: Proceedings of the 9th FDIBA Conference - Challenges of the Digital World, Sofia, Bulgaria, 28–29 November 2019

MAC-Based Symmetric Key Protocol for Secure Traffic Forwarding in Drones

Zaid Ameen Abduljabbar[1,2], Vincent Omollo Nyangaresi[3], Junchao Ma[4(✉)],
Mustafa A. Al Sibahee[4,5], Mustafa S. Khalefa[1], and Dhafer G. Honi[1]

[1] Department of Computer Science, College of Education for Pure Sciences,
University of Basrah, Basrah 61004, Iraq
{zaid.ameen,mustafa.khalefa,dhafer.honi}@uobasrah.edu.iq
[2] Huazhong University of Science and Technology, Shenzhen Institute, Shenzhen 518118, China
[3] Faculty of Biological and Physical Sciences, Tom Mboya University, Homabay 40300, Kenya
vnyangaresi@tmuc.ac.ke
[4] College of Big Data and Internet, Shenzhen Technology University, Shenzhen 518118, China
{majunchao,mustafa}@sztu.edu.cn
[5] Computer Technology Engineering Department, Iraq University College, Basrah, Iraq
mustafa.alsibahee@iuc.edu.iq

Abstract. Unmanned aerial vehicles have been deployed for surveillance in highly sensitive domains such as in the military. As such, the data exchanged between the operators and these aerial vehicles must be protected as any malicious access may lead to leakages and adversarial control of the drones. To achieve this, many schemes have been developed based on techniques such as blockchains, elliptic curve cryptography, dynamic keys, physically unclonable function, asymmetric and symmetric cryptography among others. However, majority of these protocols have been shown to be inefficient for deployment in this environment, while others have security holes that be exploited by attackers to cause mayhem in these networks. In this paper, a protocol that leverages on quadratic residues and Chinese remainder theorem is developed. Its security analysis shows that it offers mutual authentication, non-repudiation, unlinkability, identity privacy and traceability for misbehaving drones. It is also resilient against impersonation, forgery and replay attacks. In terms of performance, this protocol has the least execution time and relatively lower bandwidth requirements.

Keywords: Authentication · Drones · Encryption · MAC · Protocol · Privacy · Symmetric · UAV

1 Introduction

Unmanned Aerial Vehicles (UAVs) consist of airborne sensors and drones that communicate through wireless channels [1]. They are normally managed via radio remote control techniques and some inbuilt program control devices [2]. Due to their wider coverage, UAVs have been applied in a wide range of domains such as in the military,

D. Perakovic and L. Knapcikova (Eds.): FABULOUS 2022, LNICST 445, pp. 16–36, 2022.
https://doi.org/10.1007/978-3-031-15101-9_2

disaster monitoring, geological investigation, intelligence reconnaissance, aerial photography, television shooting and agricultural surveillance. In addition, they have been deployed to monitor roads and forests to prevent theft and forest fires. Moreover, they have facilitated the acquisition of detailed aerial images as well as the creation of detailed 3D models [3].

Despite the potential merits that UAVs present, security and privacy are major issues that need to be addressed. As explained in [4] and [5], UAVs lack communication security, and hence the need to develop protocols to secure the communication between the users and the drones. As explained in [2], attackers can forge, monitor, tamper or delete the packets being exchanged in UAV networks. In addition, authors in [6] identify Man-In-The-Middle (MITM), forgery and replay attacks as being serious issues in UAVs. Similarly, spoofing, Denial of Service (DoS), MITM and Telnet or File Transfer Protocol (FTP) attacks have been highlighted in [7] and [8] as being detrimental for UAV deployments. The reliance on open wireless channels for UAV communication has been identified in [9] and [10] as being the source of vulnerabilities and active attacks such as cloning, eavesdropping, physical capture, replays, MITM and node tampering. Further, the sensitive data in UAV devices or being exchanged over the open wireless channels need to be protected as any malicious capture, may lead to its compromise that may disrupt or interfere with normal operations [11].

Authors in [12] explain that the widespread usage of UAVs render security and computing resource utilization efficiency very crucial. Unfortunately, drones deployed in this environment are designed devoid of inbuilt security mechanisms [13, 14]. As such, privacy and security are thorny issues that require urgent solution [12, 15, 16]. As explained in [17], privacy is a major concern in UAVs owing to the sensitive data that is conveyed in these networks. One possible solution to these security challenges is strong identity authentication that must be executed before drones could commence packet exchanges [6]. In UAV networks, there is high mobility and hence the connection states keep on changing in terms of the links or serving base stations. As such, frequent authentications are required for these dynamic networks to prevent adversaries from accessing the network resources or causing any havoc [18].

In line with this, many security protocols have been developed over the recent past. However, majority of these protocols are not sufficient to curb typical UAV attacks [15]. Consequently, how to effectively protect UAVs from disruptions or unauthorized access is still an open challenge. Another setback related to security and privacy is the resource-constrained nature of the UAV sensors, which limit their computing power. As such, the sophisticated and frequent authentications may be detrimental to these devices [12]. There is therefore need to improve on operational efficiency of the UAV sensors through the deployment of lightweight security protocols [19]. The specific contributions of this paper include the following:

- A protocol that leverages on quadratic residues and Chinese remainder theorem is developed for secure traffic forwarding in UAVs.
- Message authentication codes are deployed to encipher the exchanged messages for enhanced integrity and privacy protection.
- Extensive formal and informal security analysis is carried out to show that our protocol offers mutual authentication and resilience against typical UAV attacks.

- Performance evaluation is executed to demonstrate that the proposed protocol exhibits lower bandwidth requirements and the least execution time.

The rest of this article is organized as follows: Sect. 2 presents related literature while Sect. 3 outlines the system mode. On the other hand, Sect. 4 presents the security analysis, while Sect. 5 details performance evaluation of the proposed protocol. Finally, Sect. 6 concludes the paper and gives future research directions.

2 Related Work

The ever-increasing UAV deployments and security challenges in these networks has seen the development of numerous techniques to address these issues. However, some of these protocols still have issues regarding their efficiency or susceptibility to attacks. For example, authors in [20] have introduced an authentication protocol for security enhancement. However, this scheme cannot offer sufficient privacy [21]. Similarly, the authentication protocol presented in [7] cannot provide physical security. On the other hand, the lightweight user authentication scheme in [22] fails to uphold forward key secrecy [12]. Based on temporal credentials, an anonymous authentication protocol is developed in [11]. However, it is vulnerable to traceability, impersonation and stolen verifier attacks. In addition, it has scalability issues and cannot provide anonymity [16, 23]. Moreover, although the protocols in [11] and [22] offer increased security levels, the deployment of bilinear pairing operations increase their computational complexities [10, 24]. On its part, the protocol in [23] is susceptible to de-synchronization attacks and cannot offer backward security [12]. Similarly, the protocol introduced in [25] has high communication costs, is susceptible to traceability attacks and cannot offer backward and forward key secrecy.

An anonymous lightweight authentication protocol is presented in [26] that is shown to resists many attacks, while a watermark based authentication technique is developed in [27]. Unfortunately, the scheme in [27] has high storage and computational complexities. Based on public and private keys, a Certification Authority (CA) based authentication mechanism is presented in [28]. However, this approach has high computation overheads and its reliance on CA may present a single point of failure [29]. Based on Physical Unclonable Function (PUF), a mutual authentication scheme is introduced in [30]. Unfortunately, this protocol fails to provide forward key secrecy [12]. Similarly, anonymous mutual authentication scheme is presented in [31] that is demonstrated to offer anonymity. However, the usage of Trusted Platform Modules (TPMs) render this protocol expensive. In addition, this scheme cannot resist node tampering as well as physical attacks [10]. Authors in [32] introduce a spanning tree-based protocol. Unfortunately, this scheme lacks some security features, which authors in [33] addressed. On the other hand, the lightweight protocol developed in [34] has diminished performance [4].

Using Public-Key Cryptosystem (PKC), authors in [35] present a privacy preserving protocol. However, the deployment of PKC can potentially lead to high computation complexity [36]. Although the scheme presented in [37] can resist node cloning attacks, it is only ideal in situations where error data appear more often [2]. On the other hand, the lightweight authentication scheme in [38] is robust against numerous attacks, but has high communication overheads. Similarly, the authentication protocol in [39] exhibits high performance due to its lightweight cryptographic operations, but has numerous security issues. On the other hand, the tag-based scheme in [40] potentially prevents tag compromise attacks. However, the tag is required to execute computationally expensive cryptographic operations which render it unsuitable for resource constrained tags [41]. Similarly, Elliptic Curve Cryptography (ECC) based user authentication technique presented in [42] has high communication and computation overheads. On the other hand, the authentication protocol introduced in [43] is susceptible to MITM, replay, password guessing, privileged insider attacks and cannot uphold forward security. Although the Software Define Networking (SDN) based protocol in [44] offers mutual authentication in multi-drone networks, it is vulnerable to session key violation attacks [12]. Using cryptographic identities, an authentication scheme is presented in [45] to offer privacy and device anonymity. However, this protocol cannot offer strong mutual authentication.

In order to provide privacy and security enhancements, a blockchain based protocol is developed in [46]. Unfortunately, the deployed blockchains results in high computation and storage costs [47]. Similarly, the exponential time complexities for the scheme in [48] makes it unsuitable for UAV sensors. Although the schemes in [49] and [50] offer some levels of physical security using PUFs, these protocols are unsuitable for large scale dynamic UAV networks. On the other hand, the two-way authentication protocol presented in [51] is susceptible to session key leakage, secret temporary parameter leakage, server and user emulation attacks [52]. In addition, it has scalability issues and cannot guarantee user anonymity. Based on noisy PUF, authors in [21] have introduced an authentication scheme, but the tag here is required to execute computationally expensive operations and store helper data which makes it unsuitable for UAV environment. Similarly, the authentication technique in [53] has expensive computation and communication overheads due to pairing operations [54].

Based on certificate based digital signatures, authors in [55] develop an authentication scheme, but which cannot provide protection against physical and location threats. Similarly, the user authentication scheme in [56] is insecure due to its susceptibility to numerous attacks [57]. On the other hand, the scheme in [58] is prone to impersonation and DoS attacks. Although the protocol in [59] offers forward security, it is still susceptible to offline password guessing and smart card loss attacks [60]. On the other hand, based on asymmetric key cryptography, authors in [61] have developed an authentication scheme for UAV sensors. However, asymmetric encryption has expensive computations [62] and hence this protocol is not ideal for this application. Authors in [63] present a pairing-free protocol, but which has issues with malevolent drone revocation. On the other hand, the protocol in [64] is vulnerable to de-synchronization and MITM attacks, and cannot uphold backward key secrecy. Similarly, although the scheme in [65] provides anonymity, it is vulnerable to replay, dictionary and privileged insider attacks.

Based on the discussions above, it is evident that most of the current schemes still have security issues, while others have performance challenges. For instance, in most of the PUF based protocols, there is need for exhaustive search operations during device identification. This results in high computation and storage costs, which is not ideal for large scale UAV environments. Similarly, blockchain, asymmetric key and PKC based protocols have high performance costs. The aim of this article is to address these issues by developing a lightweight symmetric key based authentication scheme that is not only secure but also has lower computation and communication overheads.

3 System Model

This section presents the mathematical preliminaries of the cryptographic primitives deployed in this paper. This is followed by the detailing of the procedures executed in the proposed protocol, as discussed in the following sub-sections.

3.1 Mathematical Preliminaries

The proposed protocol is based on some features of the Quadratic Residues (QRs) and Chinese Remainder Theorem (CRT). Here, we let m and s be any integer and natural numbers respectively. On condition that the greatest common divisor (G) of these numbers is unity, then m is a Quadratic Residue Modulo (QRM) s if the congruence q^2 can be solved in polynomial time. Mathematically, this G and congruence are expressed as in (1):

$$G(m,\ s) = 1;\ q^2 = m\ (\text{mod } s) \tag{1}$$

The solutions to the above expression are the modular square root of m (mod s). Suppose that e is an odd prime number such that $G(m, e) = 1$. In this case, m becomes a QRM of e if and only if (2) holds.

$$m^{\frac{e-1}{2}} = 1(\text{mod } e) \tag{2}$$

On condition that m is QRM of e and $e = 3 \pmod 4$, then the square roots of QR m modulo e is obtained as in (3).

$$R_{1,2} = \pm m^{\frac{e+1}{4}}\ (\text{mod } e) \tag{3}$$

Suppose that e and f are some two distinct odd prime numbers such that $e = f = 3 \pmod 4$. If we let $s = e.f$ and $G(m, s) = 1$, then m is a QRM s if and only if the conditions in (4) hold:

$$m^{\frac{e-1}{2}} = 1(\text{mod } e)\text{ and } m^{\frac{f-1}{2}} = 1\ (\text{mod } f) \tag{4}$$

Based on (3), (4) and CRT, four modular square roots $R_{1,2,3,4}$ of a QR m modulo s are derived as in (5).

$$R_{1,2,3,4} = \pm j.f.f^* \pm T.e.e^*(\text{mod } s) \tag{5}$$

In (5), $j = m^{\frac{e+1}{4}} = 1 \pmod{e}$, $T = m^{\frac{f+1}{4}} = 1 \pmod{f}$, $e^* = e^{-1} \pmod{f}$ and $f^* = f^{-1} \pmod{e}$. In this case, it is straightforward to derive e^* and f^* using the extended Euclidean algorithm (EA) since G (e, f) = 1.

Suppose that e and f are some two distinct odd prime numbers and s = e.f. The number of QRs modulo s is given in (6).

$$N = \frac{(e-1)(f-1)}{4} \tag{6}$$

Based on (6), the likelihood of any integer m being a QRM s is approximately 0.25.

3.2 The Proposed Protocol

The communicating entities that are involved in the proposed protocol include the Registration Authority (RA), the Gateway Node (GWN), the Ground Control Center (GCC) and the Unmanned Aerial Vehicles (UAVs). Figure 1 depicts the network architecture of the proposed protocol. As shown in this network, the UAVs exchange messages among themselves and these messages may then be forwarded on behalf of other UAVs. Before the onset of the message exchange process, all the UAVs are registered at the RA, after which they communicated to the GCC via the GWN. Here, the GWN contacted the RA to get updates regarding the registration details.

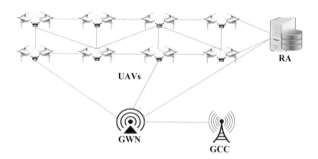

Fig.1. Network architecture.

However, the GWN and RA authentication is out of scope of the current work and hence the assumption made is that both the RA and the GWN are trusted entities. The GWN is particularly important where the GCC manages a large number of UAVs and the different UAVs could be grouped into a cluster and communicate via their respective GWNs. Table 1 presents the notations used in this paper.

The proposed protocol is executed in five major phases: parameter setting, registration, joining, UAV to GWN message signing - verification, and GWN to UAV message signing - verification phases. The details of these phases are discussed below.

Parameter Setting Phase: This phase involves the initialization of the security parameters that are utilized for the subsequent stages. It is executed in 3 steps as illustrated below.

Table 1. Symbols

Symbol	Description
ID_{UAV}	Unique identity of the UAV
ID_{GWN}	Unique identity of the GWN
SC_{UAV}	UAV secret code
SP_i	RA generated UAV secret parameters
E_k	Symmetric encryption using k
D_k	Symmetric decryption using k
T_M	Timestamp
j	Random integers
h(.)	Hashing operation
∥	Concatenation operation
⊕	XOR operation

Step 1: The registration authority chooses two large distinct odd prime numbers A_1, A_2 and derives $B_1 = (A_1. A_2)$. Next, it chooses another two large distinct odd prime numbers A_3 and A_4 for each of the gateway nodes, before computing $B_2 = (A_3. A_4)$.

Step 2: The registration authority generates two prime numbers C_1 and C_2 for each of the unmanned aerial vehicle and then derives $B_3 = (C_1. C_2)$. Next, it transmits parameters $\{A_3, A_4\}$ and $\{C_1, C_2\}$ to all GWNs and UAVs respectively.

Step 3: The RA selects some secure message authentication code (MAC) and one-way hashing function h(.) before publishing security parameters $\{MAC(.), B_1, B_2, B_3, h(.)\}$. At the same time, it privately stores security parameters $\{A_1, A_2\}$ in its database.

Registration Phase: In this phase, all the unmanned aerial vehicles are registered at the RA such that each of them is issued with some long-term secret keys. This phase is executed in 4 steps as detailed below.

Step 1: Each UAV generates its identity ID_{UAV} and secret code SC_{UAV} before sending registration request Reg_{Req} together with security parameters $\{ID_{UAV}, SC_{UAV}\}$ to the RA through some secure channels.

Step 2: Upon receipt of Reg_{Req}, the registration authority generates a set of security parameters $SP = \{SP_1, SP_2, SP_3, \dots SP_n\}$, where $SP_i \in SP$.

Step 3: The registration authority issues certificate cert = $\{SP_i, R_i, Q_i\}$ to UAV_i. Algorithm 1 illustrates the required steps for the generation of this certificate.

Algorithm 1: UAV→ GWN Certificate Generation

Begin
    a)   Input SP_i & initialize R_i to zero
    b)   Derive m = $h(SP_i, R_i)$
    c)   **IF** $m^{\frac{A_1-1}{2}} ! = 1 \pmod{A_1}$ and $m^{\frac{A_2-1}{2}} ! = 1 \pmod{A_2}$ **THEN:**
    d) $R_i = R_i + 1$
    e)   **GoTo** step c
    f)   **ELSE:**
    g)   Derive modular square roots $n_{1,2,3,4}$ of $n^2 = m \pmod{B_1}$
    h)   Select the smallest square root as Q_i
    i)   **return** cert = (SP_i, R_i, Q_i)
END

As shown in Algorithm 1, the successful computation of the four square roots in step g requires knowledge of A_1 and A_2.

Step 4: The registration authority generates a UAV list U_L and stores parameters $\{SP_i, ID_{UAV}\}$ in this list. This list is significant during the detection of malicious UAVs within the network. Finally, it sends security parameters $\{h(ID_{UAV}, SC_{UAV}), C_1, C_2, SP_i, R_i, Q_i\}$ to the UAV over some secured channels.

Joining Phase: In the proposed protocol, the identity of the UAV is verified before being allowed to join the network. To accomplish this, the following 2 steps are followed:

Step 1: The UAV utilizes its unique identity ID_{UAV} and security code SC_{UAV} to derive E = $h(ID_{UAV}, SC_{UAV})$. Next, the resulting hash value E is transmitted securely to the RA.
Step 2: On receiving E, the RA uses its stored parameter set $\{ID_{UAV}, SC_{UAV}\}$ to recomputed E^*. Next, the RA checks if $E^* \overset{?}{=} E$ such that the joining request is rejected if the two values are dissimilar. Otherwise, the UAV is legitimate and is permitted to join the network.

UAV → GWN Message Signing and Verification Phase: The three main procedures in the proposed protocol encompass Key Generation (KG), encryption and decryption. Basically, the KG step involves the sender selecting some two distinct large prime numbers e and f after which s is computed. This is followed by the publication of s but private storage of parameters e and f. During encryption, the sender composes message msg such that $msg.2^k$ is less than s. Afterwards, parameter V = $(msg.2^k)^2 \pmod{s}$ is derived and transmitted to the receiver. Upon receiving message V, the receiver derives four modular square roots of $q^2 = V \pmod{s}$ based on e and f as in (5). Finally, the original message msg is extracted from the modular square root with parameter k.

In the UAV network, messages M_i may be sent to the gateway node for subsequent transmission to the operator. During this transmission, it is important that UAV privacy is upheld, and these messages are securely delivered to their destinations. This is accomplished through message signing and verification using the 4 steps below.

Step 1: To start off message signing, the UAV generate random integer j and selects a single unused certificate $cert_U = \{SP_j, R_j, Q_j\}$. Here, $B_2^{\frac{1}{2}} < j < \frac{B_2}{2}$. It then chooses integer $k > 30$ and sets $T = 2^k$, where $2^{k-1} < B_2 < 2^k$.

Step 2: The UAV derives $Z = j^2.T^{-1} \pmod{B_2}$, $L = h(j)$, $X = MAC_L (ID_{GWN})$ and $Y = E_L (SP_j, R_j, Q_j, T_M, M_i)$.

Step 3: UAV constructs $UM = \{Z, X, Y\}$ and appends parameter set $\{SP_j, T_M\}$ in its malicious UAV list, M_{UL}. Here, the M_{UL} maintains a record of all pseudonyms of all revoked UAVs together with their respective timestamps. Finally, the UAV transmits final message UM to the GWN.

Step 4: After receiving UM from a particular UAV, the GWN validates this message to confirm whether the sending UAV is properly authenticated by the RA. To achieve this, Algorithm 2 is deployed. As shown in Algorithm 2, the GWN needs to derive four modular square roots as in step a followed by the computation of four hash values in step b which serve as the secret candidate keys.

To establish the precise secret key L, the GWN matches the received X with MAC operation in step c. In this case, the likelihood of having more than one candidate key matching is infinitesimal. In step d, the GWN deploys key L to decrypt parameter Y to obtain parameter set $\{SP_j, R_j, Q_j, T_M, M_i\}$. This is followed by the verification of timestamp T_M to thwart any packet replay attacks. To curb the re-use of any revoked certificate, the GWN extracts parameter set $\{SP_j, T_M\}$ from M_{UL} and one again validate timestamp T_M. In both cases, the verification process is terminated if T_M is invalid.

Algorithm 2: UAV→ GWN Message Verification

Begin
   a)   Derive modular square roots $n_{1,2,3,4}$ of $n^2 = Z.T \pmod{B_2}$
   b)   Compute $L_{1,2,3,4} = h(n_{1,2,3,4})$
   c)   Match received X with $X = MAC_{L_{1,2,3,4}} (ID_{GWN})$
   d)   Execute $D_L(Y) = (SP_j, R_j, Q_j, T_M, M_i)$
   e)   **IF** T_M is invalid **THEN:**
   f)   Terminate session
   g)   **ELSE:**
   h)   **IF** $Q_i^2 \ ! = h(SP_j, R_j)(\bmod B_1)$ **THEN:**
   i)   Terminate session
   j)   **ELSE:**
   k)   Permit data access

END

Otherwise, the GWN proceeds with the verification process by executing the check in step h. Provided that the authentication in step h is successful, the implication is that this UAV is legitimate and data access is allowed.

GWN → UAV Message Signing and Verification Phase: Upon sucessful message verification, the GWN examines message M_i to determine its legitimacy. If M_i is bogus, the GWN traces the particular UAV that sent this message and appends its SP_j together with timestamp T_M in its M_{UL}. Otherwise, the GWN broadcasts M_j to all UAVs within its coverage area as described in step 1–5 below.

Step 1: The GWN derives some secret certificate as illustrated in Algorithm 3. As shown in Algorithm 3, the derivation of the four square roots in step g requires knowledge of A_3 and A_4. To thwart any masquerading attacks, each secret certificate is deployed only once.

Algorithm 3: GWN$\rightarrow$ UAV Certificate Generation

Begin
a)   Input ID_{GWN} & initialize R_i to zero
b)   Derive m = $h(ID_{GWN}, R_i)$
c)   **IF** $m^{\frac{A_3-1}{2}} = 1 \pmod{A_3}$ & $m^{\frac{A_4-1}{2}} = 1 \pmod{A_4}$ **THEN:**
d) $R_j = R_j + 1$
e)   **GoTo** step c
f)   **ELSE:**
g)   Derive modular square roots $n_{1,2,3,4}$ of $n^2 = m \pmod{B_2}$
h)   Select the smallest square root as Q_i
i)   **return** cert $= (ID_{GWN}, R_i, Q_i)$
END

Step 2: Each time the GWN needs to share the received message M_j to all UAVs, it will need to sign this message before broadcasting it to all UAVs within its coverage area.

To start off the signing process, the GWN selects some random integer $B_3^{\frac{1}{2}} < j^* < \frac{B_3}{2}$, where $2^{k-1} < B_3 < 2^k$. It then sets $T^* = 2^k$.

Step 3: The GWN derives $Z^* = j^{*2}.T^{*-1} \pmod{B_3}$, $L^* = h(j^*)$, $X^* = MAC_{L^*}(ID_{GWN})$ and $Y^* = E_{L^*}(ID_{GWN}, R_j, Q_j, T_M, M_j)$.

Step 4: GWN composes GM $= \{ID_{GWN}, Z^*, X^*, Y^*\}$ before broadcasting GM to all UAVs within its range.

Step 5: Upon receiving GM from the GWN, each UAV verifies message M_j in Y^* as described in Algorithm 4. The process begins by generating four square roots as in step a with the help of C_1 and C_2.

Algorithm 4: GWN→ UAV Message Verification

Begin
   a)   Derive modular square roots $n_{1,2,3,4}$ of $n^2 = Z^*.T^*$ (mod B_3)
   b)   Compute $L^*_{1,2,3,4} = h(n_{1,2,3,4})$
   c)   Match received X^* with $X^* = MAC_{L^*_{1,2,3,4}}(ID_{GWN})$
   d)   Execute $D_{L^*}(Y^*) = (ID_{GWN}, R_j, Q_j, T_M, M_j)$
   e)   **IF** T_M is invalid **THEN:**
   f)   Terminate session
   g)   **ELSE:**
   h)   **IF** $Q_i^2 \,! = h(ID_{GWN}, R_j)$(mod B_2) **THEN:**
   i)   Terminate session
   j)   **ELSE:**
   k)   Accept & process M_j

END

This is followed by the computation of four hash values in step *b* to serve as secret keys. Next, the precise secret key L^* is established through matching the received ID_{GWN} and parameter X^* using the MAC operation in step *c*. This is followed by the decryption of parameter Y^* using key L^* to obtain the security parameters in step *d*. To curb any packet replay attacks, the timestamp verification in step *e* is executed. On the other hand, step *h* is carried out to thwart any masquerade attacks. Upon successful verification process, the UAV is assured that M_j was transmitted by a legitimate GWN and hence can accept and process its contents.

4 Security Analysis

The first part of this section presents the security analysis of the proposed protocol. This involves both formal analysis using Burrows–Abadi–Needham (BAN) logic, as well informal security analysis through some hypotheses that are formulated and proofed.

4.1 Formal Security Analysis

In this section, we deploy the widely adopted BAN logic to show that the proposed protocol attains the formulated authentications goals. To accomplish this, the BAN logic rules and notations in [4, 47] and [62] are utilized. In addition, the session –key rule is introduced during this analysis.

     Session-key rule: $\dfrac{A|\equiv\#(B), A|\equiv D|\equiv B}{A|\equiv A \overset{L}{\leftrightarrow} D}$

During this analysis, the following four goals are formulated:

G_1: GWN $|\equiv (Z, X, Y)$

G_2: GWN $|\equiv$ GWN $\overset{j}{\leftrightarrow}$ UAV
G_3: UAV $|\equiv (ID_{GWN}, Z^*, X^*, Y^*)$

$\mathbf{G_4}$: UAV $| \equiv$ UAV $\overset{j^*}{\leftrightarrow}$ GWN

Based on the message exchanges in our protocol, two sets of messages are transmitted during the message signing and verification phase. These messages include UM = {Z, X, Y} sent from the UAV towards the GWN, and GM = {ID_{GWN}, Z^*, X^*, Y^*} transmitted from the GWN to all the UAVs. In idealized form, these messages are represented as shown below.

UAV $\rightarrow$ GWN: {Z, X, Y}
{$\langle j \rangle_T$, $(ID_{GWN})_j$, {SP_j, R_j, Q_j, T_M, M_i}$_j$}
GWN $\rightarrow$ UAV: {ID_{GWN}, Z^*, X^*, Y^*}
{ID_{GWN}, $\langle j^* \rangle_{T^*}$, $(ID_{GWN})_{j^*}$, { ID_{GWN}, R_j, Q_j, T_M, M_j}$_{j^*}$}

For effective evaluation of the proposed protocol, the following six initial assumptions (IAs) are made:

IA_1: GWN $| \equiv$ GWN $\overset{T}{\leftrightarrow}$ UAV
IA2: GWN $| \equiv$ #TM
IA_3: GWN $| \equiv$ UAV $\Rightarrow$ {SP_j, R_j, Q_j}
IA_4: UAV $| \equiv$ UAV $\overset{T^*}{\leftrightarrow}$ GWN
IA5: UAV $| \equiv$ #TM
IA_6: UAV $| \equiv$ GWN $\Rightarrow$ {ID_{GWN}, R_j, Q_j}

Thereafter, the idealized form of the proposed protocol is analyzed based on the BAN logic rules and initial assumptions. This analysis is executed step-wise in the BAN logic proofs (BLPs) below.

For the case of UAV $\rightarrow$ GWN: {Z, X, Y}:
{$\langle j \rangle_T$, $(ID_{GWN})_j$, {SP_j, R_j, Q_j, T_M, M_i}$_j$}

The application of seeing rule (SR) in the above idealized message yield BLP_1:

$\mathbf{BLP_1}$: GWN $\triangleleft$ Z, X, Y: {$\langle j \rangle_T$, $(ID_{GWN})_j$, {SP_j, R_j, Q_j, T_M, M_i}$_j$}
According to the message-meaning rule (MMR), BLP_1 and IA_1, BLP_2 is yielded:
$\mathbf{BLP_2}$: GWN $| \equiv$ UAV$| \sim$ {j, $(ID_{GWN})_j$, {SP_j, R_j, Q_j, T_M, M_i}$_j$}
Based on the nonce-verification rule (NVR), fresh-promotion rule (FPR), BLP2 and IA2, BLP3 is obtained:
$\mathbf{BLP_3}$: GWN $| \equiv$ UAV $| \equiv$ {j, ID_{GWN}, SP_j, R_j, Q_j, T_M, M_i}
On the other hand, the application of the jurisdiction rule (JR) on both BLP_3 and IA_3 yields BLP_4:
$\mathbf{BLP_4}$: GWN $| \equiv$ {j, ID_{GWN}, $\langle SP_j$, R_j, $Q_j \rangle_{B_{j \to RA}}$, T_M, M_i}, hence $\mathbf{G_1}$ is achieved.
According to IA_2, BLP_4 and session-key rule (SKR), BLP_5 is obtained.

$\mathbf{BLP_5}$: GWN $| \equiv$ GWN $\overset{j}{\leftrightarrow}$ UAV, therefore $\mathbf{G_2}$ is attained.

For the case of GWN $\rightarrow$ UAV: $\{ID_{GWN}, Z^*, X^*, Y^*\}$

$\{ID_{GWN}, \langle j^* \rangle_{T*}, (ID_{GWN})_{j*}, \{ ID_{GWN}, R_j, Q_j, T_M, M_j\}_{j*}\}$.

The application of SR in this idealized message results in BLP_6:

$\mathbf{BLP_6}$: UAV $\lhd ID_{GWN}, Z^*, X^*, Y^*:\{ID_{GWN}, \langle j^* \rangle_{T*}, (ID_{GWN})_{j*}, \{ID_{GWN}, R_j, Q_j, T_M, M_j\}_{j*}\}$.

Based on BLP_6 and IA_5, NVR and FPR are applied to yield BLP_7:

$\mathbf{BLP_7}$: UAV $| \equiv$ GWN$|\sim\{ID_{GWN}, j^*, (ID_{GWN})_{j*}, \{ID_{GWN}, R_j, Q_j, T_M, M_j\}_{j*}\}$

According to IA_5, NVR and FPR are applied on BLP_7 to get BLP_8:

$\mathbf{BLP_8}$: UAV $| \equiv$ GWN $| \equiv \{j^*, ID_{GWN}, R_j, Q_j, T_M, M_j\}$

Based on BLP_8 and IA_6, jurisdiction rule (JR) is applied to yield BLP_9:

$\mathbf{BLP_9}$: UAV $| \equiv (ID_{GWN}, Z^*, X^*, Y^*)$, hence $\mathbf{G_3}$ is attained.

Finally, according to BLP_9 and IA_5, SR is applied to obtain BLP_{10}:

$\mathbf{BLP_{10}}$: UAV $| \equiv$ UAV $\overset{j^*}{\leftrightarrow}$ GWN, achieving $\mathbf{G_4}$.

The successful attainment of all the four formulated security goals imply that the UAVs and the GWNs execute strong mutual authentication amongst themselves.

4.2 Informal Security Analysis

In this section, we show that the proposed protocol offers mutual authentication, misbehaving UAAV tracing, unlinkability and non-repudiation. In addition, it provides protection against forgery, impersonation, privacy leaks and packet replays. To achieve this, the following hypotheses are formulated and proofed.

Hypothesis 1: *The proposed protocol protects against forgery attacks.*

Proof: Suppose that an attacker is interested in capturing parameter sets $\{SP_j, R_j, Q_j, T_M, M_i\}$ or $\{ ID_{GWN}, R_j, Q_j, T_M, M_j\}$. To accomplish this, messages UM $= \{Z, X, Y\}$ and GM $= \{ID_{GWN}, Z^*, X^*, Y^*\}$ must be intercepted. However, the decryption of Y and Y^* requires knowledge of secret key L which is unavailable to the adversary. If an attacker tries to forge messages UM and GM, these modifications are easily detected using Algorithm 2 and Algorithm 4 respectively.

Hypothesis 2: *Unlinkability is assured in the proposed scheme.*

Proof: In our scheme, message UM $= \{Z, X, Y\}$ is generated at the UAV, where $Z = j^2.T^{-1}$ (mod B_2), X $= MAC_L (ID_{GWN})$ and Y $= E_L (SP_j, R_j, Q_j, T_M, M_i)$. Suppose that an adversary is interested in linking messages generated by the UAV. However, the incorporation of random integer j implies that message UM will be different for each session. If an attacker decrypts parameter Y, access to $\{SP_j, R_j, Q_j, T_M, M_i\}$ is obtained. However, certificate cert $= \{ SP_j, R_j, Q_j\}$ has never been used before and timestamp T_M is still fresh. As such, these parameters cannot be linked to any previously captured messages.

Hypothesis 3: *The proposed protocol offers mutual authentication.*

Proof: Suppose that an attacker has intercepted message UM = {Z, X, Y}, where $Z = j^2.T^{-1}$ (mod B_2), X = MAC$_L$ (ID$_{GWN}$) and Y = E$_L$ (SP$_j$, R$_j$, Q$_j$, T$_M$, M$_i$). However, without knowledge of both A_3 and A_4, and encryption key L, adversary cannot decrypt Y to access message M$_i$. Here, the correct computation of secret key L requires both A_3 and A_4 as evidenced in (3), and hence only legitimate GWN can decrypt it. In addition, upon receipt of message UM = {Z, X, Y} from a particular UAV, its authenticity is confirmed by the GWN using certificate cert = {SP$_j$, R$_j$, Q$_j$} in accordance with Algorithm 2. These certificates are only issued by the RA and without RA's valid parameters A_1 and A_2, an attacker is unable to generate these certificates. Similarly, when the GWN broadcasts message GM = {ID$_{GWN}$, Z*, X*, Y*}, only UAVs with valid C_1 and C_2 can decrypt Y* to access message M$_j$. The computation of secret key L* requires knowledge of C_1 and C_2 which are only known to the legitimate UAVs. As such, without these parameters, an adversary cannot decipher Y*. To authenticate the GWN, the UAVs utilizes certificate cert = {ID$_{GWN}$, R$_j$, Q$_j$} as described in Algorithm 4.

Hypothesis 4: *The proposed protocol assures message non-repudiation.*

Proof: The assumption made here is that a particular UAV has sent message UM = {Z, X, Y} but wants to deny having sent this message. However, each message sent by a UAV is signed by certificate cert = {SP$_j$, R$_j$, Q$_j$} that is issued by the RA. As such, a particular UAV cannot deny its own sent messages. Similarly, message GM = {ID$_{GWN}$, Z*, X*, Y*} sent by the GWN is signed by its certificate cert = {ID$_{GWN}$, R$_j$, Q$_j$} and hence cannot be denied by a particular GWN.

Hypothesis 5: *Impersonation attacks are thwarted in the proposed scheme.*

Proof: To effectively masquerade as a UAV or GWN, messages UM = {Z, X, Y} and GM = {ID$_{GWN}$, Z*, X*, Y*} must be generated respectively. However, this requires that an adversary have access to certificates cert = {SP$_j$, R$_j$, Q$_j$} and cert = {ID$_{GWN}$, R$_j$, Q$_j$}, in addition to parameter set {A_1, A_2} and {A_3, A_4}. Since these security tokens are only generated by the RA, any form of impersonation fails since fake certificates will be detected in accordance with Algorithm 2 and Algorithm 4.

Hypothesis 6: *The proposed protocol upholds identity privacy.*

Proof: During the registration phase, the RA assigns each UAV a set of secret parameters SP = {SP$_1$, SP$_2$, SP$_3$,..... SP$_n$} and equivalent certificates {SP$_i$, R$_i$}. During message transmission, a single unused secret parameter is chosen and incorporated in the sent message so as to conceal its identity. Consequently, it is infeasible for the UAV's real identity to be deciphered from the intercepted messages.

Hypothesis 7: *Replay attacks are prevented in our protocol.*

Proof: In the proposed protocol, message UM = {Z, X, Y} is sent from the UAV towards the GWN. On its part, the GWN transmits message GM = {ID$_{GWN}$, Z*, X*, Y*}. Here, $Z = j^2.T^{-1}$ (mod B_2), L = h(j), X = MAC$_L$ (ID$_{GWN}$), Y = E$_L$ (SP$_j$, R$_j$, Q$_j$, T$_M$, M$_i$),

$Z^* = j^{*2}.T^{*-1} \pmod{B_3}$, $L^* = h(j^*)$, $X^* = MAC_{L^*} (ID_{GWN})$ and $Y^* = E_{L^*} (ID_{GWN}$, R_j, Q_j, T_M, M_j). Evidently, these messages incorporate timestamp T_M. During message verification in Algorithm 2 and Algorithm 4, the message freshness checks are executed. As such, any replayed message is easily detected in our protocol.

Hypothesis 8: *The proposed protocol offers traceability for misbehaving UAVs.*

Proof: During the registration phase, the certificates cert $= \{SP_i, R_i, Q_i\}$ deployed for message signing and verification are issues by the RA. In addition, the RA generates secret parameters SP_j for each UAV. Since these parameters are related to the UAV real identities, it is only the RA that has knowledge of these identities. Upon generation of a single message UM $= \{Z, X, Y\}$ using any available cert, the RA is able to relate this message to a particular secret parameter SP_i. Consequently, the RA can trace the real identity of the UAV. As such, any UAV misusing another UAV's real identity is easily identified and eliminated from the network.

5 Performance Evaluation

In typical security protocols, the execution time and bandwidth requirements are the widely adopted metrics for evaluating these protocols. As such, in this sub-section, the proposed protocol is evaluated using these metrics. In addition, the values obtained are compared with those of other related schemes.

Execution Time: During message signing and verification, the cryptographic operations executed include AES encryption (AE), Montgomery (M), AES decryption (AD), message authentication code (MA), modular square root (MS) and hashing (H) operations. The execution time (T) for these cryptographic operations are as follows: $T_{AE} = 0.006$ ms, $T_M = 0.003$ ms, $T_{AD} = 0.003$ ms, $T_{MA} = 0.002$ ms, $T_{MS} = 0.076$ ms and $T_H = 0.001$ ms. Based on the message signing and verification steps, single T_M, T_{AE}, T_{MA} and T_H operations are executed at the UAV and GWN and hence the total cost for signing is $2T_M$, $2T_{AE}$, $2T_{MA}$ and $2T_H$ operations. However, during message verification, $4T_{MA}$, $1T_M$, $5T_H$, $1T_{MS}$ and $1T_{AD}$ operations are carried out on the GWN and the UAVs. As such, the total cost for message verification is $8T_{MA}$, $2T_M$, $10T_H$, $2T_{MS}$ and $2T_{AD}$ operations. Consequently, the total execution time for signing and verification is: $4T_M + 2T_{AE} + 10T_{MA} + 12T_H + 2T_{AD} + 2T_{MS}$ operations. In overall, 0.214 ms are required for message signing and verification process as shown in Table 2.

   Based on the results presented in Table 2, the scheme developed in [42] has the longest execution time followed by the schemes in [23, 25, 64] and the proposed protocol in that order. Given that the sensors in UAVs are resource limited, it is required that the authentication protocol be lightweight in terms of the cryptographic execution time. As such, the proposed protocol is the most applicable in the UAV sensor environment.

Bandwidth Requirement: In the proposed protocol, B_1, B_2 and B_3 are 512 bits in length while A_1, A_2, C_1, C_2, A_3 and A_4 are 256 bits each. On the other hand, HMAC operation using SHA-1, timestamp, hash function, AES encryption or decryption, and identity are

Table 2. Execution time

Scheme	Execution time (ms)
[64]	2.4345
[42]	34.3225
[25]	2.4769
[23]	2.4301
Proposed	0.214

160 bits, 32 bits, 160 bits, 256 bits and 32 bits in length respectively. During message signing and verification, messages $UM = \{Z, X, Y\}$ and $GM = \{ID_{GWN}, Z^*, X^*, Y^*\}$ are exchanged. Here, $Z = j^2.T^{-1}$ (mod B_2), $X = MAC_L$ (ID_{GWN}), $Y = E_L$ (SP_j, R_j, Q_j, T_M, M_i), $Z^* = j^{*2}.T^{*-1}$ (mod B_3), $X^* = MAC_{L*}$ (ID_{GWN}) and $Y^* = E_{L*}$ (ID_{GWN}, R_j, Q_j, T_M, M_j). The required bandwidth is then computed as follows:

$UM = \{Z, X, Y\}$: $Z = 512$ bits, $X = 160$ bits, $Y = 256$ bits,
    hence UM is 928 bits long. On the other hand:
$GM = \{ID_{GWN}, Z^*, X^*, Y^*\}$: $ID_{GWN} = 32$ bits, $Z^* = 512$ bits, $X^* = 160$ bits, $Y^* = 256$ bits

As such, the total overhead for GM is 960 bits. Therefore, 1,888 bits are exchanged during the message signing and verification process, as shown in Table 3.

Table 3. Bandwidth requirements

Scheme	Bandwidth (bits)
[64]	1984
[42]	2528
[25]	1856
[23]	1696
Proposed	1888

Based on the graphs in Fig. 2, the protocol in [42] has the highest bandwidth requirements, followed by the protocols in [64], the proposed protocol, [25] and [23] in that order.

Although the scheme in [23] has the lowest bandwidth requirements, it is susceptible to de-synchronization attacks and cannot offer backward security. On the other hand, the protocol in [25] cannot offer backward and forward key secrecy, and has high communication costs. Consequently, although the proposed protocol has slightly higher bandwidth requirements than these protocols, it offers robust security features.

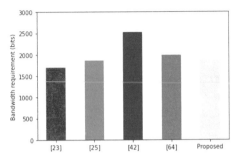

Fig.2. Bandwidth requirements.

6 Conclusion and Future Work

Many schemes have been developed for security and privacy enhancement in UAV networks. Majority of these schemes are based on PUF, ECC, PKC, blockchains, RSA certificates among other techniques. However, the noise in PUF-based schemes may lead to output bits being incorrect for some given challenges. On the other hand, the conventional authentication techniques based on dynamic keys, usernames or passwords offer low levels of security. In addition, RSA certification generates long session keys which are inefficient for UAV sensors. The dynamic topologies in UAVs owing to frequent mobility imply continuous identity authentication, hence the need for lightweight protocols. The proposed protocol has been demonstrated to fulfill this lightweight requirement, in addition to offering robust security and privacy protection. Future work lies in the deployment and evaluation of the proposed protocol in a real UAV communication environment so that the presented security and performance metrics can be validated.

Acknowledgement. This work is supported by Natural Science Foundation of Top Talent of SZTU (Grant number: 20211061010016) and National Natural Science Foundation of China under Grant 62072064.

References

1. Ozmen, M.O., Attila Yavuz, A.: Dronecrypt-an efficient cryptographic framework for small aerial drones. In: Prooceedings of IEEE Military Communications Conference (MILCOM), pp. 1–6. IEEE (2018)
2. Sun, J., et al.: A data authentication scheme for UAV ad hoc network communication. J. Supercomput. **76**(6), 4041–4056 (2017). https://doi.org/10.1007/s11227-017-2179-3
3. Giordan, D., et al.: The use of unmanned aerial vehicles (UAVs) for engineering geology applications. Bull. Eng. Geol. Env. **79**(7), 3437–3481 (2020). https://doi.org/10.1007/s10064-020-01766-2
4. Nyangaresi, V. O., Morsy, M.A.: Towards privacy preservation in internet of drones. In: 2021 IEEE 6th International Forum on Research and Technology for Society and Industry (RTSI), pp. 306–311. IEEE (2021)
5. Kwon, Y.M., Yu, J., Cho, B.M., Eun, Y., Park, K.J.: Empirical analysis of MAVLink protocol vulnerability for attacking unmanned aerial vehicles. IEEE Access **6**, 43203–43212 (2018)

6. Teng, L., et al.: Lightweight security authentication mechanism towards UAV networks. In: 2019 International Conference on Networking and Network Applications (NaNA), pp. 379–384. IEEE (2019)

7. Hooper, M., et al.: Securing commercial Wifi based UAVs from common security attacks. In: Military Communications Conference (MILCOM), pp. 1213–1218. IEEE (2016)

8. Rodday, N.M., Schmidt, R.D.O., Pras, A.: Exploring security vulnerabilities of unmanned aerial vehicles. In: Network Operations and Management Symposium (NOMS), pp. 993–994. IEEE (2016)

9. Nyangaresi, V.O., Ogundoyin, S.O.: Certificate based authentication scheme for smart homes. In: 2021 3rd Global Power, Energy and Communication Conference (GPECOM), pp. 202–207. IEEE (2021)

10. Bansal, G., Sikdar, B.: S-MAPS: Scalable mutual authentication protocol for dynamic UAV swarms. IEEE Trans. Veh. Technol. **70**(11), 12088–12100 (2021)

11. Srinivas, J., Das, A.K., Kumar, N., Rodrigues, J.J.: Tcalas: temporal credential-based anonymous lightweight authentication scheme for Internet of drones environment. IEEE Trans. Veh. Technol. **68**(7), 6903–6916 (2019)

12. Lei, Y., Zeng, L., Li, Y.X., Wang, M.X., Qin, H.: A lightweight authentication protocol for UAV networks based on security and computational resource optimization. IEEE Access **9**, 53769–53785 (2021)

13. Yahuza, M., Idris, M.Y.I., Wahab, A.W.A., Nandy, T., Ahmedy, I.B., Ramli, R.: An edge assisted secure lightweight authentication technique for safe communication on the Internet of drones network. IEEE Access **9**, 31420–31440 (2021)

14. Ever, Y.K.: A secure authentication scheme framework for mobile-sinks used in the Internet of drones applications. Comput. Commun. **155**, 143–149 (2020)

15. Lin, C., He, D., Kumar, N., Choo, K.K.R., Vinel, A., Huang, X.: Security and privacy for the Internet of drones: challenges and solutions. IEEE Commun. Mag. **56**(1), 64–69 (2018)

16. Nyangaresi, V.O., Petrovic, N.: Efficient PUF based authentication protocol for internet of drones. In: 2021 International Telecommunications Conference (ITC), pp. 1–4. IEEE (2021)

17. Yoon, K., Park, D., Yim, Y., Kim, K., Yang, S.K., Robinson, M.: Security authentication system using encrypted channel on UAV network. In: 2017 First IEEE International Conference on Robotic Computing (IRC), pp. 393–398. IEEE (2017)

18. Fang, D., Qian, Y., Hu, R.Q.: Security for 5g mobile wireless networks. IEEE Access **6**, 4850–4874 (2017)

19. Nyangaresi, V.O.: ECC based authentication scheme for smart homes. In: 2021 International Symposium ELMAR, pp. 5–10. IEEE (2021)

20. Aysu, A., Gulcan, E., Moriyama, D., Schaumont, P., Yung, M.: End-to-end design of a PUF-based privacy preserving authentication protocol. In: Güneysu, T., Handschuh, H. (eds.) CHES 2015. LNCS, vol. 9293, pp. 556–576. Springer, Heidelberg (2015). https://doi.org/10.1007/978-3-662-48324-4_28

21. Gope, P., Lee, J., Quek, T.Q.S.: Lightweight and practical anonymous authentication protocol for RFID systems using physically unclonable functions. IEEE Trans. Inf. Forensics Secur. **13**(11), 2831–2843 (2018)

22. Wazid, M., Das, A.K., Kumar, N., Vasilakos, A.V., Rodrigues, J.J.P.C.: Design and analysis of secure lightweight remote user authentication and key agreement scheme in internet of drones deployment. IEEE Internet Things J. **6**(2), 3572–3584 (2019)

23. Ali, Z., Chaudhry, S.A., Ramzan, M.S., Al-Turjman, F.: Securing smart city surveillance: a lightweight authentication mechanism for unmanned vehicles. IEEE Access **8**, 43711–43724 (2020)

24. Nyangaresi, V.O.: Hardware assisted protocol for attacks prevention in ad hoc networks. In: Miraz, M.H., Southall, G., Ali, M., Ware, A., Soomro, S. (eds.) iCETiC 2021. LNICSSITE, vol. 395, pp. 3–20. Springer, Cham (2021). https://doi.org/10.1007/978-3-030-90016-8_1

25. Dammak, M., Boudia, O.R.M., Messous, M.A., Senouci, S.M., Gransart, C.: Token-based lightweight authentication to secure IoT networks. In: Proceedings of 16th IEEE Annual Consumer Communications & Networking Conference (CCNC), pp. 1–4. IEEE (2019)
26. Li, T., Ma, J., Ma, X., Gao, C., Zhang, J.: Lightweight secure communication mechanism towards UAV networks. In: Proceedings of IEEE Globecom Workshops (GC Wkshps), pp. 1–6. IEEE (2019)
27. Shi, X., Xiao, D.: A reversible watermarking authentication scheme for wireless sensor networks. Inf. Sci. **240**(11), 173–183 (2013)
28. Nicanfar, H., Jokar, P., Leung, V.C.: Smart grid authentication and key management for unicast and multicast communications. In: 2011 IEEE PES Innovative Smart Grid Technologies, pp. 1–8. IEEE (2011)
29. Nyangaresi, V.O., Rodrigues, A.J., Taha, N.K.: Mutual authentication protocol for secure VANET data exchanges. In: Perakovic, D., Knapcikova, L. (eds.) FABULOUS 2021. LNIC-SSITE, vol. 382, pp. 58–76. Springer, Cham (2021). https://doi.org/10.1007/978-3-030-784 59-1_5
30. Pu, C., Li, Y.: Lightweight authentication protocol for unmanned aerial vehicles using physical unclonable function and chaotic system. In: Proceedings of EEE International Symposium on Local and Metropolitan Area Networks (LANMAN), pp. 1–6. IEEE (2020)
31. Chen, L., Qian, S., Lim, M., Wang, S.: An enhanced direct anonymous attestation scheme with mutual authentication for network connected UAV communication systems. China Commun. **15**(5), 61–76 (2018)
32. Asokan, N., et al.: Seda: scalable embedded device attestation. In: Proceedings of the 22nd SIGSAC Conference on Computer and Communications Security, pp. 964–975. ACM (2015)
33. Ibrahim, A., Sadeghi, A.R., Tsudik, G., Zeitouni, S.: Darpa: device attestation resilient to physical attacks. In: Proceedings of the 9th ACM Conference on Security & Privacy in Wireless and Mobile Networks, pp. 171–182. ACM (2016)
34. Zhang, Y., He, D., Li, L., Chen, B.: A lightweight authentication and key agreement scheme for Internet of drones. Comput. Commun. **154**, 455–464 (2020)
35. Lee, K., Nieto, J.G., Boyd, C.: A state-aware RFID privacy model with reader corruption. In: Xiang, Y., Lopez, J., Kuo, C.-C. J., Zhou, W. (eds.) CSS 2012. LNCS, vol. 7672, pp. 324–338. Springer, Heidelberg (2012). https://doi.org/10.1007/978-3-642-35362-8_25
36. Nyangaresi, V.O., Abduljabbar, Z.A., Al Sibahee, M.A., Abduljaleel, I.Q., Abood, E.W.: Towards security and privacy preservation in 5G networks. In: 2021 29th Telecommunications Forum (TELFOR), pp. 1–4. IEEE (2021)
37. Guan, T., Chen, Y.: A node clone attack detection scheme based on digital watermark in WSNs. In: IEEE International Conference on Computer Communication and the Internet, pp. 257–260. IEEE (2016)
38. Liang, W., Xie, S., Long, J., Li, K.C., Zhang, D., Li, K.: A double PUF based RFID identity authentication protocol in service-centric internet of things environments. Inf. Sci. **503**, 129–147 (2019)
39. Chamola, V., Hassija, V., Gupta, V., Guizani, M.: A comprehensive review of the COVID-19 pandemic and the role of IoT, drones, AI, blockchain, and 5G in managing its impact. IEEE Access **8**, 90225–90265 (2020)
40. Pandey, S., Deyati, S., Singh, A., Chatterjee, A.: Noise-resilient SRAM physically unclonable function design for security. In: IEEE 25th Asian Test Symposium, ATS, pp. 55–60. IEEE (2016)
41. Nyangaresi, V.O., Moundounga, A.R.A.: Secure data exchange scheme for smart grids. In: 2021 IEEE 6th International Forum on Research and Technology for Society and Industry (RTSI), pp. 312–316. IEEE (2021)
42. Challa, S., et al.: Secure signature-based authenticated key establishment scheme for future IoT applications. IEEE Access **5**, 3028–3043 (2017)

43. Tai, W.L., Chang, Y.F., Li, W.H.: An IoT notion-based authentication and key agreement scheme ensuring user anonymity for heterogeneous ad hoc wireless sensor networks. J. Inf. Secur. Appl. **34**, 133–141 (2017)

44. Yan, Q., Gong, Q., Deng, F.A.: Detection of DDoS attacks against wireless SDN controllers based on the fuzzy synthetic evaluation decision making model. Adhoc Sens. Wirel. Netw. **33**, 275–299 (2016)

45. Benzarti, S., Triki, B., Korbaa, O.: Privacy preservation and drone authentication using id-based signcryption. In: SoMeT, pp. 226–239 (2018)

46. Rupa, C., Srivastava, G., Gadekallu, T.R., Maddikunta, P.K.R., Bhattacharya, S.: Security and privacy of UAV data using blockchain technology. J. Inf. Secur. Appl. **55**, 102670 (2020)

47. Nyangaresi, V.O.: Lightweight key agreement and authentication protocol for smart homes. In: 2021 IEEE AFRICON, pp. 1–6. IEEE (2021)

48. Püllen, D., Anagnostopoulos, N.A., Arul, T., Katzenbeisser, S.: Using implicit certification to efficiently establish authenticated group keys for in-vehicle networks. In: Proceedings of IEEE Vehicular Networking Conference (VNC), pp. 1–8. IEEE (2019)

49. Bansal, G., Naren, N., Chamola, V.: Rama: real-time automobile mutual authentication protocol using puf. In: Proceedings of IEEE International Conference on Information Networking (ICOIN), pp. 265–270. IEEE 2020

50. Bansal, G., Naren, N., Chamola, V., Sikdar, B., Kumar, N., Guizani, M.: Lightweight mutual authentication protocol for v2g using puf. IEEE Trans. Veh. Technol. **69**(7), 7234–7246 (2020)

51. Barman, S., Shum, H.P.H., Chattopadhyay, S., Samanta, D.: A secure authentication protocol for multi-server-based e-healthcare using a fuzzy commitment scheme. IEEE Access **7**, 12557–12574 (2019)

52. Ali, Z., et al.: Itssaka-ms: an improved three-factor symmetric key based secure aka scheme for multi-server environments. IEEE Access **8**, 107993–108003 (2020)

53. Semal, B., Markantonakis, K., Akram, R.N.: A certificateless group authenticated key agreement protocol for secure communication in untrusted UAV networks. In: 2018 IEEE/AIAA 37th Digital Avionics Systems Conference (DASC), pp. 1–8. IEEE (2018)

54. Nyangaresi, V.O., Rodrigues, A.J., Abeka, S.O.: Machine learning protocol for secure 5G handovers. Int. J. Wirel. Inf. Netw.**29**, 1–22 (2022)

55. Tian, Y., Yuan, J., Song, H.: Efficient privacy-preserving authentication framework for edge-assisted internet of drones. J. Inf. Secur. Appl. **48**, 102354 (2019)

56. Turkanovi´c, M., Brumen, B., Hölbl, M.: A novel user authentication and key agreement scheme for heterogeneous ad hoc wireless sensor networks, based on the internet of things notion. Ad. Hoc Netw. **20**, 96–112 (2014)

57. Farash, M.S., Turkanovi´c, M., Kumari, S., Hölbl, M.: An efficient user authentication and key agreement scheme for heterogeneous wireless sensor network tailored for the internet of things environment. Ad Hoc Netw. **36**, 152–176 (2016)

58. Bringer, J., Chabanne, H., Icart, T.: Improved privacy of the tree-based hash protocols using physically unclonable function. In: Ostrovsky, R., De Prisco, R., Visconti, I. (eds.) SCN 2008. LNCS, vol. 5229, pp. 77–91. Springer, Heidelberg (2008). https://doi.org/10.1007/978-3-540-85855-3_6

59. Amin, R., Islam, S.H., Biswas, G.P., Khan, M.K., Leng, L., Kumar, N.: Design of an anonymity-preserving three-factor authenticated key exchange protocol for wireless sensor networks. Comput. Netw. **101**, 42–62 (2016)

60. Jiang, Q., Zeadally, S., Ma, J., He, D.: Lightweight three-factor authentication and key agreement protocol for Internet-integrated wireless sensor networks. IEEE Access **5**, 3376–3392 (2017)

61. Yao, X., Han, X., Du, X.: A light-weight certificate-less public key cryptography scheme based on ECC. In: Proceedings of 23rd International Conference on Computer Communications and Networks (ICCCN), pp. 1–8. IEEE (2014)

62. Nyangaresi, V.O., Rodrigues, A.J.: Efficient handover protocol for 5G and beyond networks. Comput. Secur. **113**, 102546 (2022)
63. Seo, S.H., Won, J., Bertino, E.: pCLSC-TKEM: a pairing free certificateless signcryption-tag key encapsulation mechanism for a privacy-preserving IoT. Trans. Data Priv. **9**(2), 101–130 (2016)
64. Das, A.K.: A secure and robust temporal credential-based three-factor user authentication scheme for wireless sensor networks. Peer-to-Peer Netw. Appl. **9**(1), 223–244 (2014). https://doi.org/10.1007/s12083-014-0324-9
65. Guo, C., Chang, C.C., Chang, S.C.: A secure and efficient mutual authentication and key agreement protocol with smart cards for wireless communications. I.J Netw. Secur. **20**(2), 323–331 (2018)

Optimal Placement of Two IRSs in Beyond 5G Indoor Network

Ahmed M. Nor[1,2]([✉]), Octavian Fratu[1], and Simona Halunga[1]

[1] Telecommunications Department, University Politehnica of Bucharest, Bucharest, Romania
{ahmed.nor,octavian.fratu,simona.halunga}@upb.ro
[2] Electrical Engineering Department, Faculty of Engineering, Aswan University, Aswan, Egypt
ahmed.nor@aswu.edu.eg

Abstract. Intelligent reflecting surfaces (IRSs) became, during the last few years a major player in beyond 5G networks because it can assist millimeter wave and terahertz transmissions to overcome their propagation and blockage issues. IRSs provide the network with alternative line of sight paths and extend the network coverage. However, deploying a single IRS seems not to be enough, specially in crowded large indoor area with multiple blocking elements. In this paper, we will discuss a scenario of the network with two implemented IRSs and compare it with the case of a single IRS, hence proving the superiority of first case to extend the coverage and reduce the effect of blockage occurrence in the network. Then, we will propose optimal placement of two IRSs in the environment to enhance the overall performance of the network. The proposed method is based on maximizing the average received power over all possible user equipment (UEs) positions within the study area. This method can guarantee larger received power for almost all UE positions. Finally, we study the performance of the network with different blockage probability of occurrence cases that effects on both the direct link between access point and UE and the alternative link between IRS and UE.

Keywords: Intelligent reflecting surfaces · Optimal placement · Beyond 5G networks · Blockage

1 Introduction

5G and beyond network gained a much interest from both industry and academia recently. Those networks come with requirements, e.g., ultra-high data rate, wider coverage and connectivity, high reliability and ultra-low latency, which cannot be handled by already existence 5G solutions [1–3]. Moreover, implementing millimeter wave (mmWave) and terahertz (THz) transmissions alone is inefficient, as their propagation highly attenuated with distance. Besides, they are susceptible to blockage, whether it is caused by static obstacles or dynamic ones due to human shadowing [4, 5], hence losing their predominant line of sight (LOS) link. Thus, intelligent reflecting surfaces (IRSs) have appeared as a promising candidate to play a role as an assistant in beyond 5G wireless communication network [1]. Because IRS can provide an alternative virtual LOS link to user equipment

D. Perakovic and L. Knapcikova (Eds.): FABULOUS 2022, LNICST 445, pp. 37–46, 2022.
https://doi.org/10.1007/978-3-031-15101-9_3

(UE) when the main link between access point (AP) and UE is blocked, i.e., AP-IRS-UE link can be used for communication and localization services. Moreover, it can extend the network coverage, improve the cannel rank and refine the channel statistics. Generally, IRS is a planner surface consists of number of passive reflecting meta elements that can be controlled to reflect the incident signal with a defined phase towards UE.

The AP-IRS-UE propagation link mainly depends on the position of IRS relative to the position of AP and UE, and thus, several recent works studied the optimal placement of IRS in the network [6–13]. In [6], the authors proposed an algorithm to maximize the coverage of cell by optimizing the orientation of IRS and the horizontal distance between IRS and AP. In [13], the placement and phase shift of aerial IRS are jointly optimized to maximize the worst case signal-to-noise ratio (SNR) in a 3 dimensional (3D) network. Moreover, the authors in [8] and [9] studied the optimal placement of IRS to maximize the SNR at UE and minimize the joint blocking probability of AP and UE in mmWave network, respectively. In [10], to extend the cell coverage and enhance the performance of air-ground networks, the authors analyzed the IRS placement problem with considering interference generated from adjacent cells. The authors of [11] discussed the problem of optimizing the IRS placement and designing multiple access scheme in a multi-user network and proved that optimizing the deployment position of a single IRS can improve the performance gain of the network. In [7], the placement of IRS is studied in terms of achieving minimum desired power level at UE taking into consideration the available gains from AP and possible positions of both AP and IRS in a mobile user scenario in indoor environment. This work proved that, implementing single IRS in the middle of a wall opposite to the AP is the desirable choice to maximize the received power. Moreover, in [1, 12], multiple IRSs implementations to enable cooperative beamforming to provide larger gain is discussed, but no insight about the placement of multiple IRSs in the network is given, specially in non-cooperative case.

In [6–11, 13], the placement of a single IRS in the network is only studied by assuming that the IRS-UE link is not liable to be blocked and only the AP-UE link is blocked. However, this scenario is not a realistic one, specially in indoor environment, where mmWave and THz paths can be blocked with a probability of occurrence [5, 14, 15] whether they are AP-UE or IRS-UE links. For example, if the probability of blocking occurrence is assumed to be 0.5 in an indoor environment, only $(1–0.5 \times 0.5 = 0.75 \times 100\%)$ 75% of UEs on the average can be served with LOS paths, whether they are actual or virtual, when one IRS aided AP while deploying two IRSs can guarantee LOS path for 87.5% of UEs on the average and so on. Hence, implementing more than one IRS in the network can provide alternative links to UE. In addition, multiple IRSs can guarantee wider coverage of the network with providing larger received power at UEs. Although studies in [1, 12] discussed the scenario of two implemented IRSs, they only considered the case of cooperative beamforming, while the case where each IRS can provide a LOS link to UE in a non-cooperative manner has been neglected.

In this paper, we will consider implementing two IRSs to aid beyond 5G network thus reducing the blockage effect and extending the network coverage. Additionally, the blocking phenomena, which will be considered with different probabilities of occurrence, will be assumed to occur not only in AP-UE link but also in IRS-UE link which is more realistic scenario than considering blockage for an actual LOS link between AP and

UE. Moreover, a search on all suitable positions for locating pairs of IRSs is performed to find their optimal placement in the network. This search will aim to maximize the average received power overall possible UE positions within the study area. The study in this paper proves the superior performance of using more than one IRS in the network specially with high blockage probability. In addition, the optimal placement of two IRSs is studied under different cases of link blockage.

The reminder of this work is organized as following: Sect. 2 describes the system model of IRS aided mmWave for beyond 5G network. In Sect. 3, we discuss the blockage effect on IRS-UE link which requires implementation of multiple IRSs in the network to handle this effect instead of using one single IRS. Section 4 discuss the optimal placement of two IRSs to extend the coverage of the network with and without blockage then shows the performance of the network in different scenarios. Finally, we summarize this work in Sect. 5.

2 System Model

The system model of IRS assisted mmWave network is described in Fig. 1, where the AP and RIS can be placed in any position in an indoor area, e.g., small room with dimensions. The AP is hanged by the room ceil while the IRS can be placed on the wall because of its flat surface. The red beam refers to the direct AP-UE link while the blue beam indicates to the reflected beam by IRS, i.e., AP-IRS-UE link. Here, we present the blockage caused by a human body, either static or dynamic, as well as blocking due to obstacles is considered in our study. The configuration of IRS is presented in Fig. 2, where the IRS is centered in the origin of coordinates system and IRS elements are represented as a green-colored rectangular shapes, which are distributed along x and y directions. The distance between AP and IRS center is d_{AP} while the elevation and azimuth angles seen by IRS are θ_{AP} and φ_{AP}, respectively. The RIS reflects the incident beam comes from AP to the direction of UE by adjusting the phases of RIS elements. The distance between UE and IRS center is d_{UE} while the elevation and azimuth angles seen by IRS are θ_{UE} and φ_{UE}, respectively.

The received power P_r at UE position w, can be expressed as [7]:

$$P_r = A_r S_r \tag{1}$$

where A_r is UE effective aperture and presented as [7]:

$$A_r = \frac{G_r \lambda^2}{4\pi} \tag{2}$$

where G_r indicates to UE antenna gain and λ is the wavelength of free space. While, S_r is the power density at UE whether it is direct AP-UE link density S_r^{AP-UE} or reflected AP-IRS-UE link density $S_r^{AP-IRS-UE}$ which can be expressed as [16]:

$$S_r^{AP-UE} = \frac{2P_t G_t}{8\pi D^2} \tag{3}$$

$$S_r^{AP-IRS-UE} = \frac{\frac{2P_t}{\lambda Z_R}|R|^2}{\sqrt{\left(1 + \frac{d_{UE}^2}{Z_R^2}\right)\left(1 + \frac{d_{UE}^2}{Z_R^2 \cos^4 \theta_{UE}}\right)}} \tag{4}$$

where P_t is the AP transmitted power, G_t indicates to AP antenna gain and D is the distance between AP and UE. Here, $|R|$ refers to the common reflection amplitude of all elements of IRS while Z_R is the Rayleigh length and can be written as:

$$Z_R = \frac{4k_o d_{AP}^2}{G_t} \tag{5}$$

where k_o is the free space wavenumber and G_t indicates to the antenna gain of AP.

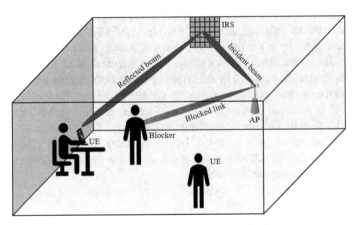

Fig. 1. IRS aided mmWave communication.

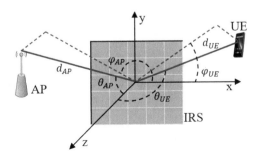

Fig. 2. The configuration of intelligent reflecting surface.

3   Implementing Multiple IRSs to Reduce Blockage Probability

MmWave blockage happens when an obstacle or a human body is located within the direct AP-UE link or reflected AP-IRS-UE link. In case of AP-UE link is in LOS, AP uses this link to establish a connection between AP and UE, while if it is blocked AP will depend on the reflected link between first IRS and UE; if this link is also blocked, the second reflected link between second IRS and UE is used. In case when all links are susceptible to blockage, we assume UE connects with AP using non line of sight link though received power from this link is too small. Let us assume that E_B is the event that the link from UE to AP or IRS is blocked. Hence, the probability that AP-UE or IRS-UE link to be blocked, $P(E_B/d)$, can be written as:

$$P(E_B/d) = 1 - exp\left(-\lambda_B d \frac{h_B}{h}\right) \tag{6}$$

where λ_B is a constant, d is the distance from user to AP or IRS, h_B is the height of blocker and h is the height of AP or IRS. The occurrence of blockage between UE and AP or IRSs is independent, i.e., blockage occurs to one link without effecting on the occurrence of blockage to other links, hence the probability of blockage occurrence to LOS link, whether actual or virtual, in a network with 2 IRS aided AP will be:

$$P_B = P(E_B/d_{AP-UE})P(E_B/d_{IRS_1-UE})P(E_B/d_{IRS_2-UE}) \tag{7}$$

This probability will decrease when the number of deployed IRSs in the network is increasing at the expense of increasing the complexity of the system.

Figure 3 shows CDF of the received power at UE if the AP-UE link is totally blocked, i.e., with blocking probability equals to 1, in case of implementing one IRS and two IRS in the network. This result is obtained assuming blockage probability equals to 0.5 and IRSs are deployed in the middle of the wall following the setup described in [7]. The case in which two IRS are used outperforms the previous one as alternative links will be available to UE if the link between AP, first IRS and UE is blocked. For example, using 2 IRS guarantees $P_r > -15$ dBm to all UEs in the area while one IRS can provide 87.5% of UEs with received power larger than -15 dBm. Overall, two IRSs can provide UEs with larger received power comparable to the case with one IRS.

4   Optimal Placement of Two IRSs

In this section, we will study the optimal placement of more than one IRS in the network. The aim of implementing multiple IRSs is to increase the coverage of beyond 5G network, hence IRSs placement should consider providing a suitable average received power to all UEs in the area. To do this, we will search on all available space to implement the two IRSs in position that maximizes average received power within the area A, where UEs are assumed to be in any position within the room. We assume indoor environment with dimension $5 \times 5 \times 3 \, m^3$, an AP with a 150 GHz central frequency is implemented at the center of the room, while IRSs can be placed anywhere in the top wall at height of 3 m. We discretized the wall with a step of 0.1 m and deploy the pairs of IRSs

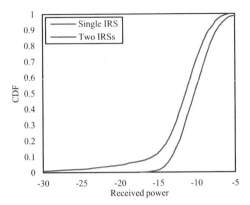

Fig. 3. CDF of received power at all UEs if implementing one IRSs versus two IRSs.

in all possible positions and calculate the average received power of all possible UEs locations. Simulation parameters are summarized in Table. 1. The analysis is performed with 100,000 Monte Carlo trials to handle blockage probability and all possible positions of UEs. First, we assume only AP-UE link can be blocked to find the optimal positions of the two IRSs. Then, the blockage is assumed for all links when we study the performance of the network. We compare our results with a reference work presented in [7].

Table 1. Simulation parameters.

Parameter	Value
AP transmitted power, P_t	1 W
AP transmitted antenna gain, G_t	45 dBm
UE received antenna gain, G_r	20 dBm
Height of AP, IRSs, UEs	3 m, 3 m, 1 m
Probability of blockage occurrence	0.3, 0.5, 0.7
Operating frequency	150 GHz
Common reflection amplitude, $|R|$	0.9

Figure 4. a. and b. show the received power at all UE positions in case of the implementation of IRSs based on the scheme proposed in [7] that depends on maximizing the minimum received power at UE and our proposal, i.e., maximizing average received power obtained by all UEs, respectively. Also, Fig. 5. Presents the CDF of the received power for the two proposals. The reference proposal selected the middle of the wall for deploying the two RISs. On contrast, our proposed scheme will place the two IRSs in the positions that extends the coverage of the network. Hence, it guarantees more alternative paths to UE if main link is blocked, and better average received power to all UEs network. The optimal placement of the two IRSs pairs is in locations (0, 3.75) and (5, 1.25), which indicated with the largest received power in Fig. 4. b. Of course, the IRSs

can be placed on the other two walls, but we show only this option as an example. The proposed scheme can guarantee $P_r > 5$ dBm to 56% of UEs while reference work in [7] can guarantee this for only 40% of UEs. Moreover, the proposed method outperforms the reference one for almost all possible UEs positions in the area.

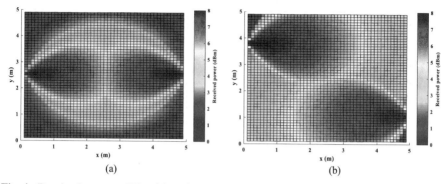

Fig. 4. Received power at UEs with optimal IRSs placement: (a) using reference [7] method, (b) based on proposed method, considering no blockage to IRS-UE link.

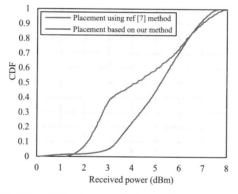

Fig. 5. CDF of P_r at UEs with considering no blockage to IRS-UE link.

In Fig. 6. a. and b., the P_r of all possible UEs positions by IRSs in the network is presented if reference method or our method are, respectively, used for deploying IRSs. While Fig. 7. Shows the CDF of these received power. In this scenario, we assume AP-UE link is fully blocked while IRSs-UEs links are blocked with probability of occurrence equals to 0.5. These figures clarify the effect of blockage on virtual LOS links between IRSs and UEs where blocking highly attenuates the signal power of reflected beam from IRS. For example, comparable to the scenario whose results are represented in Fig. 4 and 5., the received power is decreased with nearly 15 dBm for all possible positions. Moreover, blockage determines large variations of the distribution of P_r, which increases the importance of optimal placement of two IRSs to extend coverage. Hence, blockage on both AP-UE and IRS-UE link should be considered when studying the performance of IRSs aided beyond 5G network. Also, the proposed method guarantees $P_r > -10$ dBm to 58% of UEs while comparable method guarantees this to only 42% of UEs.

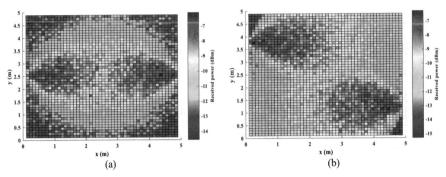

Fig. 6. Received power at UEs with optimal IRSs placement: (a) using reference [7] method, (b) based on proposed method, considering blockage probability equals 0.5 to IRS-UE link.

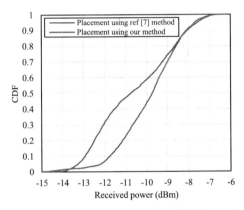

Fig. 7. CDF of P_r at UEs with considering blockage probability equals 0.5 to IRS-UE link.

In Fig. 8, the CDF of overall network performance in terms of P_r at UEs is presented, for different probability of blockage occurrence and in two scenarios where one IRS is deployed, and when we place two IRSs in the network using our method. It's clear that the network with two IRSs outperforms the overall performance of network with single IRS specially when the blockage increases. For instance, the difference of average received power between the two cases is 1.8 dBm when blockage probability is 0.3 while increasing blockage to 0.5 and 0.7, rises the difference to 3 dBm and 3.5 dBm, respectively. In addition, implementing two IRSs guarantees larger received power for all UEs comparable to network with single IRS scenario. For example, optimal deploying for two IRSs provides 90% of UEs with received power larger than 9.5 dBm, 6 dBm and 0 dBm for blockage probability equals to 0.3, 0.5 and 0.7, respectively. On contrast, deploying single IRS can provide the same percentage of UEs with only 8 dBm, 3.5 dBm and -3.2 dBm for blockage probability equals to 0.3, 0.5 and 0.7, respectively.

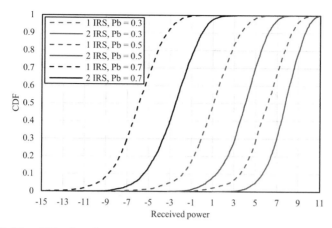

Fig. 8. CDF of P_r at UEs when single versus two IRSs is deployed in the network with considering different blockage probabilities to IRS-UE link.

5   Conclusion

In this paper, we proved the superiority of deploying multiple IRSs in the network to reduce the blockage probability and extend the coverage comparable to deploy a single IRS. Also, we considered blockage occurrence to both AP-UE and IRS-UE links which is more realistic scenario. Moreover, the optimal placement of the two IRSs is discussed, and an optimization problem based on maximizing average received power overall UEs within study area is proposed. This method can guarantee larger received power at almost all UEs comparable to the method based on maximizing the minimum received power at UEs where IRSs are placed in the middle of the wall opposite to transmitted AP. For instance, our proposal provides nearly 56% of UEs with $P_r > 5$ dBm and $P_r > -10$ dBm in case of blockage occurrence probability equals 0 and 0.5, respectively. On contrast, the reference method provides these power levels to only 42% of UEs. In addition, we study the performance of the network with one and two IRSs with different blockage probabilities cases and found that the proposed method can guarantee $P_r > 6$ dBm for 90% of UEs while network with single IRS can provide $P_r > 3.5$ dBm for the same percent of UEs in case the blockage probability is 0.5. In future, authors can study the scenario where other multi APs, whether homogenous or non-homogenous, exist in the environment. Also, optimal placement of multiple IRSs aided multi input multi output (MIMO) AP seems to be a promising direction.

Acknowledgment. This study has been conducted under the project 'MObility and Training fOR beyond 5G ecosystems (MOTOR5G)'. The project has received funding from the European Union's Horizon 2020 programme under the Marie Skłodowska Curie Actions (MSCA) Innovative Training Network (ITN) under grant agreement No. 861219.

References

1. Wu, Q., Zhang, S., Zheng, B., You, C., Zhang, R.: Intelligent reflecting sur-face-aided wireless communications: a tutorial. IEEE Trans. Commun. **69** (2021). https://doi.org/10.1109/TCOMM.2021.3051897
2. Nor, A.M., Mohamed, E.M.: Li-Fi positioning for efficient millimeter wave beamforming training in indoor environment. Mob. Netw. Appl. **24**(2), 517–531 (2018). https://doi.org/10.1007/s11036-018-1154-4
3. Nor, A.M., Mohamed, E.M.: Millimeter wave beamforming training based on Li-Fi localization in indoor environment. In: 2017 IEEE Global Communications Conference, GLOBECOM 2017 - Proceedings (2017)
4. Nor, A.M.: Access point selection in beyond 5G hybrid MmWave/Wi-Fi/Li-Fi network. Phys. Commun. **46** (2021). https://doi.org/10.1016/j.phycom.2021.101299
5. Gapeyenko, M., et al.: Analysis of human-body blockage in urban millimeter-wave cellular communications. In: 2016 IEEE International Conference on Communications (ICC), IEEE (2016)
6. Zeng, S., Zhang, H., Di, B., Han, Z., Song, L.: Reconfigurable intelligent sur-face (RIS) assisted wireless coverage extension: RIS orientation and location optimization. IEEE Commun. Lett. **25** (2021). https://doi.org/10.1109/LCOMM.2020.3025345
7. Stratidakis, G., Droulias, S., Alexiou, A.: An analytical framework for recon-figurable intelligent surfaces placement in a mobile user environment. In: Proceedings of the 19th ACM Conference on Embedded Networked Sensor Systems, ACM, New York (2021)
8. Ntontin, K., Boulogeorgos, A.-A.A., Selimis, D.G., Lazarakis, F.I., Alexiou, A., Chatzinotas, S.: Reconfigurable intelligent surface optimal placement in millimeter-wave networks. IEEE Open J. Commun. Soc. **2** (2021). https://doi.org/10.1109/ojcoms.2021.3068790
9. Ghatak, G.: On the placement of intelligent surfaces for RSSI-based rang-ing in mm-Wave Networks. IEEE Commun. Lett. **25** (2021). https://doi.org/10.1109/LCOMM.2021.3063918
10. Hashida, H., Kawamoto, Y., Kato, N.: Intelligent reflecting surface placement optimization in air-ground communication networks toward 6G. IEEE Wirel. Commun. (2020). https://doi.org/10.1109/MWC.001.2000142
11. Mu, X., Liu, Y., Guo, L., Lin, J., Schober, R.: Joint deployment and multiple access design for intelligent reflecting surface assisted networks. IEEE Trans. Wirel. Commun. **20** (2021). https://doi.org/10.1109/TWC.2021.3075885
12. Han, Y., Zhang, S., Duan, L., Zhang, R.: Cooperative double-iRS aided communication: beamforming design and power scaling. IEEE Wirel. Commun. Lett. **9** (2020). https://doi.org/10.1109/LWC.2020.2986290
13. Lu, H., Zeng, Y., Jin, S., Zhang, R.: Enabling panoramic full-angle reflection via aerial intelligent reflecting surface. In: 2020 IEEE International Conference on Communications Workshops, ICC Workshops 2020 - Proceedings (2020)
14. Rappaport, T.S., Xing, Y., MacCartney, G.R., Molisch, A.F., Mellios, E., Zhang, J.: Overview of millimeter wave communications for fifth-generation (5G) wireless networks-with a focus on propagation models (2017)
15. Nor, A.M., Esmaiel, H., Omer, O.A.: Performance evaluation of proportional fairness scheduling in MmWave network. In: 2019 International Conference on Computer and Information Sciences, ICCIS 2019 (2019)
16. Stratidakis, G., Droulias, S., Alexiou, A.: Analytical performance assessment of beamforming efficiency in reconfigurable intelligent surface-aided links. IEEE Access (2021). https://doi.org/10.1109/ACCESS.2021.3105477

An Auction-Based Mechanism for Task Offloading in a Secure Fog-Cloud Environment

Branka Mikavica$^{(\boxtimes)}$ ⓘ and Aleksandra Kostić-Ljubisavljević ⓘ

Faculty of Transport and Traffic Engineering, University of Belgrade, Belgrade, Serbia
b.mikavica@sf.bg.ac.rs

Abstract. With the rapid growth of terminal devices, fog-cloud systems become promising for solving delays and congestions in task provisioning. When the fog computing resources are insufficient, task offloading to the remote cloud can be performed to improve performances. Auctions are considered as a convenient tool to provide incentives for task offloading, and efficiently allocate resources in the fog-cloud environment. However, due to virtualization, the cloud segment in the fog-cloud system is prone to malicious attacks. Security requirements are often in contrast with performance requirements since the operation of security mechanisms consumes a part of computation capacities. Therefore, a comprehensive study is needed to address resource allocation with a security assessment. In this paper, we propose a novel simulation model for resource allocation in the hierarchical fog-cloud system with task offloading. To improve the experience and prevent performance deterioration, we introduce task differentiation into delay-sensitive and delay-tolerant tasks. Resource allocation of the fog and the cloud layer is based on the truthful double auction. A Vicrey-Clarke-Grove (VCG) driven resource allocation is established for winner determination. The proposed simulation model is used to analyze utility functions in the observed fog-cloud environment depending on the offered security level.

Keywords: Fog-cloud environment · Auction-based offloading · Security

1 Introduction

The number of Internet of Things (IoT) entities and IoT related services shows ever-increasing expansion [1]. These devices generate enormous data that need to be processed. The majority of IoT entities have limited computation and storage capacities. Hence, submitted tasks are sent to remote cloud data centers for processing and analysis. However, numerous tasks running on the cloud have specific deadlines. Furthermore, the networks' bandwidth is limited, thus posing an additional challenge for delay-sensitive and context-aware IoT applications [2]. To overcome these issues, computation offloading can be applied. Tasks from IoT entities are first sent to fog nodes, instead of being submitted directly to the cloud data center. The fog node executes the submitted task if there are sufficient computing resources. Otherwise, the task will be offloaded to the remote cloud. Introduction of fog provides timely-response service with local awareness

© ICST Institute for Computer Sciences, Social Informatics and Telecommunications Engineering 2022
Published by Springer Nature Switzerland AG 2022. All Rights Reserved
D. Perakovic and L. Knapcikova (Eds.): FABULOUS 2022, LNICST 445, pp. 47–63, 2022.
https://doi.org/10.1007/978-3-031-15101-9_4

and supports mobility and wireless access. The offloading problem can be analyzed at three levels, including the IoT entities layer, the fog layer, and the cloud layer. The aim of offloading is to optimize operations so that total costs are reduced [3]. In general, offloading depends not only on the single entity decision but also on the interactions of other entities. It is considered that fog nodes are reluctant to offload tasks to cloud nodes, thus deteriorating network performances. To solve this issue, fog nodes should be motivated to participate in offloading operations.

Due to virtualization, the security of a cloud segment in the fog-cloud system is an important issue to be addressed. In general, cloud resources are organized as pre-configured Virtual Machines (VMs), individually accessible over the Internet. The majority of cloud-specific attacks occur via compromised VM. There are numerous types of VM-based attacks with different effects on the VM under attack [4]. Delays and failures in task provisioning are possible. Depending on the attacks' severity, the number of available VMs can be reduced. Implementation of a security mechanism may be a promising solution to alleviate the performances degradation. However, security mechanisms consume some computation resources and sometimes may extend the processing time. Therefore, an appropriate security evaluation is needed to support efficient resource allocation.

Auction-based mechanisms are often recommended as a promising solution to improve efficiency and support fair distribution in various edge-computing domains, including mobile-edge computing, content delivery networks, fog computing, and cloud computing [5–8]. In an auction process, there are three essential participants: buyer, seller, and auctioneer. The buyer aims at acquiring resources with minimum expenses. The seller offers its resources with the main goal to maximize revenues by selling resources to buyers that value them the most. The auctioneer acts as an intermediate agent that determines the winners. There are numerous types of auction mechanisms [9], including English auction, Dutch auction, Vickrey auction and its modification to Vicrey-Clarke-Grove (VCG) auction, combinatorial, double, etc. It is considered that double auctions can efficiently balance buyers' and sellers' benefits. During a double auction process, buyers place bids (buyers' willingness to pay), while sellers place asks (the required price). If the bids are greater than or equal to the ask, an auctioneer settles the hammer price, and the process terminates. Auctions are also proposed as an efficient tool to provide incentives for offloading in a fog-cloud environment [3].

The main contributions of this paper are the following: (i) we formulate the system model that comprises an IoT layer, a fog layer, and a cloud layer; to allocate resources in both fog and cloud layer, double auction-based mechanisms are performed in the two stages: between IoT layer and fog layer (I stage), and between fog layer and cloud layer (II stage); (ii) we set truthful VCG-based double auctions that satisfy individual rationality and provide incentives for task offloading; (iii) to improve experience and resource utilization in task provisioning on the fog layer, we distinguish delay-sensitive and delay-tolerant tasks; the highest priority in task provisioning on fog layer is assigned to delay-sensitive tasks, thus preventing performance degradation; (iv) a VM security modeling on the cloud layer in introduces, with the malicious VM-based attack and the complexity of the security mechanism as critical factors affecting the VMs availability.

The remainder of the paper is organized as follows. Section 2 reviews related works on the problems of auction-based offloading optimization and resource allocation in a fog-cloud environment. The system model and problem formulation comprising cloud layer security modeling, establishing double VCG-based auction-mechanisms between the layers, and the utility functions formulations are presented in Sect. 3. In Sect. 4, we present performance evaluation and discuss simulation results. Finally, Sect. 5 provides concluding remarks and future research directions.

2 Related Work

Auction-based resource allocation in a fog environment is addressed in various studies. In [10], a decentralized auction-based fog node allocation that improves the utilization of fog resources is proposed. The major advantage of the proposed model is that allows fog resource providers to participate in more than one auction simultaneously. Moreover, the model reduces the number of exchanged messages and represents an application of 5G due to decentralization and requirements in terms of bandwidth. In [11], the authors propose two types of truthful mechanisms for resource allocation and pricing in a fog environment, Fixed Price based Fog Node Allocation Mechanism, and Combinatorial Auction based Fog Service Allocation Mechanism. It shows that a combinatorial auction-based mechanism can improve resource allocation with high proficiency and higher revenues for fog providers. A dynamic resource allocation model based on the overbooking mechanism is proposed in [12]. The model considers the Quality of Service (QoS) requirements and provides individual rationality, computation efficiency, and truthfulness. The results show that the auction achieves the preferred properties, and the given resource allocation maximizes the profit of nodes with a high degree of QoS satisfaction.

Cloud resource allocation and pricing strategies using auction-based mechanisms are widely studied in the literature. In [13], a comprehensive survey on auction-based mechanisms in a cloud environment is provided. VCG auction mechanism is very often used since it provides a socially optimal solution [14]. Relations between security and cloud resource allocation are analyzed in [15, 16]. An auction-based mechanism that provides incentives for customers to reveal their actual requests and security valuations is proposed in [15]. The mechanism applies a greedy allocation rule, where customers are prioritized depending on their valuation of the security. The results show acceptable performance compared to the offline VCG-based auction mechanism. A truthful VCG-based auction mechanism addressing revenues, security, and energy consumption in a cloud environment is proposed in [4]. The VMs security model is proposed to assess the security level of VMs. The simulation results show that investment in security increases revenues and reduces rejection rate, but concurrently, increases energy consumption and the provider's lost revenue.

Numerous studies addressed the problem of offloading in fog computing. Comprehensive surveys on fog-cloud offloading are provided by [17, 18]. Auction mechanisms are often used to provide incentives for participants in the fog-cloud system to offload tasks. Thus, an incentive-compatible offloading mechanism in a fog-cloud environment can be performed by using a second-price sealed-bid auction [3]. The proposed system considers fog nodes and cloud data centers as bidders and auctioneers, respectively. The observed auction mechanism provides incentive compatibility and individual rationality. The problem is formulated using the queuing theory in both the edge layer and the cloud layer. The results show that the method proposed in [3] outperforms other state-of-the-art methods in terms of execution time, energy consumption, and network usage.

An ascending-bid auction mechanism is proposed in [9] to relieve the strict requirements of cloud computing on delays, congestion and energy consumption. The fog network is divided into several clusters. In each cluster, a fog controller acts as an auctioneer and schedules the idle fog nodes for task provisioning. The proposed model guarantees the QoS requirements of task nodes. The fog controller takes the reward prices as their strategy, while the fog nodes take task sizes as their strategies. The utility function on the fog nodes is proposed, with the analysis of the cost of task computation delay and energy consumption. The results show satisfactory performance and a win-win solution under the condition of meeting the QoS.

An auction-based optimization method for modeling the offloading interactions in a fog-cloud environment is proposed in [19]. The interactions between fog nodes and the cloud entities are modelled with consideration of the specifications and limitations of the underlying physical infrastructure, with the bandwidth as a commodity.

A multi-attribute combinatorial reverse auction-based model for resource allocation in a system that includes customer, auctioneer, fog provider, cloud provider, and fog & cloud provider together as auction participants, is proposed in [20]. The model distinguishes three types of resources, local fog, remote fog, and cloud. The proposed auction model is a truthful, robust, and fair allocation method that considers response time, data source mobility requirements, and fog resource limitations. To support truthful bidding, the Vicrey model is extended.

In this paper, the proposed simulation model analyzes resource allocation, security, and task offloading in the fog-cloud environment. To the best of our knowledge, this is the first paper addressing the following issues jointly: (i) truthful double auctioning between all participants in the fog-cloud system; (ii) cloud layer security modeling, where the complexity of the security mechanism and malicious attacks are used to assess the security level in various scenarios; (iii) introducing prioritization in the offloading task process to the remote cloud.

3   System Model and Problem Formulation

As shown in Fig. 1, the hierarchical architecture of the proposed system comprises three layers: the IoT entities layer, the fog layer, and the cloud layer.

The IoT entities include mobile devices, sensors, or end devices that require computation resources to run their heavy computation tasks.

The fog layer contains fog nodes. In general, fog nodes can be categorized as Fog Computational Nodes (FCNs) and Fog Broker Nodes (FBNs). FCNs provide the computation resource to run tasks of IoT entities. Compared to IoT entities, these nodes have some moderate computation and storage capabilities. FBNs act as mediators between FCNs and IoT entities [10]. It is assumed that the fog layer provides the highest level of security.

The cloud layer comprises cloud resources and Cloud Broker Nodes (CBNs). The resources are organized in the form of pre-configured virtual machines (VMs). VMs are individually accessible over the network. Hence, they are vulnerable to malicious attacks. Attacks may cause delays and failure in tasks' provisioning, or reduce the number of available VMs, thus deteriorating performances. These effects may be alleviated by the implementation of security mechanisms. Depending on the security level provided, in this paper, we divide all VMs into several Trust Zones (TZs). The term TZ can be described as a combination of network segmentation and identity access management controls that define physical, logical, or virtual boundaries in network resources [21]. CBNs act as mediators between the fog layer and the cloud layer.

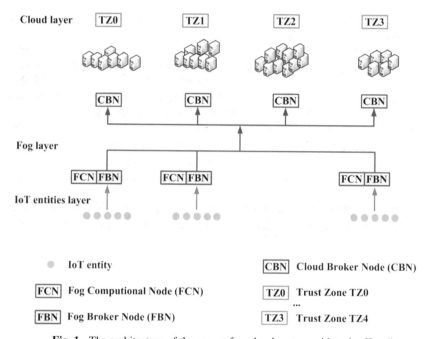

Fig. 1. The architecture of the secure fog-cloud system with task offloading

Resources on the fog and cloud layer are considered as a commodity for a double auction. IoT entities take the role of the bidders for task provisioning to parenting FCN. Each task is characterized depending on requirements in terms of delay and security level. Concurrently, FCNs place asks for fog resources via FBNs. Dedicated FBNs are auctioneers in the auction process. The role of FBNs is to match values of bids and asks, to prioritize the arriving tasks and proceed winning delay-sensitive tasks to FCNs for further processing. If the capacity of the FCN is not exceeded after allocation of the winning delay-sensitive tasks, the FBN can perform a double auction for delay-tolerant tasks and allocate those tasks for provisioning in the fog. The remaining delay-tolerant tasks are offloaded to the remote cloud. It should be emphasized that the fog layer is neutral in offloading since the offloading costs are considered while delegating tasks for offloading. Depending on the required security level, tasks are offloaded to the corresponding TZ. CBNs are auctioneers in auction-based task offloading.

3.1 Security Modeling in the Cloud Layer

Similar to [22], the term intensity will be used to describe the algorithm complexity or security level of the implemented security mechanism. TZs facilitate the management and tasks' processing in the cloud layer. An example of cloud network segmentation in TZs is shown in [4]. Similar security interpretation applies in Amazon Web Virtual Private Clouds (Amazon VPC) [23]. The security of a TZ is built upon an adequate configuration of domain controllers, firewalls, switches and routers, thus supporting segmentation and protecting access to cloud resources. Within a TZ, all VMs apply the unitive security mechanism with the same intensity. Thus, the TZ depicts a certain security level.

In this paper, we assume that all VMs are of the same computation and storage capabilities. The analysis is performed in N consecutive time slots. There are three assumed intensities for the corresponding security mechanism: high, middle and low. Higher intensity of the security mechanism implies higher complexity of the implemented algorithm, and consequently, higher security level. Four TZs can be distinguished depending on the provided security level, namely, TZ0, TZ1, TZ2 and TZ3. TZ0 provides the highest security level and all VMs in this TZ apply the security mechanism with high intensity. Accordingly, VMs in TZ1 and TZ2 use the security mechanism with medium and low intensity, respectively. TZ3 does not provide guarantees in terms of security, since VMs in this TZ do not apply a security mechanism.

It is considered that most attacks are unorganized, spontaneous, with a random arrival rate [22]. In this paper, the probability that a VM is threatened by a malicious attack is denoted by $p_a \in (0, 1)$. The probability that a VM remains available under an attack is denoted by $\beta_j \in (0, 1)$, where $j \in \{0, 1, 2, 3\}$ denotes the corresponding TZ. There are m_j available VMs in TZ j at the beginning of each time slot. It applies, $\beta_0 > \beta_1 > \beta_2 > \beta_3$, i.e., lower security level causes higher probability of a successful attack on a VM.

3.2 Auction Mechanisms

The dynamic resource allocation and pricing in the analyzed fog-cloud environment is performed using a two-stage VCG-based double auction mechanism. Thus, the double auction mechanisms are established between the IoT entities layer and the fog layer, and between the fog layer and the cloud layer.

VCG-Based Double Auction – I Stage. We assume there are F fog nodes with the role of the FCN. A FBN is assigned to each FCN in this architecture. The average number of IoT entities connecting to its parenting FCN is denoted by E. The number of active IoT entities generating request in time slot $i \in [1, N]$ for task execution on the FCN $f \in [1, F]$ is denoted by $E_{i,f}$. Furthermore, we assume that the arrival rate of requests for task execution follows a Poisson distribution with the average input rate λ [3].

All requests generated by IoT entities are computationally independent. To initiate task execution, an IoT entity creates and submits a bid to the FBN. We assume that each active IoT entity in a given time slot generates a single request for task execution, and each task can be executed within a single time slot. Each request that an active IoT entity generates in a given time slot i, $e_{i,f} \in [1, E_{i,f}]$ can be described as the following tuple:

$$e_{i,f} = \left(\tau_{e_{i,f}}, \psi_{e_{i,f}}, \theta_{e_{i,f}}, \upsilon_{e_{i,f}} \right) \tag{1}$$

The parameter $\tau_{e_{i,f}}$ in (1) is introduced to classify the task in terms of sensitivity to delays. Thus, $\tau_{e_{i,f}} = 0$ if the task can be classified as delay-sensitive. These tasks have the priority in the execution queue, so FCN primarily allocates its resources for their execution. If the task is delay-tolerant, it applies $\tau_{e_{i,f}} = 1$. Delay-tolerant tasks are executed on FCN if there are enough computing resources on the FCN. Otherwise, these tasks are offloaded to the cloud. The probability that task is delay-sensitive is denoted by ρ_s, while the probability that task is delay-tolerant is denoted by $\rho_t = 1 - \rho_s$.

To indicate preferred security level for task execution, the parameter $\psi_{e_{i,f}}$ is used in (1). Since the fog layer provides the highest security level, as indicated previously, it applies $\psi_{e_{i,f}} = 0$, if the task is delay-sensitive, i.e., $\tau_{e_{i,f}} = 0$, or the task is delay-tolerant, i.e., $\tau_{e_{i,f}} = 1$, but intended for execution on FCN f. If the task is delay-tolerant, and it is offloaded to the cloud, $\psi_{e_{i,f}}$ corresponds to the preferred TZ. Thus, for offloaded tasks it applies $\psi_{e_{i,f}} = j \in \{0, 1, 2, 3\}$. The probability that task will choose a certain security level for task provisioning is denoted by π_j, and it applies $\sum_j \pi_j = 1$.

The parameter $\theta_{e_{i,f}}$ in (1) is used to denote the resources that task $e_{i,f}$ occupies. If the task executes on FCN f, $\theta_{e_{i,f}}$ is expressed in capacity units. Here, the term capacity unit refers to the predefined unit of the computation or storage capacity. Moreover, we assume that each offloaded task requires a single VM for execution. Therefore, in the case of offloading, $\theta_{e_{i,f}} = 1$ VM.

The bid value is a nonnegative value, expressed by the parameter $\upsilon_{e_{i,f}}$ in (1), and represents the true willingness to pay per task for its execution. It should be noted that an IoT entity is not being charged by the bid value, but the value that is less or equal to the bid. The value to be paid is defined in an auction process. Bids are independent, and there is no information on others' bids. The assumed maximum bid value is the on-demand price for the given VM with appropriate security level, i.e., $\upsilon_{e_{i,f}} \in (0, p_{o,j}]$.

At the beginning of each time slot, each FBN defines FCN f asks per capacity unit for task provisioning in current time slot, denoted by $\alpha_{i,f} \in (\alpha_{i,f,\min}, \alpha_{i,f,\max})$. Minimum ask represents the FCN f'cost per capacity unit for task provisioning. To prevent FCN f from posing to high asks per capacity unit, the maximum ask is limited to the $\alpha_{i,f,\max}$.

Once the bids are submitted by all active IoT entities, FBNs collect those bids and determine the set of winning bids for corresponding FCNs. At first, a FBN creates separate queues for delay-sensitive and delay-tolerant tasks for its dedicated FCN. Delay-sensitive tasks are of the highest priority and are intended for processing in the fog layer. To determine candidates for the set of winning delay-sensitive tasks, each FBN calculates the value of the unit bid for each task, i.e., the bid value per capacity unit of the FCN:

$$v_{e_{i,f}} = \frac{\upsilon_{e_{i,f}}}{\theta_{e_{i,f}}} \tag{2}$$

The candidates for the winning set are the tasks with unit bid is greater than or equal to the FCN f ask, i.e., the candidate is each task $e_{i,f}$ if it applies $v_{e_{i,f}} \geq \alpha_{i,f}$. Afterwards, the candidate tasks are sorted in the non-increasing order by the values of the unit bids. Tasks from the sorted set of candidate tasks are added to the winning set of tasks until there is enough capacity for task provisioning. The winning set of delay-sensitive tasks for the FCN f in the time slot i is denoted by $W_{i,f}^S$. Therefore, each winning delay-sensitive task

$\omega_{i,f}^S \in W_{i,f}^S$ satisfies the following:

$$\omega_{i,f,l}^S \geq \omega_{i,f,l+1}^S, \quad v_{\omega_{i,f,l}^S} \geq \alpha_{i,f}, \quad \sum \theta_{\omega_{i,f,l}^S} \leq Q \tag{3}$$

In (3), l denotes the position of the winning task in the $W_{i,f}^S$, and Q denotes the capacity of the FCN expressed in capacity units.

The price to be paid per task provisioning is determined using the VCG-based double auction. Each winning delay-sensitive task is charged depending on the unit bid value of the next winning task in the ordered set $W_{i,f}^S$ and the required resources. Thus, the price for each winning task in the $W_{i,f}^S$ can be expressed as:

$$P_{\omega_{i,f,l}^S} = \begin{cases} v_{\omega_{i,f,l+1}^S} \cdot \theta_{\omega_{i,f,l}^S}, & if \ \exists \omega_{i,f,l+1}^S \\ v_{\omega_{i,f,l}^S} \cdot \theta_{\omega_{i,f,l}^S}, & otherwise \end{cases} \tag{4}$$

As shown in (4), the price per task execution is always less than or equal to the value of the bid for the given task.

If the capacity of the FCN f is not exceeded by provisioning of delay-sensitive tasks, $\sum \theta_{\omega_{i,f,l}^S} \leq Q$, the dedicated FBN analyses the queue of the delay-tolerant tasks. To determine candidates for the set of winning delay-tolerant tasks that will be provisioned by FCN f, the FBN determines the unit bid per each delay-tolerant task using (2). Similar to the delay-sensitive tasks, the candidates for winning are the tasks with unit bid greater than or equal to the FCN f's ask per capacity unit. Afterwards, the candidate tasks are sorted in the nonincreasing order by the value of the unit bid. Tasks in this sorted list are added to the set of the winning delay-tolerant tasks by the value of the unit bid, from the highest to the lowest, until there are unutilized resources on FCN f available for task provisioning. The set of winning delay-tolerant tasks that are provisioned by FCN f is denoted by $W_{i,f}^T$. For each winning delay-tolerant task $\omega_{i,f}^T \in W_{i,f}^T$ applies:

$$\omega_{i,f,m}^T \geq \omega_{i,f,m+1}^T, \quad v_{\omega_{i,f,m}^T} \geq \alpha_{i,f}, \quad \sum \theta_{\omega_{i,f,m}^T} \leq Q, \tag{5}$$

where m in (5) denotes the position of the winning task in the $W_{i,f}^T$.

Similar to the case with the provisioning of delay-sensitive tasks by FCN f, the price to be paid per task provisioning is determined using the VCG-based auction. Each winning delay-sensitive task is charged depending on the unit bid value of the next winning task in the ordered set $W_{i,f}^T$ and the required resources. Thus, the price for each winning task in the $W_{i,f}^T$ can be expressed as:

$$P_{\omega_{i,f,m}^T} = \begin{cases} v_{\omega_{i,f,m+1}^T} \cdot \theta_{\omega_{i,f,m}^T}, & if \ \exists \omega_{i,f,m+1}^T \\ v_{\omega_{i,f,m}^T} \cdot \theta_{\omega_{i,f,m}^T}, & otherwise \end{cases} \tag{6}$$

If the FCN f's capacity Q is exceeded, the dedicated FBN collects all remaining delay-tolerant tasks, including those with unit bid lower than the FCN f ask, and creates a new queue intended for provisioning in the cloud layer.

VCG-Based Double Auction – II Stage. At the beginning of each time slot, dedicated CBNs determine asks per VM in each TZ j, denoted by $\gamma_{i,j} \in (\gamma_{i,j,\min}, \gamma_{i,j,\max})$. Minimum ask per task provisioning on a VM in the TZ j, $\gamma_{i,j,\min}$, represents the cost for task provisioning. To prevent too high asks, the upper bound for cloud asks is set to be $\gamma_{i,j,\max} = p_{o,j}$. Due to the same computation and storage capabilities, we assume that cloud provider sets the same asks for each VM in the TZ j.

Delay-tolerant task in a queue for offloading to the cloud can be expressed as follows:

$$e_{i,f}^{off} = \left(\psi_{e_{i,f}^{off}}, \upsilon_{e_{i,f}^{off}} \right) \tag{7}$$

In (7), $\psi_{e_{i,f}^{off}}$ denotes the requested security level for task provisioning, i.e., the selected TZ j, and $\upsilon_{e_{i,f}^{off}}$ denotes the bid value. These tasks are sorted in the nonincreasing order, not by the unit bid value, but their actual bid for the given task. The tasks intended for offloading to the cloud are tasks whose bids are greater than or equal to the FCN f's offloading cost per task, i.e., $\upsilon_{e_{i,f}^{off}} \geq \chi_{i,f}$. Thus, the fog layer does not incur losses due to task offloading. Each FBN delegates the tasks to the corresponding CBN, depending on the selected security level. Hence, each CBN generates the queue of the tasks intended for cloud processing on the selected TZ.

The set of candidate tasks comprises all tasks intended for offloading, whose bids are higher than the cloud provider's ask for given TZ, i.e., $\upsilon_{e_{i,f}^{off}} - \chi_{i,f} \geq \gamma_{i,j}$. The winning set for each TZ j, $W_{i,j}$, is defined depending on the length of the corresponding set of the candidate tasks, and the number of the available VMs.

The price to be paid per task provisioned on the cloud VM in the selected TZ is determined using the VCG-based double auction. Each winning task is charged by the value of the next highest bid (if the one exists), or the value of its bid, as long as there are available VMs in the given TZ. Therefore, the price for each winning task in the $W_{i,j}$ provisioned on the VM $k_j \in [1, m_j]$ can be expressed as follows:

$$p_{i,j,k_j} = \begin{cases} \omega_{i,j,k_{j+1}} \cdot \mu_{i,j,k_j}, & \text{if } k_j < |W_{i,j}| \\ \omega_{i,j,k_j} \cdot \mu_{i,j,k_j}, & \text{if } k_j = |W_{i,j}| \\ 0, & \text{otherwise} \end{cases} \tag{8}$$

In (8), we introduce the parameter μ_{i,j,k_j} to indicate VM availability, and it takes the value 0, if the VM k_j is unavailable due to the malicious attack in the current time slot; and the value 1, if the is no malicious attack, or the security mechanism prevented the failure due to the attack.

3.3 Utility Functions

We define utility functions for each layer in the analyzed hierarchical fog-cloud structure. In this paper, the term utility refers to the difference between the ask/bid for task provisioning and the revenue/cost. Due to the settings of the VCG-based double auctions established between the layers, the utility is always a non-negative value.

IoT Layer Utility. The utility function for the IoT layer comprises the utility for all provisioned delay-sensitive tasks on FCNs, the utility for all provisioned delay-tolerant tasks on FCNs, and the utility for tasks offloaded to the cloud:

$$U_{IoT} = U_{IoT}^S + U_{IoT}^T + U_{IoT}^{off} \tag{9}$$

The utility for provisioning of delay-sensitive tasks can be expressed as follows:

$$U_{IoT}^S = \sum_i \sum_f \sum_l \omega_{i,f,l}^S - P_{\omega_{i,f,l}^S} \tag{10}$$

The utility for provisioning delay-tolerant tasks by FCNs can be expressed as:

$$U_{IoT}^T = \sum_i \sum_f \sum_m \omega_{i,f,m}^T - P_{\omega_{i,f,m}^T} \tag{11}$$

The utility for tasks offloaded to the cloud can be expressed as follows:

$$U_{IoT}^{off} = \sum_i \sum_j \sum_{k_j} \gamma_{i,j} - p_{i,j,k_j} \tag{12}$$

Fog Layer Utility. The utility for the fog layer comprises utility for all delay-sensitive and delay-tolerant tasks provisioned by FCNs, as indicated by (13). It should be noted that the fog layer does not incur costs for tasks offloading to the cloud and obtains zero utility for offloading. Therefore, it is not included in the fog layer utility function.

$$U_{FOG} = U_{FOG}^S + U_{FOG}^T \tag{13}$$

The utility for provisioning delay-sensitive tasks by FCNs can be expressed as:

$$U_{FOG}^S = \sum_i \sum_f \sum_l \alpha_{i,f} - P_{\omega_{i,f,l}^S} \tag{14}$$

Accordingly, the utility for provisioning delay-tolerant tasks can be expressed as:

$$U_{FOG}^T = \sum_i \sum_f \sum_m \omega_{i,f,m}^T - P_{\omega_{i,f,m}^T} \tag{15}$$

Cloud Layer Utility. The utility for the cloud layer comprises utilities for tasks provisioned by VMs in each TZ, as indicated by (16). Compared to task provisioning on the fog layer, where the highest security level is provided, the cloud layer is exposed to potential malicious attacks, thus affecting the overall utility.

$$U_{Cloud} = \sum_i \sum_j \sum_{k_j} \gamma_{i,j} - p_{i,j,k_j} \tag{16}$$

4   Performance Evaluation

To analyze the proposed system model, we conducted a set of simulation experiments in the open-source programming language Python 3.7 in 100 iterations.

4.1 Simulation Setup

To investigate the utilities off all layers in the proposed VCG-based double auctions, and the effects of the cloud layer security, we set several scenarios. The analysis is performed in $N = 24$ time slots of one-hour duration. The number of fog nodes with the role of FCNs takes values from the set (25, 50, 75, 100). Since each FCN has a dedicated FBN, it applies the same number of FBNs. The average number of IoT entities connecting to its parenting FCN takes values from the set (10, 20, 30, 40, 50). There are 1200 available VMs available at the beginning of each time slot.

IoT Layer Setup. The number of active IoT entities initiating requests for tasks provisioning in each time slot is modeled by the Poisson distribution, with the average input rate $\lambda = 2$. The classification into delay-sensitive and delay-tolerant tasks is performed by the probability $\rho_s = \rho_t = 0.5$. The preferred security level is selected with the probability $\pi_j = 0.25$. The required FCN's resources per task are set randomly from the set (1 cu, 20 cu), where cu refers to the capacity unit. The bid value is also assigned randomly, with upper bound defined as the price for the equivalent on-demand VM instance.

Fog Layer Setup. For simplicity, we assume that all FCNs have the same computation and storage capabilities, with $Q = 100$ cu. Due to the same characteristics, the costs per capacity unit are the same for each FCN. Minimum ask for for task provisioning per capacity unit equals to the costs per capacity unit, and it applies $\alpha_{i,f,\min} = 0.05\$/cu$. To prevent seting too high asks in the double auction process, the upper bound for asks is set as $\alpha_{i,f,\max} = 0.25$ \$/cu. The cost of task offloading to the cloud is $\chi_{i,f} = 0.25$ per task.

Cloud Layer Setup. Depending on the VM allocation per TZ, we set 4 scenarios, as shown in Table 1.

Table 1. VMs allocation per TZ

Scenario	The number of VMs per TZ			
	TZ0	TZ1	TZ2	TZ3
The highest security	540	360	180	120
High security	420	280	140	360
Medium security	300	200	100	600
Low security	180	120	60	840

The probability of a VM malicious attack takes values from the set $p_a = \{0.1, 0.2, 0.3\}$. Simulation parameters relevant for TZs are listed in Table 2. Selected prices for equivalent on-demand VM instances are in the range of Amazon EC2 prices [24].

Table 2. Simulation parameters for TZs

Parameter	Trust Zones			
	TZ0	TZ1	TZ2	TZ3
Security mechanism's intensity	High	Medium	Low	–
Probability of VM's availability, β_j	0.84	0.75	0.66	0.5
VM's on-demand price per time slot [\$/h]	32.576	16.288	8.144	4.072
VM's minimum ask per time slot [\$/h]	9.773	4.886	2.443	1.222

4.2 IoT Entities Layer Utility

IoT entities layer utility mainly depends on the number of active IoT entities that generate requests for task provisioning. Figure 2. Shows the effects of variations in the number of connected IoT entities per FCN, for 50 FCNs. Overall utility for an IoT layer increases as the number of IoT entities per FCN increases. However, the utility significantly increases as the number of FCNs increases in the observed fog-cloud structure. Figure 3 shows the effects of variations of the number of FCNs in the given structure containing 30 connected IoT entities per FCN.

Since the large majority of requests are provisioned by FCNs, the utility slightly decreases for lower security provided. Thus, for the given number of IoT entities, the low-security scenario with the probability of 0.3 for malicious attack occurrence generates the lowest utility.

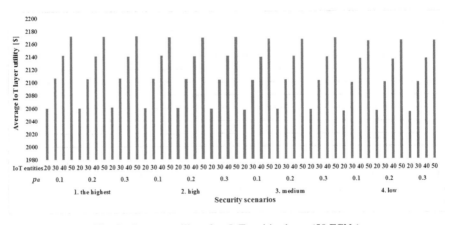

Fig. 2. Average utility of an IoT entities layer (50 FCNs)

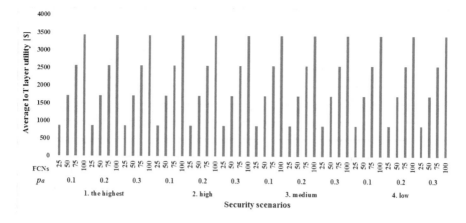

Fig. 3. Average utility of an IoT layer (30 IoT entities per FCN)

4.3 Fog Layer Utility

The fog layer, in general, is not affected by the security level provided by the cloud layer. However, the number of FCNs and the number of connected IoT entities induce utility to the large extent.

Figure 4 shows the average utility of a fog layer with variations in the number of FCNs in the fog-cloud system and variations in the number of connected IoT entities. Since overall security on the cloud layer does not affect the fog layer significantly, the results are shown for the medium-security scenario and the probability of malicious attack occurrence of 0.2. Notably, utility is directly proportional to the number of FCNs. As the number of connected IoT entities increases, the utility increases as well, but at a slower pace compared to the number of FCNs in the system.

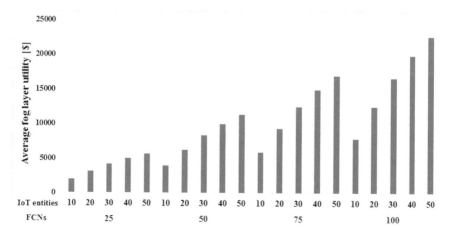

Fig. 4. Average utility of a fog layer

4.4   Cloud Layer Utility

Due to the VMs exposure and easy access over the Internet, the cloud layer is prone to malicious threats. The VMs vulnerability and effects on utility reduction are noticeable for both small and large network scenarios. As the probability of malicious attack occurrence increases, a low-security scenario is an undesirable solution.

Figure 5 shows the average cloud layer utility for 50 FCNs and variations in the number of connected IoT entities per FCN. A greater number of connected IoT entities per FCN significantly increases the cloud layer utility, especially for the highest and high-security scenarios.

Figure 6 shows the average cloud layer utility with 30 IoT entities per FCN and variations of the number of FCNs on the fog layer. The number of FCNs is the major driver of cloud layer utility enhancement. The utility is directly proportional to the number of FCNs in the network. Moreover, the investment in security is highly recommended, especially for large network scenarios.

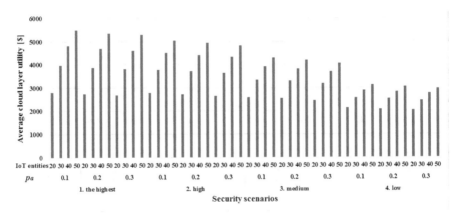

Fig. 5. Average utility of a cloud layer (50 FCNs)

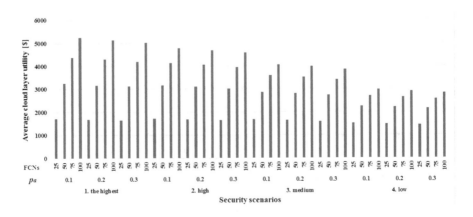

Fig. 6. Average utility of a cloud layer (30 IoT entities per FCN)

5 Conclusion

In this paper, the problem of task offloading in the fog-cloud environment is jointly addressed with security assessment and resource allocation. A truthful double VCG-based auction mechanism that provides individual rationality is established for winning tasks determination. The auction mechanism is performed in two stages. The first stage represents an auction between the IoT entities layer and the fog layer, while the second stage represents the auction process for task offloading to the cloud layer. The winning tasks in the first stage of the auction are executed in the fog. To improve performances, we introduce task prioritization on the fog layer depending on the delay requirements. Thus, winning delay-sensitive tasks are primarily executed. Offloading to the cloud requires security consideration. VM security modeling is introduced to assess the provided security level of VMs. The proposed simulation model is used to analyze the utility function of all participants in the fog-cloud environment.

Simulation results show that investment into security significantly increases the cloud layer utility in both small and large network scenarios. Due to task prioritization and forcing fog resources utilization improvements, the majority of the tasks are provisioned on the fog layer. Therefore, the utility of the IoT entities layer slightly decreases for lower security scenarios. The proposed model provides incentives for the fog layer to participate in task offloading since the operational offloading costs are covered in the auction process. Furthermore, the model intensifies resource utilization on the fog layer and offloads tasks to the remote cloud only in the fog resources are exceeded.

There are several future research directions. The proposed model can be extended to address potential penalties for failures. Also, the buffer size can be introduced in the fog and cloud layer to analyze effects on the execution time and network utilization. Another important issue to be solved is energy consumption. Since the operation of the security mechanism consumes computation resources, delays and energy consumption increase. Therefore, relations between energy consumption and network performance in the fog-cloud environment are subjects for future research.

References

1. Baranwal, G., Vidyarthi, D.: Admission control policies in fog computing using extensive form game. IEEE Trans. Cloud Comput., 1–14 (2020)
2. Singh, M., Baranwal, G.: Quality of service (QoS) in internet of things. In: 2018 3rd International Conference on Internet of Things: Smart Innovation and Usages (IoT-SIU), pp. 1–6. IEEE. Bhimtal (2018)
3. Besharati, R., Rezvani, M.H., Sadeghi, M.M.G.: An incentive-compatible offloading mechanism in fog-cloud environments using second-price sealed-bid auction. J. Grid Comput. **19**(37), 1 (2021)
4. Mikavica, B., Kostic-Ljubisavljevic, A.: A security-driven approach for energy-aware cloud resource pricing and allocation. Adv. Electr. Comput. Eng. **21**(4), 99–106 (2021)

5. Wang, Q., Guo, S., Liu, J., Pan, C., Yang, L.: Profit maximization incentive mechanism for resource providers in mobile edge computing. IEEE Trans. Serv. Comput. **15**(1), 138–149 (2022)
6. Garmehi, M., Analoui, M., Pathan, M., Buyya, R.: An economic mechanism for request routing and resource allocation in hybrid CDN-P2P networks. Int. J. Netw. Manag. **25**(6), 375–393 (2015)
7. Tasiopoulos, A., Ascigil, O., Psaras, I., Toumpis, S., Pavlou, G.: FogSpot: spot pricing for application provisioning in edge/fog computing. IEEE Trans. Serv. Comput. **14**(6), 1781–1795 (2021)
8. Mikavica, B., Kostic-Ljubisavljevic, A.: Auction-based pricing in cloud environment. In: Khosrow-Pour, M. (eds.) Encyclopedia of Organizational Knowledge, Administration, and Technologies, pp. 86–97. IGI Global (2021)
9. Zu, Y., et al.: An auction-based mechanism for task offloading in fog networks. In: 2019 IEEE 30th Annual International Symposium on Personal, Indoor and Mobile Radio Communications (PIMRC), pp. 1–6. IEEE. Istanbul (2019)
10. Baranwal, G., Kumar, D.: DAFNA: decentralized auction based fog node allocation in 5G era. In: 2020 IEEE 15th International Conference on Industrial and Information Systems (ICIIS), pp. 575–580. IEEE. Rupnagar (2020)
11. Bandyopadhyay, A., Roy, T.S., Sarkar, V., Mallik, S.: Combinatorial auction-based fog service allocation mechanism for IoT applications. In: 2020 10th International Conference on Cloud Computing, Data Science & Engineering (Confluence), pp. 518–524. IEEE. Noida (2020)
12. Zhang, F., Tang, Z., Chen, M., Zhou, X., Jia, W.: A dynamic resource overbooking mechanism in fog computing. In: 2018 IEEE 15th International Conference on Mobile Ad Hoc and Sensor Systems (MASS), pp. 89–97. IEEE. Chengdu (2018)
13. Sheikholeslami, F., Navimipour, N.J.: Auction-based resource allocation mechanisms in the cloud environments: a review of the literature and reflection on future challenges. Concurrency and Comput. Pract. Experience **30**(16), 1–15 (2018)
14. Wang, X., Chen, X., Wu, W.: Towards truthful auction mechanisms for task assignment in mobile device clouds. In: IEEE Conference on Computer Communications (IEEE INFOCOM), pp. 1–9. IEEE. Atlanta (2017)
15. Halabi, T., Bellaiche, M., Abusitta, A.: Cloud security up for auction: a DSIC online mechanism for secure IaaS resource allocation. In: 2018 2nd Cyber Security in Networking Conference (CSNet), pp. 1–8. IEEE. Paris (2018)
16. Mikavica, B., Kostic-Ljubisavljevic, A., Popovic, D.: A security-driven approach to the auction-based cloud service pricing. Int. J. Transp. Traffic Eng. **11**(2), 213–228 (2021)
17. Yi, S., Li, C. and Li, Q.: A survey of fog computing: concepts, applications and issues. In: Proceedings of the 2015 Workshop on Mobile Big Data, pp. 37–42. ACM (2018)
18. Mahmud, R., Kotagiri, R., Buyya, R.: Fog computing: a taxonomy, survey and future directions. In: Di Martino, B., Li, K.-C., Yang, L.T., Esposito, A. (eds.) Internet of Everything. IT, pp. 103–130. Springer, Singapore (2018). https://doi.org/10.1007/978-981-10-5861-5_5
19. Besharati, R., Rezvani, M. H.: A prototype auction-based mechanism for computation offloading in fog-cloud environments. In: 2019 5th Conference on Knowledge Based Engineering and Innovation (KBEI), pp. 542–547. IEEE. Tehran (2019)
20. Aggarwal, A., Kumar, N., Vidyarthy, D.P., Buyya, R.: Fog-integrated cloud architecture enabled multi-atributive combinatorial reverse auctioning framework. Simul. Model. Pract. Theory **109**(2021), 102307 (2021)
21. Gonzales, D., Kaplan, J., Saltzman, E., Winkelman, Z., Woods, D.: Cloud-trust – a security assessment model for infrastructure as a service (IaaS) clouds. IEEE Trans. Cloud Comput. **5**(3), 523–536 (2017)
22. Xu, H., Qiu, X., Sheng, Y., Luo, L., Xiang, Y.: A QoS-driven approach to the cloud service addressing attributes of security. IEEE Access **6**, 34477–34487 (2018)

23. Amazon Virtual Private Clouds (Amazon VPC). https://aws.amazon.com/vpc/?nc2=h_ql_p rod_fs_vpc&vpc-blogs.sort-by=item.additionalFields.createdDate&vpc-blogs.sort-order= desc. Accessed 15 Dec 2021
24. Amazon EC2 On-Demand Pricing. https://aws.amazon.com/ec2/pricing/on-demand/. Accessed 15 Dec 2021

Exploring the Applicability of Open-Source Tools for Web Application Cybersecurity Improvement

Ivan Cvitić⬤, Dragan Peraković(✉)⬤, Marko Periša⬤, and Mario Sekondo

Faculty of Transport and Traffic Sciences, University of Zagreb, Vukelićeva 4,
10000 Zagreb, Croatia
{ivan.cvitic,dragan.perakovic,marko.perisa}@fpz.unizg.hr

Abstract. The security of the information-communication system is crucial to avoid potential cyber-attacks. Web applications are most vulnerable to attacks, so it is very important to determine the most common vulnerabilities and the best tools to improve the security of such applications. Vulnerabilities are potential flaws in the system that make it prone to potential attacks. These vulnerabilities can stem from various sources, such as programming languages with inherited security flaws, bad security coding practices, outdated or unpatched services etc. In order to improve security of web applications, the system as a whole needs to be assessed. One of the ways to improve the security is to hire a third-party company that specializes in pen-testing and security of such systems. But since security is complex and needs to be thoroughly tested, this service is rather expensive. So for a smaller web applications and projects this may not be the best or the smartest option. So in order to improve security one of the options is use of vulnerability assessment tools such as open-source vulnerability scanners. This paper will analyze technologies that are used for the development of web applications, the most common vulnerabilities encountered and open source tools that can be used to improve web application security.

Keywords: Web application · Security · Open source tools · Vulnerability

1 Introduction

In today's world, technology is an indispensable part of human lives. The development of the Internet and information technology has changed the way of life in which people now devote more and more free time to use various information and communication services for entertainment and personal needs or use them to do remote work. Businesses are expanding or changing the way they do business precisely because of the development of these technologies. Whether businesses are building their own web solutions or hiring companies to develop such solutions, it is important to keep in mind that the security and protection of the information and communications system is a key component.

© ICST Institute for Computer Sciences, Social Informatics and Telecommunications Engineering 2022
Published by Springer Nature Switzerland AG 2022. All Rights Reserved
D. Perakovic and L. Knapcikova (Eds.): FABULOUS 2022, LNICST 445, pp. 64–79, 2022.
https://doi.org/10.1007/978-3-031-15101-9_5

Web applications are increasingly the victims of cyber-attacks, and thus endanger their end users. Therefore, more and more businesses are hiring companies whose services are based on improving the security of information systems in order to validate and test their systems. Such companies typically have their own security assessment methodology developed and their own tools to implement their services, which ultimately results in costly service which may not be acceptable for smaller businesses in terms of cost. Therefore, it is important to consider alternative ways in which businesses could improve the security of their own applications or websites.

Web application vulnerabilities can arise from various sources, and addressing security vulnerabilities requires a certain amount of knowledge and resources to improve system security successfully. One way to improve the security of web applications is to use open source software to detect vulnerabilities. Usually such tools are free or have a reasonable price that suits smaller businesses. The main tasks of such tools are to find vulnerabilities and shortcomings in web applications, and they can provide automatic scanning or configured scanning parameters to match the needs of the web application.

The aim of this research is to determine the level of applicability of various vulnerability scanners in improving the security of web applications.

2   Previous Research

The field of web application development is fast growing. New technologies applicable in this area are developing rapidly, so there is a need to develop the security aspect of web applications and study existing vulnerabilities. Therefore, it is important to follow scientific research papers in order to be able to record trends and make recommendations for security solutions. In addition, many tools try to solve the issue of web application security by applying them. The fact is that any tool cannot completely solve the security issue of web applications, so the research can try to approximate the applicability of individual tools so that their potential can be maximized.

Statistical data collected through relevant research is an indicator of the prevalence of individual vulnerabilities in web applications and the trends that are developing in this area. Thus, such data can be used to improve the security of web applications and potentially select the appropriate tool to be used to improve security.

OWASP (The Open Web Application Security Project) is a non-profit organization that finds its purpose in improving software security. OWASP collects network security data from a variety of sources, and their OWASP Top Ten document is one of the most popular documents that acts as an indicator of the most critical security risks faced by web applications. The document is updated on average every third or fourth year, and the last edition is from 2017. According to this document, the most critical risks for web applications are Injections, Broken Authentication, Sensitive Data Exposure, XML External Entities, Broken Access Control, Security Misconfiguration, XSS - Cross Side Scripting, Insecure Deserialization, Components with Known Vulnerabilities, Insufficient Logging & Monitoring [1].

In addition to these common security risks, as many as 20% of businesses and organizations often encounter denial-of-service attacks, which was noted as a trend in a study by the European Union Agency for Cyber Security (ENISA). This research found that in 2019, the number of attacks on web applications increased by 52%, and it was found that as much as 84% of vulnerabilities stem from security configuration errors. Figure 1 shows the data correlated with OWASP Top Ten safety risks [2].

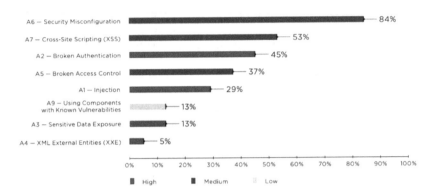

Fig.1. Statistical data correlated to OWASP top ten vulnerabilities [2]

The prevalence of denial-of-service attacks is also confirmed by the scientific paper *Cyber Security Threats and Vulnerabilities: A Systematic Mapping Study*, which maps data from scientific articles from publicly available sources. In this article, a total of 78 scientific articles that passed the final selection were analysed and it was found that a denial-of-service attack occurs in 37% of cases [3].

Security testing of web applications or websites requires pre-defined strategy and planning due to the choice of tools and constant new challenges in the security sector in the information industry. Therefore, the choice of the tool itself must correspond to the ultimate goal for which the security testing is carried out. In order to choose a tool, it is important to know the vulnerabilities and how the average web application works.

Web applications are considered any program that runs in a browser and can be accessed over the Internet. Web applications provide various functionalities to users, and due to the development of new technologies they are becoming more and more complex. Applications are usually divided into three layers. The first layer is the user, which may consist of a browser through which the user loads the web application's content. Then the second layer is the server, which serves the user and dynamically loads the content. The third layer consists of the final structure of the web application, i.e. "backend", which is used to store data [4].

Security tools that perform penetration testing are usually defined as scanners. They are considered automated tools that analyse web applications and websites, and thus try to find potential security vulnerabilities. In addition to simple search and scanning, such tools can also search for source code errors that could allow other attack vectors, such as buffer overflows. Web application scanners typically use the black box method in penetration testing [5].

In the work of *Baykar, M. Investigation and Comparison of Web Application Vulnerabilities Test tools*, six different tools were analysed. The tools consisted of commercial and open source tools, and a vulnerable application created by the Netsparker team at http://aspnet.testsparker.com was used for testing. The tools Netsparker, Acunetix, Vega, OWASP ZAP, Wapiti and Iron WASP were tested. Comparative work analysis is divided into nine categories: tool scanning time, number of scanned vulnerabilities, tool report capabilities, module scan capabilities, manual scan capabilities, graphical interface availability, availability on specific operating systems, tool fee, and using area [5].

Looking solely at performance, the Vega tool had the fastest scan time of 45 min, while the Wapiti tool had the longest scan time of 13 h. The IronWASP tool detected the most vulnerabilities, 213, while the OWASP ZAP tool detected only 7 vulnerabilities, the least of all tools. Although free open source tools have achieved the best performance in this research, the author of the paper suggests that the choice of tools is not so simple, but that each tool has its purpose [5].

A similar suggestion is found in the work of *A. Alzahrani, A. Alqazzaz, Y. Zhu, H. Fu and N. Almashfi, "Web Application Security Tools Analysis"*, where the authors tested ten types of security tools depending on their purposes. In this tool, tools that are more focused on individual areas of vulnerability, such as deficiencies in transport layer protection, information leakage vulnerabilities, XSS vulnerabilities, and injection vulnerabilities, are tested. The authors of this paper concluded that security testing of web applications or pages requires a carefully designed testing process and plan, and careful selection of tools given that each tool has advantages and disadvantages [4].

3   Related Technologies and Security Threats in Web Applications

Most of today's web applications and websites are designed through a group of technologies. Technology groups or more commonly referred to as "stacks" are groups of tools used to implement certain ideas in terms of web applications. Stacks consist of programming languages, frameworks, programming libraries, and various development tools. The choice of a particular technology group will depend on the application itself and the web application's needs, which may include its functionality, scalability, sustainability, security, etc. [6].

3.1   Web Application Architecture

The web application architecture can be divided into two parts, the client part and the server part. The client part, better known as the frontend, is responsible for presenting data to the user, receiving requests and data from the user, and directing it to the server. The server part of the web application, better known by the term backend, is credited with request processing, client management, storage and data processing. Different technologies are often used to make frontends and backends [6].

Programming languages such as HTML/HTML5, CSS, and JavaScript are used to create the front-end interface and working environments and programming libraries such as ReactJS, AngularJS, React, Node.js jQuery.

For the server, backend part, programming languages such as C#, Java, PHP, Python, Objective-C and many other programming languages are used, along with web server frameworks created through programming languages in order to enable scalability and easier application development. Examples of such frameworks are Node.js, .NET,

Django, etc. Databases such as SQL, MySQL, PostgreSQL, Oracle, MongoDB are used to store and manage data. Applications such as Apache and Nginx are used to run web servers, and cloud servers are often used for additional services such as AWS, Microsoft Azure, Google Cloud [6].

Currently the two most popular stacks are MERN and MEAN. These two technology stacks refer to a collection of technologies based on the JavaScript programming language. In the StackOverflow survey, as many as 68.62% of respondents use JavaScript in a professional environment for a long time, which makes this programming language the most used for the ninth year in a row especially in web development. For the web server framework, the choice in these technology groups is Node.js (36.19%), and for web development environments the most commonly used are React.js (41.4%), jQuery (34.52%), Angular (26, 23%) and Express.js (23.6%). MongoDB (28.03%) is the main choice of tools for working with databases in these technological groups [7].

MEAN and MERN are technology stacks that are based on JavaScript programming language. These technology stacks are both free and open source, and are used as a framework for development and design of web applications. The main benefit of using these stacks is that they allow developers to work in one programming language, applying already existing programming concepts for that language [8, 9].

These technology stacks are consisted of four key technologies and they represent layers of the stack respectfully.

MEAN stack is consisted of [8]: MongoDB - database, Express.js - web application framework, Angular.js – client-side framework, Node.js - web server.

MERN stack is consisted of [9]: MongoDB - database, Express.js - web application framework, React.js – client-side framework, Node.js - web server.

3.2   Security Aspects of Web Applications

The principles of information system security are important to maintain in order to protect the information and communication systems. This implies the application of a series of measures, standards and procedures in order to maintain the desired level of security of the information and communication system [10].

There are six basic principles of security according to [10]:

- **Confidentiality** is a characteristic of an information system that ensures the disclosure of information and data exclusively to authorized persons, entities and processes, at a defined time and by a defined procedure.
- **Integrity** of system and information means protection against intentional or accidental unauthorized modification caused by human influence or system malfunction.
- **Availability** refers to the availability of information to authorized users at the requested time and under specified conditions.
- **Authentication** is the verification of the legitimacy of a user who requests access to certain information system resources.
- **Authorization** refers to the assignment of a certain level of access rights to the system after the user has been authenticated.
- **Audit** is a process of evaluating the effectiveness of implemented security mechanisms.

Web application security threats are any possible occurrences, malicious or not, that could harm web applications in some way. Vulnerability is the weakness that makes a threat possible. Vulnerabilities can be caused by poor design, configuration error, or insecure and untested coding techniques. An attack is an action that exploits vulnerabilities in a web application.

4 Open-Source Tools Evaluation and Analysis of Applicability

Vulnerability scanners are automated tools used to detect vulnerabilities within computers, networks, or applications. Depending on the type of tool, scanners may have different functionalities and different vulnerability detection techniques. Some of the key features will be analysed later in this paper. The tools that are going to be used for applicability analysis are security scanners for dynamically testing the security of web applications. The tools to be analysed are OWASP ZAP, Vega, Arachni and Nikto. The main division of application security testing is divided into static and dynamic analysis. Static Application Security Testing (SAST) often uses various types of static analysis techniques to detect vulnerabilities, while Dynamic Application Security Testing (DAST) uses attack graph implementation techniques.

Static analysis is a fast and reliable technique. This technique focuses on the analysis of the program structure within the application, primarily on the source code itself in order to detect possible vulnerabilities within the application. This technique is considered very effective for detecting vulnerabilities. Static analysis often uses program libraries or databases for comparison with analysed code to verify program code. One of the disadvantages of such an analysis is that in the case of discovering a new unknown vulnerability it is not possible to make any comparison with the program library to verify the security of the program code [11].

An attack graph is defined as a summary of all the paths an attacker follows in the network to achieve the desired state. The desired condition may include network corruption, theft of network packets, or full access to it to determine what is happening on the network. Attack graphs help identify security vulnerabilities that lie within an application, they are usually quite large because they represent the entire application, so they are quite complex to understand and analyse. Attack graph generation is implemented within the vulnerability scanner to identify underlying application vulnerabilities, and then establish overall attack graphs to analyse the strength of an individual attack [11].

Vulnerability assessment means identifying vulnerabilities in the system before they can be exploited by anyone whose intentions are malicious. This is a proactive approach to security where vulnerabilities are detected and addressed so that no one can exploit them maliciously. Vulnerabilities do not only arise from the application, the platforms on which the application is located, operating systems, middleware that connects various parts of the application system, etc. can also be vulnerable. Therefore, it is necessary to scan the entire system including the network and software used by the application [11].

4.1 Vulnerable Application Configuration

This research aims to determine the level of applicability of various vulnerability scanners in improving the security of web applications. In order to obtain objective results when scanning vulnerabilities on a web application, a predefined intentionally vulnerable web application OWASP Mutilidae II was used.

OWASP Mutilidae II is a free, intentionally vulnerable open source web application, which provides a simulation service of a real vulnerable web application and serves as a target of attack for potential users who want to learn more about web security. Mutilidae can be installed on Linux and Windows operating systems using one of a group of server solutions for serving at a local address, such as LAMP, WAMP, or XAMPP [12].

For the purposes of this paper, the web application will run in XAMPP on Windows 7 (x64). XAMPP is a free cross-platform server solution package with multiple open source platforms developed by Apache Friends, and consists mainly of Apache HTTP servers, a MariaDB database, and an interpreter for scripts written in the PHP and Perl programming languages [13].

To serve a vulnerable web application at a local address, it is needed to run the Apache server and MySQL database in the XAMPP user interface. After starting the server and database, it is necessary to move the directory with the source code of the Mutilidae application to the XAMPP executable directory on the local disk. In this case, it's at the C:\xampp\htdocs location in the Windows 7 operating system called mutilidae. The application can then be accessed at the local URL address 127.0.0.1/mutilidae.

4.2 OWASP Zed Attack Proxy (ZAP)

Zed Attack Proxy (ZAP) is a free open source tool used for penetration testing developed and maintained under the OWASP organization. ZAP is designed and developed specifically to test the security of web applications and be very flexible and extensible. ZAP works on the principle of man-in-the-middle proxy. In this way, ZAP intercepts and reviews requests and responses between the tester's browser and the web application, and can modify the contents of the request as needed and forward it to the destination. If there is a network proxy between the ZAP tool and the web application, then ZAP can be configured to connect to the proxy as shown in Fig. 2 [14].

Fig. 2. Demonstration of ZAP tool operation between web application and browser [14]

ZAP offers a number of functionalities that advanced developers can use, but also beginners in security testing. It is available on every popular operating system such as Linux, Windows and OS X, and is expandable through additional features that can be downloaded freely from the ZAP Marketplace.

To start automatic scanning, user needs to press the Automated Scan button. User is then prompted to enter the desired scan target and select additional scan options. After selecting the options, it is necessary to press the Attack button to start scanning. After running the scan, the tool first performs a passive scan, exploring possible attack pathways along with application and system information. After the passive scan is complete, the tool switches to the active scan. During the active scanning, it is possible to monitor information about the operation of the tool, and already found vulnerabilities are available via the Alerts menu in the information window. It is also possible to monitor the detailed progress of the scan by pressing the Show scan progress details button in the Active Scan menu.

Upon completing the automatic scan, the results are arranged in the Alerts menu in the information window. The total scan time was 30 min, and the ZAP tool found a total of 44 vulnerabilities in the Mutilidae application. The Alerts menu sorts vulnerabilities by severity and priority from high, medium and low levels, and information vulnerabilities that can potentially be vulnerabilities or reveal unnecessary information about the web application. Figure 3 represents the Alerts menu showing the vulnerabilities found in the Mutilidae web application.

Fig. 3. Vulnerabilities shown in alerts menu after automatic scan

For a more detailed analysis of individual vulnerabilities, it is possible to obtain more information by clicking on the vulnerabilities and selecting a specific application request or response. In addition to information about the attack, the information window also contains auxiliary information for resolving the vulnerability in that case. In addition to that, additional resources are included so that web application users can investigate specific vulnerabilities and find an adequate solution for their own applications.

4.3 Vega

Vega is a platform for testing the security of web applications. Vega is a free open source tool written in the Java programming language and can run on Windows, Linux and OS X operating systems. It is based on a graphical interface and can be easily extended using modules written in Javascript. It was developed by Subgraph, a company that deals exclusively with open source information security [15].

The total scan time was 18 min, and the Vega tool found 198 different vulnerabilities within the Mutilidae application. The Vega tool also ranks vulnerabilities by severity and sorts them by priority in the Scan Alerts window as shown in Fig. 4. Within this window it is possible to view all vulnerabilities found within the application, and the requests or responses used to find them.

Fig. 4. Vulnerabilities shown in the *Scan Alerts* windows after automated scan

For more information on each vulnerability, user has to click on the request or vulnerability within the Scan Alerts window. The Scan Info window then provides the user with a more detailed overview of the vulnerability and information about that vulnerability and links to potential solutions to prevent such vulnerabilities. If the user wants to analyse in more detail the request or response sent that revealed the application vulnerabilities, then it is necessary to click on the request within the Request section in the Scan Info window.

4.4 Arachni

Arachni is a high-performance modular Ruby framework filled with features designed to help penetration testers and administrators assess the security of modern web applications. It is free and open source, supported on Linux, Windows and OS X operating systems and distributed through portable packages that allow immediate deployment. Implementation options are via the Ruby program library, available through Command Line Interface (CLI), the WebUI, and the distributed system using remote agents [16].

Arachni is a very flexible and versatile tool that covers many use cases for web application security. It can be used as a simple utility tool via the command-line interface for scanning, up to a global network of high-performance scanners, thanks to the REST API, integration is easy [16].

The user can start automated scanning via the header menu or by clicking the New scan button on the workspace. User is then asked to enter the URL of the scan target, and in addition, can select the scan profile, additional advanced options and scan description, and with whom to share the scan. Arachni cannot scan via a local address, and requires entering the private IP address of the computer on which the application is served. In

Fig. 5. Arachni scanner performance after automated scan

this case, the application will be scanned at the URL http://192.168.8.129/mutillidae/. After that it is necessary to press the Go! and the scan will begin.

During the automated scan, the user can observe the scanning process and the found vulnerabilities are available for inspection. In addition, Arachni offers a simpler display of information about scan performance such as the number of requests sent and responses received, response time, pages found, etc. Upon completing the active scan, Arachni conducts a meta-analysis of the scanned results to potentially identify possible false-positive vulnerabilities.

The total scan time was 9 h and 28 min and Arachni found a total of 390 potential vulnerabilities. In addition, Arachni discovered 599 different pages or paths within the application, and recorded a large number of requests and responses, as shown in Fig. 5.

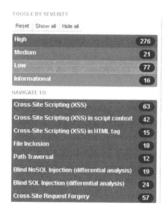

Fig. 6. Vulnerabilities shown in the Arachni *WebUI*

Similar to other tools, vulnerabilities are ranked by severity as shown in Fig. 6. Within this menu, all vulnerabilities can be searched and more detailed information about the vulnerability found can be accessed in the main menu. Within the vulnerability information window, an explanation of the vulnerability is available and the location in the web application where the vulnerability was found. For a more detailed analysis, user can click the button next to the request to determine the entire request and response process.

4.5 Nikto

Nikto is a free open source tool for scanning web server vulnerabilities. Nikto conducts extensive testing of web servers for multiple items, including more than 6,700 potentially dangerous files/programs, checking outdated versions of over 1250 servers, and version-specific issues on more than 270 servers. It also checks for server configuration items, such as the presence of multiple index files, HTTP server options, and will try to identify installed web servers and software. Scan items and plugins are frequently updated and can be updated automatically. Nikto is written in the Perl programming language and can run on all Unix-based operating systems. Nikto is used exclusively through the command line interface [17].

The goal of the Nikto is to examine a web server to find potential problems and security vulnerabilities that include incorrect server and software configurations, default files and programs, insecure files and programs, outdated servers and programs etc. Nikto points to some information about found vulnerabilities if the report saving function is used in some of the formats available, but serves more as a tool that provides pointers to users to get a better result via manual pen-testing [17].

To scan a web server, the user needs to enter the URL of the web application, the IP address of the server, and the port number. In this case, the URL of the Mutilidae application will be scanned by entering the command nikto.pl -h https://127.0.0.1/mutilidae.

Nikto reported 166 different potential vulnerabilities in just 59 s of scanning. Scanning time on a local server is slightly faster than scanning on a web server due to the use of local resources. Nikto prints the results and information within the command-line interface, if the results are printed in one of the possible formats, then the results remain saved and can be accessed at any time in a more accessible format. Nikto prints the IP address and target port number information first, followed by the SSL information and the start time of the scan.

Nikto recognized the type of server, operating system, and programming language used within the web application. After that, Nikto prints out the vulnerabilities. When analysing the results, it is important to pay attention to the OSVDB vulnerabilities. These are already discovered vulnerabilities in similar open source technologies that can be explored within the Open Source Vulnerability Database Project repository.

5   Results Analysis and Discussion

The analysis of statistics from relevant research concluded that the number of attacks on web applications is increasing, and the most common vulnerabilities stem from security configuration errors. Four different open source tools were analyzed to examine their applicability to improve web applications' security. The research aims to determine whether open source tools can be an alternative to commercial tools or third-party penetration testing. The tool research was conducted on the vulnerable web application Mutillidae. Through the research, an automated scanning method was used to show the tools' functionalities and get a rough overview of the performance of the tools. Table 1 maps the data on the basic functionalities of these tools.

The selection of tools within this research was based on potential applications of these tools within the web application development process. The intentionally vulnerable Mutillidae application was selected as an indicator of the capabilities of these tools, and the data on the scans performed will serve as suggestions on how to implement the tools

Table 1. Basic functionalities of tools used in research

Tool name	Scan mode	Operating system	Module extensibility	User interface	Report generation
OWASP Zap	Automated and manual scanning	Linux Windows OS X	Yes	GUI	Yes
Vega	Automated scanning	Linux Windows OS X	Yes	GUI	Yes
Arachni	Automated scanning	Linux Windows OS X	Yes	WebUI	Yes
Nikto	Automated scanning	Unix-based systems	Yes	CLI	Yes

before producing the applications to improve their security. Table 2 maps the Mutillidae application scan data.

In the first case, the ZAP tool developed by the OWASP organization was used. ZAP offers automated and manual scanning capabilities. Through an automated scan on the Mutilidae application, ZAP found 44 types of different vulnerabilities in a 30-min scan. ZAP offers manual application scanning capabilities which can be useful for penetration testing in different steps within the application development process making it a very flexible tool. In addition, it offers report generation, access to in-depth information and documentation on vulnerabilities, and the tool itself, which can make it easier for developers with very little experience in security testing to make an application more secure.

Table 2. Results of the scan performed on the Mutilidae application

Tool name	Number of vulnerabilities found	Scan time	Types of vulnerabilities found	Number of vulnerabilities by severity
OWASP Zap	44	30 min	• SQL injection, • XSS injection, • Directory traversal, • Security misconfiguration, • Sensitive data disclosure, • Broken access control, • Source code and error detection	**High level** 10 **Medium level** 12 **Low level** 13 **Information level** 9

(*continued*)

Table 2. (*continued*)

Tool name	Number of vulnerabilities found	Scan time	Types of vulnerabilities found	Number of vulnerabilities by severity
Vega	198	18 min	• Security misconfiguration, • SQL injection, • URL injection, • XSS injection, • Sensitive data disclosure, • Cookie information, • Source code and error detection	**High level** 15 **Medium level** 124 **Low level** 44 **Information level** 15
Arachni	390	9 h and 28 min	• SQL injection, • XSS injection, • CSRF attacks, • OS and URL injection, • Sensitive data disclosure, • Unsafe cookies, • Security misconfiguration, • Broken access control, • Broken authentication	**High level** 267 **Medium level** 21 **Low level** 77 **Information level** 16
Nikto	166	59 s	• Insecure cookies, • Sensitive data disclosure, • Detection of unsafe configurations, • Remote command execution, • XST vulnerabilites	N/A

In the second case, the Vega tool was used. Vega has proven to be a very simple tool for dynamically scanning the security of web applications. It offers a very simple user interface and scanning which can also help developers in analyzing the security of a web application. Vega found 198 different vulnerabilities in just 18 min. The ability to scan and intercept proxy requests allows it to tactically analyze the security of web applications, which can later be used to cross-check vulnerabilities with other security tools.

In the third case, the Arachni security framework was used. Arachni offers a wide range of features and functionalities that can be implemented within the project. This makes Arachni a somewhat more complex tool to use, but offers advantages such as automation of penetration testing within the entire lifecycle of a web application. Arachni is a very thorough tool, as evidenced by the fact that the automated scan of the Mutilidae application took 9 h and 28 min, and Arachni found 390 different vulnerabilities.

In the fourth case, the Nikto tool was used to scan the web server of the Mutilidae application. Nikto is simple enough for initial use, but flexible enough for more complex scans. In this case, Nikto scanned the web server for only 59 s and found 166 potential vulnerabilities. Although Nikto offers the ability to automatically scan, the lack of a user interface makes it harder to access vulnerability information.

It is important to note that the security of a web application itself will depend on several factors. This may include the choice of technologies to be used to create the web application, the expertise and competence of the developers and other contributors, the resources available, the complexity of the project, and many other factors. When it comes to the choice of technologies, it is important to choose technologies for creating a web application that will be consistent with the size and complexity of the project and the capabilities of developers who will use these technologies. Therefore, it is important to thoroughly explore the possibilities of individual technologies in order to avoid unnecessary complications and select appropriate tools. After selecting the appropriate tools, it is important to adhere to best source code writing practices, and acceptable security coding techniques to avoid security vulnerabilities. In this paper, dynamic web application security scanners were researched, so the proposal to implement open source tools will be based on them. But along with dynamic scanners, it is essential to explore and consider the use of other types of security scanners, such as static security scanners that analyze source code.

After researching and selecting appropriate tools to be used for security testing, open source tools can be implemented in the initial steps of application design. When the application is first served to the server, Nikto can scan for vulnerabilities within the active server. Scan results can be used to manually fix vulnerabilities, and it is possible to keep documentation of scan reports after each implementation of new components within the web application to the server. Depending on the complexity of the project and application, there may be multiple servers and domains used, so Nikto security scans provide a way to implement a security audit overall servers within a project.

During web application design, ZAP and Vega can be used to scan vulnerabilities within a web application. Designing a web application is a complicated process that can involve writing a large number of components and functionalities within the application. Using the ZAP tool, it is possible to manually test new components that are implemented within the application and conclude whether there are vulnerabilities that potential attackers can use as an attack vector. This allows developers to determine if there are security vulnerabilities within the source code before the application is produced, thus giving them the ability to implement a better security coding technique. In addition, the advantage of combining multiple dynamic security scanners within a web application allows cross-analysis of scan results, which can provide a better insight into the security of the web application.

Arachni tool can serve as a security framework for full security scanning and monitoring of web application security. As a tool, Arachni offers the ability to automate the entire security system. It is also possible to adjust the performance and use the "intelligence" of the tool to obtain extensive scan results for the purpose of analyzing the security of the web application. This allows developers to perform a thorough web application security audit after each stage of the application development process. And with additional features such as writing new modules and add-ons, it allows developers to tailor security testing to the needs of the application and the entire project.

6   Conclusion

The Internet has undoubtedly become a daily occurrence for a large number of people. A large number of websites have been redesigned in recent years into interactive web applications that attract an increasing number of users. Web applications can have different purposes, but they often have in common that they request certain information from the user in order to use the web application, which later in the event of an attack can result in negative consequences for both the user and the application owner.

With the popularity of the Internet and web applications, the risk of cyber attacks has also increased. Trends show that attacks on web applications are on the rise, and the only parameters that are changing are the ways in which attackers exploit vulnerabilities in web applications. Given the already mentioned popularity, businesses are often forced to expand their business in the form of web applications. Often having limited resources the security of web applications is not a priority. Open source security tools are often free, so this paper aimed to show their applicability to improve the security of web applications.

Through this paper, four different open source tools ZAP, Vega, Arachni and Nikto were analyzed. These tools were chosen because of their availability and different ways of application, which can be a very advantageous solution for businesses with limited resources. Chapter 4 presents the tools and their scan results. Using the vulnerable application, tools were used to understand their application in improving the security of web applications. The data from the research of these tools were then mapped to better understand their applicability and propose implementing these tools for the application development process.

The final conclusion is that the security of users, their data, but also the security of the web application itself is very important, so it is necessary to protect it as much as possible. Before developing an application, it is necessary to research technologies that will suit the function and size of the application, apply appropriate security techniques for writing source code, and apply open source tools to improve security through the application development process. Developers can use security tools to implement security protections to prevent attacks and remove vulnerabilities based on scan results to improve the security of web applications.

References

1. OWASP Top Ten. https://owasp.org/www-project-top-ten/. Accessed 31 July 2021
2. ENISA Threat Landscape 2020 - Web application attacks. https://www.enisa.europa.eu/pub lications/web-application-attacks. Accessed 31 July 2021
3. Humayun, M., Niazi, M., Jhanjhi, N.Z., Alshayeb, M., Mahmood, S.: Cyber security threats and vulnerabilities: a systematic mapping study. Arab. J. Sci. Eng. **45**(4), 3171–3189 (2020). https://doi.org/10.1007/s13369-019-04319-2
4. Alzahrani, A., Alqazzaz, A., Zhu, Y., Fu, H., Almashfi N.: Web application security tools analysis. In: IEEE 3rd International Conference, pp. 237–242 (2017)
5. Baykara, M.: Investigation and comparison of web application vulnerabilities test tools. Int. J. Comput. Sci. Mob. Comput. (IJCSMC) **7**(12), 197–212 (2018)
6. Suschevich, A., Birukova, D.: What is a technology stack? Choosing the right tech stack for your web project. https://www.intexsoft.com/blog/post/tech-stack.html. Accessed 2 Aug 2021
7. StackOverflow: 2021 Developer Survey. https://insights.stackoverflow.com/survey/2021. Accessed 5 Aug 2021
8. MongoDB: What is MEAN Stack? https://www.mongodb.com/mean-stack. Accessed 5 Aug 2021
9. MongoDB: What is MERN Stack? https://www.mongodb.com/mern-stack. Accessed 6 Aug 2021
10. Cvitic, I., Perakovic, D., Perisa, M., Botica, M.: Definition of the IoT device classes based on network traffic flow features. In: Knapcikova, L., Balog, M., Perakovic, D., Perisa, M. (eds.) 4th EAI International Conference on Management of Manufacturing Systems. EICC, pp. 1–17. Springer, Cham (2020). https://doi.org/10.1007/978-3-030-34272-2_1
11. Bairwa, S., Mewara, B., Gajrani, J.: Vulnerability scanners: a proactive approach to assess web application security. Int. J. Comput. Sci. Appl. **4** (2014). https://doi.org/10.5121/ijcsa. 2014.411. Accessed 23 Aug 2021
12. GitHub: OWASP Mutilidae II. https://github.com/webpwnized/mutillidae. Accessed 24 Aug 2021
13. XAMPP Official Page. https://www.apachefriends.org/index.html. Accessed 24 Aug 2021
14. OWASP Zed Attack Proxy (ZAP) Official page. https://www.zaproxy.org/. Accessed 24 Aug 2021
15. Vega Official page. https://subgraph.com/vega/. Accessed 25 Aug 2021
16. Arachni Official page. https://www.arachni-scanner.com/. pristupljeno 26 Aug 2021
17. Nikto Official page. https://cirt.net/Nikto2. Accessed 30 Aug 2021

BloHeS Consensus Mechanism – Introduction and Performance Evaluation

Jovan Karamachoski[✉] and Liljana Gavrilovska

Ss. Cyril and Methodius University in Skopje, Skopje, Republic of North Macedonia
jovankaramac@yahoo.com, liljana@feit.ukim.edu.mk

Abstract. Consensus mechanisms are important instruments of Blockchain based systems. The consensus mechanism performance depends on its capability to balance the security, scalability and decentralization of the network. The Proof-of-work and Proof-of-stake are the most accepted consensus mechanisms. However, despite the highest level of protection they are struggling to scale with the increased transaction demand. Comparably, the Tendermint consensus mechanism has better scaling property, but decreased protection capabilities. This paper introduces the BloHeS consensus mechanism that is based on the Tendermint consensus mechanism. The BloHeS is capable to reduce the message complexity, still keeping the protection capabilities on par with the Tendermint consensus mechanism.

Keywords: Consensus mechanism · Tendermint · BloHeS · Message count · Protection capacity

1 Introduction

The problem of scaling the Blockchain networks in terms of transaction throughput, latency, user space and storage is more or less present in all Blockchain technologies. The Blockchain technologies are not one solution to fit all the applications and in the same time obtain optimal operation processes. Certain improvements and optimization can be achieved depending on the implementation scenario. Generally, the scaling problem comes from the requirement for all nodes to have knowledge of common truth and participate in the consensus mechanism. This imposes that the nodes are getting familiar with all transactions that are traversing the network, which generates pressure on the network throughput. The peer-to-peer nature of the Blockchain technologies generates high redundancy of the packages due to the requirement for sharing the common truth between the participants. The package redundancy fills up the network bandwidth especially at the router points.

There are plenty of consensus mechanisms found in the literature. Every consensus mechanism has its strong and weak characteristics. Generally, the consensus mechanism is a trade-off between the transaction throughput, the system security and the network segmentation, which optimization falls under the Blockchain trilemma problem, initially introduced by Vitalik Buterin. As described in [1] the trilemma is not formally defined

D. Perakovic and L. Knapcikova (Eds.): FABULOUS 2022, LNICST 445, pp. 80–94, 2022.
https://doi.org/10.1007/978-3-031-15101-9_6

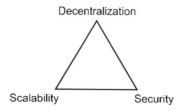

Fig. 1. Blockchain trilemma

in the literature but defines the challenge problem to obtain network's decentralization, scalability and security (see Fig. 1).

The most accepted Blockchain technologies, Bitcoin [2] and Ethereum [3], are implementing Proof-of-work (PoW) [4] consensus mechanism that offers a strong security aspect in a highly decentralized network, but lacks scalability potential for massive adoption. On top of that, the PoW consensus mechanism has compute-intensive algorithm to manage the consensus among the peers in the network, which consumes a lot of electricity, making the PoW an expensive consensus mechanism for Blockchain-based applications.

The main alternative to the PoW is the Proof-of-stake (PoS) [5] consensus mechanism that mimics the PoW consensus achievement, but requires less computation power and consumes less electricity. The PoS consensus mechanism requires the peers to stake a certain amount of assets in order to participate in the process of transaction validation. The whole process of transaction validation with the PoS consensus mechanism finishes faster, compared to the PoW, and gives room for more transactions to pass the validation process. This makes the PoS more scalable than the PoW regarding the transactions throughput. Both, the PoW and PoS are having strong protection capabilities. The networks implementing PoW and PoS can withhold 1/2 of the participants to act maliciously, and still achieve correct consensus over the data circulating in the network.

Another alternative to the PoW and PoS consensus mechanism is the Practical Byzantine Fault Tolerant (PBFT) [6] based consensus mechanisms. The PBFT is the first consensus mechanism that implements the Byzantine Fault Tolerant [7] algorithm in practice. The most prominent algorithms of this family of consensus mechanisms are PBFT and Tendermint [8]. The PBFT-based algorithms are having short voting rounds, which are finalizing in 1–3 s, resulting in faster transaction validation, thus obtaining faster transaction throughput. In the context of the Blockchain trilemma triangle, the PBFT-based consensus mechanisms are inclined toward enhanced scalability, but are lacking decentralization factor and are having reduced security. The protection capability of the PBFT and Tendermint consensus mechanisms are having reduced protection factor compared to the PoW and PoS. Systems implementing PBFT or Tendermint can withhold 1/3 malicious participants in the network. To improve the protection from malicious participants, an additional security measure, like user authentication, may enhance the overall security.

In the same performance range of the PBFT and Tendermint are the Directed Acyclic Graph (DAG) based consensus mechanisms [9]. The DAG-based consensus mechanisms are managing the consensus over a mesh-chain structure by endorsing past transactions using directional gossiping. The transaction throughput and the protection capabilities are in the range of the PBFT and Tendermint consensus mechanisms. The most prominent Blockchain technologies using the DAG-based consensus achievement are IOTA [10] and Hashgraph [11].

2   BloHeS Consensus Mechanism

The Tendermint consensus mechanism, per definition [8], progresses in rounds, where each round consists of three stages: prevote, precommit and commit. After a successful consensus over a certain voting round, the mechanism increases the height for the next block. Contrary, the unsuccessful voting round will keep the same block height and will enter a new voting round. The Tendermint consensus mechanism diagram in Fig. 2 shows the transition between the stages of the voting round [12]. This simple voting mechanism offers fast block finalization and high transaction throughput, as proven by [13, 14 12]. The Tendermint consensus mechanism can protect the network from 1/3 faulty nodes, which in turn requires the number of validators in the network to be $n = 3 * f + 1$ where f is the maximum number of faulty nodes for a given number of validators [15].

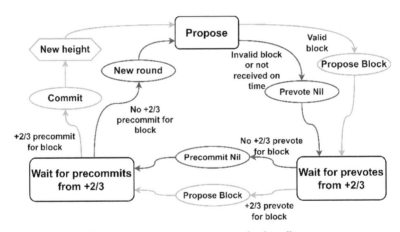

Fig. 2. Tendermint consensus mechanism diagram

The validators in the network are exchanging voting messages extensively, in order to achieve consensus, which creates a message storm between the validators in the network. The validators are voting positively for a block that is correct, and the vote messages are sent to other validators in the networks. Even if the block is incorrect or delayed, the validators will vote with nil votes, which again generates a message storm between the validators. The number of exchanged messages increases exponentially with the increasing number of validators. This affects the network bandwidth and is significant in scenarios with large numbers of validators. The papers [16, 17] are pointing out the problem of the Tendermint consensus mechanism with a large number of validators in the network. Generally, the problem in the scenarios with large numbers of validators is a result from the limited processing power of the validators, the limited network bandwidth and the increased complexity of the consensus achievement due to the increased number of the exchanged messages among the validators. Because of these limitations, the Tendermint network recommended maximum number of validators is 100, where this number can vary depending on the validators' performance, network bandwidth and transaction load. The recommended maximum number of validators is an approximative value, experimentally determined. It can be more precisely determined according the implementation scenario and participants' performance.

The single-layer architecture of the Tendermint network obviously will not scale accordingly, regarding the number of validators in a large-scale network. In order to make the network to scale, a new dimension for scaling has to be introduced. The BloHeS architecture [18] introduces a multilayer hierarchy that enables the extensive network's scaling for large-scale scenarios. This paper introduces the BloHeS consensus mechanism for the multilayer BloHeS architecture. Figure 3 shows the BloHeS consensus mechanism diagram.

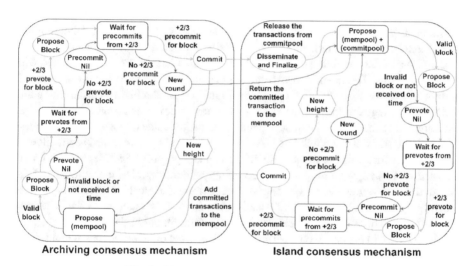

Fig. 3. BloHeS consensus mechanism diagram

The BloHeS consensus mechanisms design is based on the Tendermint consensus mechanism. It considers layered architecture and consists of two interrelated and modified Tendermint consensus mechanisms that are orchestrating the Archiving and Island domains of the BloHeS network. The network organization is presented in Fig. 4. The Island domain is the layer in the BloHeS network built from multiple Islands. An Island is a cluster of validators orchestrating independent Island consensus mechanism, which submits validated blocks for archiving to the validators in the Archiving domain. The Archiving domain is a single cluster of validators in the BloHeS network managing the Archiving consensus mechanism, which is ordering and verifying the records submitted by the Islands.

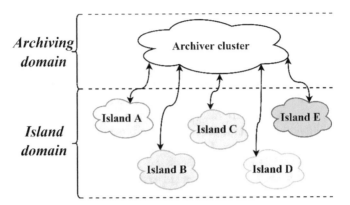

Fig. 4. Network organization of the BloHeS system

In addition to the mempool memory, [19], defined by the Tendermint consensus mechanism, the BloHeS consensus mechanism introduces a commitpool memory. Every Island manages a separate commitpool where the validators are storing the committed blocks until they are committed by the Archiving cluster. The independent consensus mechanisms of the Archiving cluster and the individual Islands are interconnected with forwarding links. The Islands' committed blocks are sent to the Archiving cluster validators, where the block is stored in the mempool of the Archiving cluster validators and will be integrated into the proposal of the next block. The Archiving cluster has two forwarding links to the Islands, depending on the outcome of the validation process of the transactions. If the block in the Archiving consensus mechanism is committed, a notification is forwarded to the corresponding Islands' proposers in order to clear up the transactions from the commitpool and accordingly the mempool of the validators of the Island. If the Archiving cluster validators cannot commit the block, the Archiving cluster proposer informs the corresponding Islands' proposers of the outcome of the validation process and the transactions are cleared from the commitpool of the Islands.

A new stage in the Island consensus mechanism is the dissemination and finalization stage, which occurs after the Islands receive a commit from the Archiving cluster. During this stage, the Island proposers are informing the Island participants to finalize the validation process by inserting the transactions in the Blockchain record and remove the transactions from the commitpool and mempool of the Island validators.

Figure 5 presents the time line of the BloHeS consensus mechanism. It shows that all committed packets from the independent Island are collected in the mempool of the Archiving cluster, in order to be integrated in the next block.

The BloHeS design and the appropriate BloHeS consensus mechanism can be implemented as a particular use case in a public healthcare system. In such case the Archiving cluster consists of dedicated validator nodes, which are under governmental management. Other independent bodies may also participate in this cluster. The validators from the Island domain are the actual healthcare practitioners from the healthcare network. They are major content creators, creating medical records for every visit from the patients, under the patients' consent.

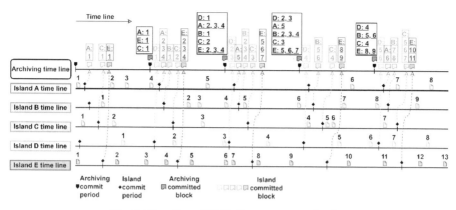

Fig. 5. Time line of BloHeS consensus mechanism

The process of transaction generation and finalization (or archiving of the transaction) starts at the healthcare practitioner's office. The patient visits the healthcare provider and gives permission to the healthcare practitioner to insert new medical record in his medical file. After the record is generated and signed by the healthcare practitioner, the transaction is sent to the Island members for validation. Actually, the validators from the Island are checking the correctness of the transactions through the Island consensus mechanism. After the transaction is validated, proof for transaction validity and its address are inserted in a consolidated transaction that is forwarded to the Archiving cluster. The validators from the archiving cluster are conducting Archiving consensus mechanism to vote for the correctness of the transactions. The output of the Archiving consensus mechanism is a consolidated list of addresses for the transactions in the system in a single consensus cycle. The address of the consolidated list of addresses for the transactions is sent to the appropriate Islands in order to finalize the transactions. The healthcare practitioner receives the finalization signal for the actual transaction and informs the patient.

3 Tendermint and BloHeS Message Exchange Diagrams

For a successful validation process of the Tendermint consensus mechanism, the number of active validators n has to be in the range $[2 * f + 1, 3 * f + 1]$, which results that the number of faulty nodes are in range $[0, f]$, [15]. All active validators contribute with their votes to achieve consensus and finalize the block during the process of consensus achievement. The number of exchanged messages between the validators in every stage of the voting process is called *message count*. The total message count for block finalization in a single round may range between minimum message count M_{min} and maximum message count M_{max}, respectively to the scenarios of f and 0 faulty nodes. The message exchange diagram of the Tendermint consensus mechanism is shown in Fig. 6.

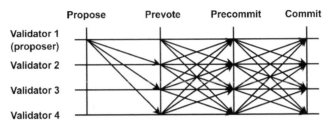

Fig. 6. Tendermint consensus mechanism message exchange

The total message count for a single block finalization in a Tendermint consensus mechanism is the sum of the message count values for three stages of the consensus mechanism. During the propose stage the message count is:

$$M_{propose} = n - 1 = 3f + 1 - 1 = 3f \tag{1}$$

where n is the number of validators in the network and f is the maximum number of the faulty nodes for the given n.

The capability of the consensus mechanism to protect the network from f faulty nodes, gives the possibility to manage correct consensus when the number of correct validators in the network is between $n - f$ and n. Accordingly, the message count for the prevote and precommit phase may range between their minimum and maximum values depending on the number of correct validators in the network. The message count for the prevote and precommit phases are calculated as:

$$M_{prevote}^{min} = M_{precommit}^{min} = (n-1)*(n-f) = 3f*(2f+1) \tag{2}$$

$$M_{prevote}^{max} = M_{precommit}^{max} = (n-1)*n = 3f*(3f+1). \tag{3}$$

Respectively the formulas for the total minimum message count M_{min} and maximum message count M_{max} are:

$$M_{min} = M_{propose} + M_{prevote}^{min} + M_{precommit}^{min} \tag{4}$$

$$M_{max} = M_{propose} + M_{prevote}^{max} + M_{precommit}^{max}. \tag{5}$$

From the analysis of the message exchange diagram of the BloHeS consensus mechanism (see Fig. 7), it is obvious that the message count consists of messages exchanged inside the Islands or intracluster messages, and messages exchanged between the Islands and the Archiving cluster or intercluster messages.

The total message count M of a single round of the BloHeS consensus mechanism is:

$$M = M_{intracluster} + M_{intercluster}. \tag{6}$$

The *intracluster message count*, $M_{intracluster}$, is:

$$M_{intracluster} = n_i * M_{island} + M_{archiving\ cluster} \tag{7}$$

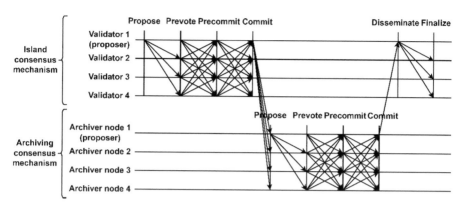

Fig. 7. BloHeS consensus mechanism message exchange

and the *intercluster message count*, $M_{intercluster}$, is:

$$M_{intercluster} = M_{request} + M_{response} = n_a * n_i + n_i. \tag{8}$$

The variable n_i represents the number of Islands in the network and n_a is the number of validators in the Archiving cluster.

The intercluster communication in the Islands has an additional communication stage represented by the dissemination phase, so the message count inside the Island is:

$$M_{island} = M_{propose}^{island} + M_{prevote}^{island} + M_{precommit}^{island} + M_{disseminate}. \tag{9}$$

Further, the message exchange pattern inside the Archiving cluster is the same as the traditional Tendermint consensus mechanism:

$$M_{archiving\ cluster} = M_{propose}^{arch} + M_{prevote}^{arch} + M_{precommit}^{arch} \tag{10}$$

where the actual message count is equal to (4) and (5) respectively, for the minimum message count and maximum message count inside the Archiving cluster.

The message count of the propose, prevote and precommit phases are following the Tendermint consensus mechanism pattern and are calculated as:

$$M_{propose} = n - 1 = 3f + 1 - 1 = 3f \tag{11}$$

$$M_{prevote}^{min} = M_{precommit}^{min} = (n - 1) * (n - f) = 3f * (2f + 1) \tag{12}$$

$$M_{prevote}^{max} = M_{precommit}^{max} = (n - 1) * n = 3f * (3f + 1) \tag{13}$$

and the dissemination phase message count is:

$$M_{disseminate} = n - 1 = 3f + 1 - 1 = 3f. \tag{14}$$

The message count of the prevote and precommit phases is also related to the number of correct validators in the consensus mechanism. Accordingly, there are minimum and maximum message count values. Therefore, the consensus mechanism inside the Archiving cluster and inside the Islands can manage correct consensus between the validators if the number of correct validators ranges between $n - f$ and n, this means that the total message count may range between minimum message count M_{min} and maximum message count M_{max}, respectively. So, the total minimum message count M_{min} and maximum message count M_{max} are:

$$M_{min} = M_{intercluster} + n_i * \left(M_{propose} + M_{prevote}^{min} + M_{precommit}^{min} + M_{disseminate} \right)$$

$$+ M_{archivingcluster} \tag{15}$$

$$M_{max} = M_{intercluster} + n_i * \left(M_{propose} + M_{prevote}^{max} + M_{precommit}^{max} + M_{disseminate} \right)$$

$$+ M_{archivingcluster} \tag{16}$$

where n_i is the number of Islands in the network.

4 Protection Capacity

The novel parameter *protection capacity* P determines the capability of the consensus mechanism to protect the consensus achievement in presence of faulty nodes. The protection capacity is related to the number of faulty nodes that can be endured by the consensus mechanism, while keeping the correctness of the consensus in the system. It is calculated as a sum of the maximum number of faulty nodes that can be tolerated by every cluster in the network:

$$P = \sum_{k=1}^{n_i} f_k \tag{17}$$

where the f_k is the maximum number of faulty nodes that can be tolerated by every Island and n_i is the number of Islands in the network.

The Tendermint network is a single cluster network, which implies the number of Islands to be $n_i = 1$. The Tendermint consensus mechanism by definition can protect the consensus in the system from f faulty nodes that is calculated as:

$$f = \frac{n - 1}{3} \tag{18}$$

where n is the number of validators in the Tendermint network [15]. By implementation of this relation in (17), the protection capacity for the Tendermint consensus mechanism will be:

$$P_T = f = \frac{n - 1}{3} \tag{19}$$

where P_T is the protection capacity of the Tendermint consensus mechanism.

The network organization of the BloHeS system is multi-clustered. The clusters, also known as Islands, implement the Island consensus mechanism, which is based on Tendermint consensus mechanism so they can achieve the same level of protection on an Island level. The distinct Islands can provide different protections from faulty nodes due to different sizes. The protection against faulty nodes on an Island level is given with (18). The validators are participating in the Islands by autonomous decision, which creates non-uniform, and random distribution of the validators among the Islands, so the number of faulty node protection on the Island level will be different for different Islands. The non-uniform validator distribution makes the definition of the protection capacity hard. The protection capacity of the BloHeS system is calculated under assumption of uniform validator distribution, i.e.:

- All Island in the network are of the same size;
- The number of faulty nodes in every Island is the same.

Implementing these assumptions in the formula for protection capacity gives:

$$P_B = P_A + n_i * P_i \tag{20}$$

where P_B is the protection capacity of the BloHeS consensus mechanism, P_A is the protection capacity of the Archiver cluster, n_i is the number of Islands in the network, and P_i is the protection capacity of the Island.

5 Performance Evaluation

To determine the improvement of the BloHeS consensus mechanism over the Tendermint consensus mechanism, a comparison of the message count and protection capacity between the two consensus mechanisms is conducted using MATLAB [20] software.

5.1 Evaluation Scenarios

The performance is evaluated over the same-sized networks of validators, respecting the structural difference between two networks implementing Tendermint and BloHeS consensus mechanisms. The number of validators in the network ranges between $V =$ [1, 1000].

Tendermint network is a single cluster network, so the number of Islands equals n_i = 1 and the number of validators in the Island is equal to the number of validators in the network $n = V$. The number of validators in the Tendermint scenario forms a discrete set of validators following the relation:

$$n = 3 * f + 1, for \ \ f = \left(\frac{n-1}{3}\right) \in N \tag{21}$$

where n is the number of validators in a cluster, f is the maximum number of faulty validators in the network for a given n and N is the set of natural numbers.

In the simulation scenarios for the BloHeS network the Archiving cluster is part of the calculations as a single cluster of 4 validators, $n_a = 1$, and $f = 1$ where $n = 3 * f$ + 1 = 4 assuming a fully functional cluster of validators. Furthermore, the distribution of validators in the BloHeS scenario is following the uniformity criterion (see Sect. 4).

Accordingly, the number of Islands n_i in the simulation increases with the increment of the number of validators in the network in discrete steps as:

$$n_i = \frac{V - 4}{n} \in N \tag{22}$$

where $n = 3 * f + 1$ is the number of validators in a single Island, V is the number of validators in the network and N is the set of natural numbers.

The maximum number of faulty nodes per Island is f = {1, 3, 7, 21} and it determines the evaluated scenarios for the BloHeS consensus mechanism. The number of validators in a single Island is n = {4, 10, 22, 64}, according (21).

5.2 Evaluation Results

The simulation results for the message count, comparing the Tendermint network and BloHeS network scenarios, are presented in Fig. 8. There is obvious improvement and significant message count reduction in the scenarios where the same numbers of valida-tors in both of the networks are participating in the consensus achievement. The results for the message count of the Tendermint consensus mechanism are showing a faster increment rate than the message count of the BloHeS consensus mechanism, which becomes significant as the number of validators in the network increases. The most significant reduction in message count is achieved in the scenario where the number of validators in the Island is $n = 4$. The message count reduction is less significant as the number of validators in the Island increases. For scenarios of $n = 64$ validators in the Islands, the improvement brought by the BloHeS consensus mechanism is small when there is small number of Islands in the network and the improvement is gaining significance as the number of Islands increases.

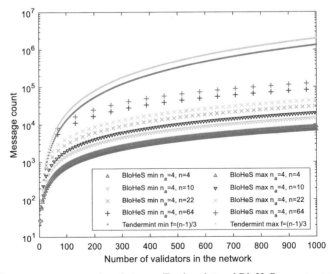

Fig. 8. Message count comparison between Tendermint and BloHeS consensus mechanism

The better performance of the BloHeS consensus mechanism regarding the message count is result of the increased segmentation of the communication in the cluster. The message exchange between the Islands and the Archiving cluster is significantly smaller than the message exchange pattern inside the Islands.

Regarding the simulation of the protection capacity for the Tendermint consensus mechanism the discrete set of the values for number of validators in the network satisfies the formula:

$$P_T = f = \frac{n-1}{3} \in N \tag{23}$$

where f is a maximum number of faulty validators, n is the number of validators in the network and N is the set of natural numbers.

The simulation for the BloHeS consensus mechanism assumes protection capacity of the Archiver cluster $P_A = 1$, protection capacity of the Islands $P_i = \{1, 3, 7, 21\}$, size of the Islands $n = \{4, 10, 21, 64\}$ and discrete set of Islands in the network calculated according to (22).

Figure 9 shows the protection capacity of the BloHeS and Tendermint consensus mechanism. The results for the protection capacity are showing decreased protection against faulty nodes in the networks implementing BloHeS consensus mechanism compared to the Tendermint consensus mechanism. It is important to note, that the protection capacity rapidly increases in the simulation scenarios where the number of validators in the Islands increases. This means that the BloHeS network participants should tend to self-organize in bigger Islands, with an upper limit of around 100 validators per Island, in order to achieve better protection capacity and reduced total message count. The Fig. 9 shows that the protective property of the Tendermint consensus mechanism is better than the BloHeS consensus mechanism, except for marginal values in the scenarios with bigger Islands in the network.

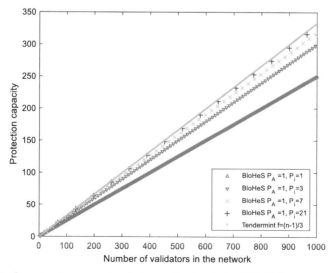

Fig. 9. Protection capacity comparison between Tendermint and BloHeS consensus mechanism

A novel parameter *ratio between the message count and the protection capacity* is determined to provide a sense if the protection gain is sufficient compared to the increased communication complexity of the Tendermint consensus mechanism. Figure 10 presents the results of the ratio between the message count and the protection capacity, where it is obvious that the Tendermint consensus mechanism has a linear increasing factor. This means that the Tendermint's communication complexity increases faster compared to the protection capacity of the Tendermint consensus mechanism when the number of validators in the network increases. The constant ratio between the message count and protection capacity of the BloHeS consensus mechanism shows that there is no increment in the message complexity over the protection capacity as the validators' number increases.

The results in Fig. 9 show that the BloHeS consensus mechanism with bigger Islands gains similar protection capacity with the Tendermint network. Moreover, the ratio between the message count and protection capacity shows that the BloHeS consensus mechanism obtains similar protection capacity to the Tendermint consensus mechanism for less complex message communication.

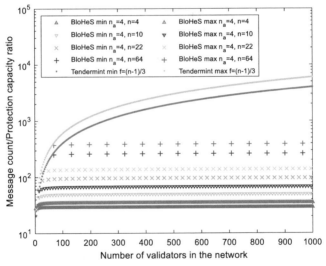

Fig. 10. Message count/Protection capacity ratio comparison between Tendermint and BloHeS consensus mechanism

6   Advantages and Disadvantages of the BloHeS Consensus Mechanism

The main advantage of the BloHeS consensus mechanism is the *reduced message complexity* in the process of consensus achievement. The addition of the new dimension, more precisely the introduction of *multi-layered structure* of the BloHeS consensus mechanism, cuts down the requirements for message exchange with all participants in the network. This advantage is achieved with the price of a *slight reduction of consensus mechanism protection*, which asymptotically approaches the protection achieved by the Tendermint consensus mechanism, when the number of the validators in the Islands increases.

A main disadvantage of the BloHeS consensus mechanism is the *extended time required for consensus finalization*, due to the requirement for consensus finalization in the two stages of the independent consensus cycles. In the best case scenario the time required for consensus finalization of the BloHeS consensus mechanism will be approximately two-times longer than the Tendermint consensus mechanism.

7 Conclusion

The flat architecture of the general Blockchain technologies shows a scaling problem. Independent of the implemented technology, the requirement for peer-to-peer communication creates a burden for the network expansion. An improvement of the network scaling can be achieved by addition of a new dimension. Accordingly, the transaction throughput of the Tendermint consensus mechanism and the scaling performances can be enhanced.

The novel BloHeS consensus mechanism implements the Tendermint consensus mechanism as a base for the segmented consensus mechanisms in each individual cluster in the network. The two-way forwarding links between the higher-layer Archiving cluster and the lower-layer Islands in the network significantly reduce the need for message exchange for consensus achievement. The communication pattern of the Tendermint consensus mechanism shows an exponential increase in the message count as the number of validators increase. The BloHeS consensus mechanism has a linear increment in the message count achieving significant difference for a high number of validators in the network.

The Tendermint consensus mechanism is capable to protect the consensus achievement process from 1/3 malicious nodes. Due to clustered architecture of the BloHeS consensus mechanism the determination of the protection capabilities is hard to be obtained due to the non-uniform distribution of the validators in the Islands. The determination of the protection capabilities is easier under assumption for uniformity in the validator distribution in the Islands. The protection capacity is introduced, to compare the protection capabilities. The analysis shows smaller protection capacity of the BloHeS consensus mechanism in small Island scenarios. However, for bigger Island scenarios of the BloHeS consensus mechanism asymptotically approaches the Tendermint's protection capacity performance.

The ratio of the message count and the protection capacity gives the relation between the message complexity and the protection capabilities of the consensus mechanism. The linearly increasing ratio of the message count and protection capacity by the Tendermint consensus mechanism shows faster increasing of the message complexity compared to the steady protection capacity increment. This performance of the Tendermint consensus mechanism in large networks will create an unusable network due to extreme message storm generated by the validators. On the other side, the constant ratio of the message count and the protection capacity of the BloHeS consensus mechanism shows the capability to obtain constant increment of the message complexity by the constant increment of the protection capacity of the BloHeS consensus mechanism. Comparison of the same-sized Tendermint and BloHeS networks (under assumption of big Islands and uniformity for the BloHeS network) shows that both networks will perform with protection capacity of almost the same level, but the Tendermint network will have more complex message pattern and bigger message count than the BloHeS network. That allows the BloHeS network to scale better than the Tendermint network.

References

1. Del Monte, G., Pennino, D., Pizzonia, M.: Scaling blockchains without giving up decentralization and security. arXiv preprint arXiv:2005.06665 (2020)
2. Nakamoto, S.: Bitcoin: a peer-to-peer electronic cash system (2008)
3. Buterin, V., et al.: Ethereum white paper: a next-generation smart contract and decentralized application platform. Ethereum (2014). http://blockchainlab.com/pdf/Ethereum_white_paper-a_next_generation_smart_contract_and_decentralized_application_platform-vitalik-buterin.pdf
4. Debus, J.: Consensus methods in blockchain systems. Frankfurt School of Finance & Management, Blockchain Center, Technical report, pp. 1–58 (2017)
5. Nguyen, C.T., Hoang, D.T., Nguyen, D.N., Niyato, D., Nguyen, H.T., Dutkiewicz, E.: Proof-of-stake consensus mechanisms for future blockchain networks: fundamentals, applications and opportunities. IEEE Access **7**, 85727–85745 (2019)
6. Castro, M., Liskov, B., et al.: Practical Byzantine fault tolerance. In: OSDI, pp. 173–186 (1999)
7. Lamport, L., Shostak, R., Pease, M.: The Byzantine generals problem. ACM Trans. Programm. Lang. Syst. (TOPLAS) **4**, 382–401 (1982)
8. Kwon, J.: Tendermint: Consensus without mining. Draft v. 0.6, fall. 1 (2014)
9. He, J., Wang, G., Zhang, G., Zhang, J.: Consensus mechanism design based on structured directed acyclic graphs. Blockchain Res. Appl **2**, 100011–100040 (2021)
10. Popov, S.: The tangle. https://assets.ctfassets.net/r1dr6vzfxhev/2t4uxvsIqk0EUau6g2sw0g/45eae33637ca92f85dd9f4a3a218e1ec/iota1_4_3.pdf
11. Baird, L.: The Swirlds hashgraph consensus algorithm: fair, fast, Byzantine fault tolerance. Swirlds Tech Reports SWIRLDS-TR-2016-01, Technical report (2016)
12. Karamachoski, J., Gavrilovska, L.: Extended performance evaluation of the tendermint protocol. In: ETAI 2021 (2021)
13. Buchman, E.: Tendermint: Byzantine fault tolerance in the age of blockchains (2016). https://allquantor.at/blockchainbib/pdf/buchman2016tendermint.pdf
14. Dib, O., Brousmiche, K.-L., Durand, A., Thea, E., Hamida, E.B.: Consortium blockchains: overview, applications and challenges. Int. J. Adv. Telecommun. **11** (2018)
15. Amoussou-Guenou, Y., Del Pozzo, A., Potop-Butucaru, M., Tucci-Piergiovanni, S.: Dissecting tendermint. In: International Conference on Networked Systems, pp. 166–182 (2019)
16. Kwon, J., Buchman, E.: Cosmos - A Network of Distributed Ledgers. Cosmos, dated, pp. 1–41 (2018)
17. Arora, S.K., Kumar, G., Kim, T.: Blockchain based trust model using tendermint in vehicular adhoc networks. Appl. Sci. **11**, 1998 (2021)
18. Karamachoski, J., Gavrilovska, L.: An optimal storage organization for blockchain-based public healthcare system. J. Electr. Eng. Inf. Technol. **5**, 143–152 (2020)
19. Miletic, L.: Formal and simulation analysis of data dissemination algorithms in a blockchain network (2018)
20. MATLAB website. https://www.mathworks.com/products/matlab.html

Designing a Cloud Based Platform for Monitoring Well-Being and Public Health in Areas with Natural Based Solutions

Parisis Gallos[1,2](✉) [ID], Andreas Menychtas[1,2] [ID], Christos Panagopoulos[1] [ID], Eftychios Protopapadakis[3] [ID], Nikolaos Doulamis[3] [ID], Anastasios Doulamis[3] [ID], Emmanuel Sardis[3] [ID], Manthos Bimpas[3], Maria Kaselimi[3] [ID], and Ilias Maglogiannis[2] [ID]

[1] BioAssist S.A, Athens, Greece
parisgallos@bioassist.gr
[2] Computational Biomedicine Research Lab, Department of Digital Systems, University of Piraeus, Piraeus, Greece
[3] National Technical University of Athens, Athens, Greece

Abstract. Nature-Based Solutions (NBS) are innovative, eco-friendly actions aiming to protect, manage and restore natural or modified ecosystems. Urban areas with NBS provide a healthier environment, which can have positive outcomes for health of the citizens, while positively affects their well-being and Public Health. The aim of this paper is to present the specifications and the design of an artificial intelligence (AI) enabled platform for monitoring the citizens' well-being and public health in areas with NBS. The euPOLIS platform's architecture is designed to measure physical activity and collect health related, as well as, environmental data, from multiple data sources to examine the impact of the NBS in the citizens well-being and Public Health. Data analysis and visualization will be conducted using appropriate services and visualization toolboxes. Future work includes the platform development and evaluation coupled with the analysis of the collected data, using specific criteria to assess the improvement of citizens' well-being.

Keywords: eHealth · eCare · Natural Based Solutions (NBS) · Mobile systems · Well-being · Pervasive computing

1 Introduction

1.1 Nature-Based Solutions (NBS)

According to International Union for Conservation of Nature (IUCN), Nature-Based Solutions (NBS) are innovative, eco-friendly solutions which include actions to protect, manage and restore natural or modified ecosystems [1]. The aim of NBS is to address societal challenges effectively and adaptively, while providing human well-being and biodiversity benefits [1]. NBS can offer a sustainable environmental management using solutions with the aim of "bringing nature into cities" by applying interventions for more

D. Perakovic and L. Knapcikova (Eds.): FABULOUS 2022, LNICST 445, pp. 95–102, 2022.
https://doi.org/10.1007/978-3-031-15101-9_7

"green" spaces in urban environment, to decrease the ambient temperature and to reduce pollution [2]. Urban areas with NBS could create a healthy environment which can have positive outcomes for mental and physical health of the citizens, while positively affects their well-being and public health [2]. NBS can also be applied for restoring and protecting forests, seas, and coastal areas.

Since 2016, the European Union recognizes the benefits of NBS application in urban environment and a lot of large-scale demonstration projects have taken place in this field [3]. At the same time, the European Union is investing in NBS to achieve economic targets of job creation, growth, and low-carbon technology innovations while protecting the environment [4]. In addition, several NBS have been tested and implemented across the world, to face environmental, health and socioeconomic challenges [1, 2].

1.2 NBS Value and Contribution to Climate Management and Health

Multiple studies acknowledge the contribution of NBS to climate change mitigation and to climate crisis management. Specifically, research indicates that the application of NBS can not only create environmental benefits but also have multiple benefits for society against climate change [5]. In addition, NBS seem to decrease the vulnerability of the urban environment and enhance the resilience of cities against climatic change [6]. Scientists advise to include NBS in climate policy and urban planning for affective climate control [7].

In addition to NBS' contribution to climate control, the effect of NBS is also significant on public health, as living in areas with NBS appears to be related to the reduction of cardiovascular diseases prevalence and mortality [8]. Studies also present the benefits of NBS interventions on citizen's well-being. Inhabitants seems to be more active in areas with NBS as they increase their daily physical activity visiting "green" sites.

1.3 Information Systems, Public Health and Well-Being

Research outcomes indicate that eHealth services, provided by health information systems and mobile health (mHealth) applications, have a positive impact on the improvement of public health [9, 10]. eHealth solutions appear to be valuable to patients with cardiovascular diseases, providing remote care with very promising results [12]. In addition, eHealth and mHealth can be used for monitoring people's well-being [11–13]. eHealth looks to play a significant role in the well-being of patients with mental diseases as it can provide solutions to support the patients' needs in a non-clinical environment [14–16].

Currently, there are several health information platforms, eHealth solutions and mHealth applications offer remote monitoring of physical activity, based on data which are recorded by wearable devices [17–22]. In addition, mHealth applications can be used to promote physical activity; people are motivated to increase their activity by setting a schedule to workout, reminders to exercise and specific individual goals [23–25].

The aim of this paper is to present the specifications and the design of a holistic platform for monitoring the citizens' well-being and public health in areas with nature-based solutions in the context of the euPOLIS EU research project.

The rest of the paper is organized as follows: Section 2, "The euPOLIS Project", briefly presents the scope of the project and the implementation areas. Section 3, "The euPOLIS Platform", outlines the specifications and the design of the suggested platform. Continuously, Sect. 4, "Discussion", presents the intentional usage of the platform, its value, and its contribution to this field of study. Finally, Sect. 5, "Conclusions", presents a discussion on the proposed platform and future work in the current field.

2   The euPOLIS Project

The euPOLIS (Integrated NBS-based Urban Planning Methodology for Enhancing the Health and Well-being of Citizens: the euPOLIS Approach) project [26] aims to regenerate and rehabilitate urban ecosystems, by creating inclusive and accessible urban spaces, focusing on investigating the impact over citizens well-being.

euPOLIS' scientific and implementation paradigm is based on the Blue Green Solution (BGS) methodology [27] of systemic urban development for sustainability, climate resilience and cost efficiency. The project will address key challenges such as low environmental quality and low biodiversity in public spaces, water-stressed resources, and undervalued use of space. Adopted solutions will be tested in four Front Runner (FR) cities: Belgrade (Serbia), Lodz (Poland), Piraeus (Greece) and Gladsaxe (Denmark). Towards that direction, the project will deploy natural systems to enhance public health and well-being and create resilient urban ecosystems.

One of the main objectives is the implementation of a new urban planning methodology, based on BGS and NBS, enriched with cultural, geographic, and societal aspects of each demo-site. FR cities have different size and climatic characteristics and are situated in different countries in northern and southern Europe. Deployed NBS and monitoring schemes need to adapt appropriately.

Thus, multiple benefits attributed to NBS implementation are expected. Yet, deployment in open public spaces, for enhancing human health and well-being, has many aspects that need consideration, including the type of intervention, appropriate adjustments to the local needs, and monitoring the impact. Additionally, analysis of local micro-climate and environmental conditions will help to identify needs for supportive/complementary measures to be taken in the euPOLIS project.

To assess the impact of BGS and NBS interventions on citizens' well-being and public health, the euPOLIS platform will be utilized based on the user needs as these recorded in the requirements analysis phase of the project.

3   The euPOLIS Platform

The euPOLIS platform's architecture is designed in a way to fulfill the user requirements, as well as to adapt to the ongoing rapid ICT technological progress in the field of personal health and well-being. A dynamic architectural design [28] can support such changes. Specifically, the middleware services are based on the Coodexx platform [29], which enclose a generic database application that can reduce considerably the cost of implementation and maintenance.

The specifications of the proposed platform for monitoring citizens' well-being in areas where NBS are applied include the collection of citizen's physical activity and health related data, and environmental data. The euPOLIS platform will be able to collect recorder data from different data sources and other information systems dedicated to specific types of data (see Fig. 1). Figure 1 also illustrates the euPOLIS platform various data sources such as (a) wearable device and mobile software, (b) installed (or going to be installed) cities' sensors, and (c) any available (or going to be) participatory tools.

Regarding the collection of citizen's activity data, an integrated to the euPOLIS platform mHealth application will be used to track the users' location, to record the date and the time of the visits in the areas, as well as to collect specific user data, such as physical activity (number of steps, daily exercise, walking/running etc.), heartrate, SpO_2, sleep quality, stress levels and other health related information. Regarding environmental parameters, the euPOLIS platform will be also integrated with environmental surveillance systems to receive data from the demo sites such as, temperature, humidity, wind speed and direction, solar radiation, atmospheric pressure, evaporation, water quality, and air quality.

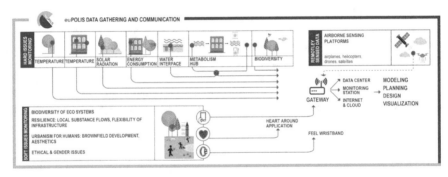

Fig. 1. euPOLIS data gathering, communication and implementations

To collect citizen's data, the "euPOLIS by BioAssist" [30] mHealth application will be used in combination with a smartphone and a wearable device, such as smartwatch or smartband (see Fig. 2). The aforementioned mobile application is a cross-platform release (available for Android and iOS), and it is compatible with several smart devices and wearables. The users' physical activity and health data are recorded by the wearable devices and the users' location is recorded by the mobile application running on the smartphone using the phone's integrated GPS module. Users can complete health related questionnaires through the mobile application. Both users' data and their location are transferred to the platform where data analysis takes place to merge and combine the data from the different sources.

To collect the required environmental data, advanced information systems with sensor networks will be installed to gather data from the surrounding environment. The aggregated data from the various integrated sources will be further analyzed to examine the impact of the NBS on the citizens' well-being and public health.

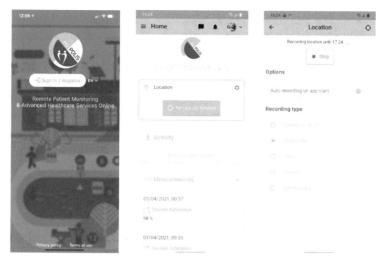

Fig. 2. "euPOLIS by BioAssist" mobile application screenshots

For data analysis and visualization, middleware services will be developed along with an additional visualization toolbox. Specifically, a Data Management System (DMS) will host all related data flows from the different sources. The DMS should support various analytics, accept data form additional sources, and communicate with 3rd party implementations, like simulation or other toolkits. Finally, a visualization toolbox will be used to provide a dynamic interface adjustable to the users' needs and capable of illustrating various information, stored in the DMS or other integrated information systems, including 3D models, advanced analytics, figures, and timeseries data.

4   Discussion

For the design of the euPOLIS platform, a multimodal approach is adopted, capable of providing a vast resource of related data values, spanning multiple categories. Gathered values are paired with location data, facilitating the evaluation of the appropriateness for applied NBS. According to the aforementioned description of the platform, data could be of human nature (e.g., heartrate), environmental conditions (e.g., temperatures), 3D models (e.g., trees), water quality metrics, or any other type capable to facilitate the assessment of implemented NBS. The flexibility of the proposed platform is that individual information systems with sensors can be operated using their software, providing values at any granularity level. The only limitation, on which the euPOLIS project emphasizes, is the capability to access the necessary values using open-source tools.

The mobile app developed in the frame of euPOLIS will be used in combination with wearable devices to support the assessment of the effectiveness and to validate the impact of NBS on public health and the well-being of the citizens. The euPOLIS platform will integrate various data sources, including (a) wearable devices and mobile software, (b) environmental sensors installed in the cities, and (c) available participatory tools, as well as, middleware services and visualization toolkits. The mobile app has been designed to offer an attractive, multilingual, easy-to-use front-end interface, considering usability and accessibility guidelines, to promote inclusivity and user acceptance. According to the international scientific literature, health information systems have been used before to collect data and to assess the well-being of people and public health [10, 13]. The expected value of the proposed platform is to establish an integrated solution to support decision making based on true world data with minimum user engagement, addressed to urban planners, civil engineers, healthcare and other professionals.

5 Conclusions

Urban planners and engineers are integrating nature-based solutions (NBS) to address contemporary environmental, social, and economic challenges. In the context of the EU-funded EuPOLIS project the proposed ecosystem will be developed to examine the deployment of natural systems in the enhancement of public health and well-being and creation of resilient urban ecosystems. The euPOLIS platform stands on the notion of a unified solution, capable to parse, gather, merge, and analyze data from multiple sources, helping city authorities to assess the effectiveness and appropriateness of adopted NBS solutions with regard to bolstering citizens' well-being and public health.

Citizens, city authorities, policy makers, psychologists, sociologists, and communication experts will be engaged in the development of the euPOLIS platform to ensure it is practical and user-friendly, while respecting all relevant privacy issues. The "euPO-LIS by BioAssist" application can be used as a health and other data collection tool. The euPOLIS project will aim to regenerate and rehabilitate urban ecosystems to create inclusive and accessible urban spaces. It will address key challenges, such as low environmental quality and low biodiversity in public spaces, water-stressed resources, and undervalued use of space. Future work includes the platform development and evaluation as well as, the analysis of the collected data using specific criteria to assess the improvement of citizens' well-being and public health.

Acknowledgements. This work is a part of the euPOLIS project. euPOLIS has received funding from the European Union's Horizon 2020 research and innovation program under grant agreement number: 869448 - *Integrated NBS-based Urban Planning Methodology for Enhancing the Health and Well-being of Citizens: the euPOLIS Approach.* The authors would like to thank all partners within euPOLIS project for their cooperation and valuable contribution.

References

1. Cohen-Shacham, E., Walters, G., Janzen, C., Maginnis, S.: Nature-Based Solutions to Address Global Societal Challenges, vol. 97. IUCN, Gland (2016)
2. Eggermont, H., et al.: Nature-based solutions: new influence for environmental management and research in Europe. GAIA-Ecol. Perspect. Sci. Soc. **24**(4), 243–248 (2015)
3. Faivre, N., Fritz, M., Freitas, T., de Boissezon, B., Vandewoestijne, S.: Nature-based solutions in the EU: innovating with nature to address social, economic and environmental challenges. Environ. Res. **159**, 509–518 (2017)

4. Maes, J., Jacobs, S.: Nature-based solutions for Europe's sustainable development. Conserv. Lett. **10**(1), 121–124 (2015)
5. Kabisch, N., Korn, H., Stadler, J., Bonn, A.: Nature-Based Solutions to Climate Change Adaptation in Urban Areas: Linkages Between Science, Policy and Practice. Springer, Cham (2015). https://doi.org/10.1007/978-3-319-56091-5
6. Kabisch, N., et al.: Nature-based solutions to climate change mitigation and adaptation in urban areas: perspectives on indicators, knowledge gaps, barriers, and opportunities for action. Ecol. Soc. **21**(2), 39 (2016)
7. Seddon, N., Chausson, A., Berry, P., Girardin, C.A., Smith, A., Turner, B.: Understanding the value and limits of nature-based solutions to climate change and other global challenges. Philos. Trans. R. Soc. B **375**(1794), 20190120 (2020)
8. Van den Bosch, M., Sang, Å.O.: Urban natural environments as nature-based solutions for improved public health–a systematic review of reviews. Environ. Res. **158**, 373–384 (2017)
9. Grady, A., Yoong, S., Sutherland, R., Lee, H., Nathan, N., Wolfenden, L.: Improving the public health impact of eHealth and mHealth interventions. Aust. N. Z. J. Public Health **42**(2), 118–119 (2018)
10. Freudenberg, N.: Assessing the public health impact of the mHealth app business. Am. J. Public Health **107**(11), 1694–1696 (2017). https://doi.org/10.2105/AJPH.2017.304083.PMID:29019765;PMCID:PMC5637691
11. Saner, H., van der Velde, E.: eHealth in cardiovascular medicine: a clinical update. Eur. J. Prev. Cardiol. **23**(2_suppl), 5–12 (2016)
12. Khorakhun, C., Bhatti, S.N.: Wellbeing as a proxy for a mHealth study. In: 2014 IEEE International Conference on Bioinformatics and Biomedicine (BIBM), pp. 32–39. IEEE, November 2014
13. Kampmeijer, R., Pavlova, M., Tambor, M., Golinowska, S., Groot, W.: The use of e-health and m-health tools in health promotion and primary prevention among older adults: a systematic literature review. BMC Health Serv. Res. **16**(5), 467–479 (2016)
14. Nedungadi, P., Jayakumar, A., Raman, R.: Personalized health monitoring system for managing well-being in rural areas. J. Med. Syst. **42**(1), 1–11 (2018)
15. Ben-Arieh, A., Kaufman, N.H., Andrews, A.B., George, R.M., Lee, B.J., Aber, L.J.: Measuring and Monitoring Children's Well-Being, vol. 7. Springer, Dordrecht (2013). https://doi.org/10.1007/978-94-017-2229-2
16. Hensel, J.M., Ellard, K., Koltek, M., Wilson, G., Sareen, J.: Digital health solutions for indigenous mental well-being. Curr. Psychiatry Rep. **21**(8), 1–9 (2019)
17. Patel, S., Saunders, K.E.: Apps and wearables in the monitoring of mental health disorders. Br. J. Hosp. Med. **79**(12), 672–675 (2018)
18. Majumder, S., Mondal, T., Deen, M.J.: Wearable sensors for remote health monitoring. Sensors **17**(1), 130 (2017)
19. Block, V.A., Pitsch, E., Tahir, P., Cree, B.A., Allen, D.D., Gelfand, J.M.: Remote physical activity monitoring in neurological disease: a systematic review. PLoS ONE **11**(4), e0154335 (2016)
20. Kallipolitis, A., Galliakis, M., Menychtas, A., Maglogiannis, I.: Affective analysis of patients in homecare video-assisted telemedicine using computational intelligence. Neural Comput. Appl. **32**(23), 17125–17136 (2020). https://doi.org/10.1007/s00521-020-05203-z
21. Panagopoulos, C., et al.: Utilizing a homecare platform for remote monitoring of patients with idiopathic pulmonary fibrosis. In: Vlamos, P. (ed.) GeNeDis 2016. AEMB, vol. 989, pp. 177–187. Springer, Cham (2017). https://doi.org/10.1007/978-3-319-57348-9_15
22. Menychtas, A., Doukas, C., Tsanakas, P., Maglogiannis, I.: A versatile architecture for building IoT quantified-self applications. In: 2017 IEEE 30th International Symposium on Computer-Based Medical Systems (CBMS), pp. 500–505. IEEE, June 2017

23. Panagopoulos, C., Menychtas, A., Tsanakas, P., Maglogiannis, I.: Increasing usability of homecare applications for older adults: a case study. Designs **3**(2), 23 (2019)

24. McGarrigle, L., Todd, C.: Promotion of physical activity in older people using mHealth and eHealth technologies: rapid review of reviews. J. Med. Internet Res. **22**(12), e22201 (2020)

25. Dobkin, B.H., Dorsch, A.: The promise of mHealth: daily activity monitoring and outcome assessments by wearable sensors. Neurorehabil. Neural Repair **25**(9), 788–798 (2011)

26. Zafeiropoulos, C.: An introduction to the euPOLIS project. In: Novelties in Intelligent Digital Systems, pp. 197–206. IOS Press (2021)

27. Bozovic, R., Maksimovic, C., Mijic, A., Smith, K.M., Suter, I., Van Reeuwijk, M.: Blue green solutions. A Systems Approach to Sustainable and Cost-Effective Urban Development (2017)

28. Jawhar, I., Mohamed, N., Al-Jaroodi, J.: Networking architectures and protocols for smart city systems. J. Internet Serv. Appl. **9**(1), 1–16 (2018). https://doi.org/10.1186/s13174-018-0097-0

29. Hussels, U., Camarinopoulos, S., Lüdtke, T., Pampoukis, G.: Database application for changing data models in environmental engineering. EnviroInfo, 569–575 (2013)

30. Gallos, P., Menychtas, A., Panagopoulos, C., Bimpas, M., Maglogiannis, I.: Quantifying citizens' well-being in areas with natural based solutions using mobile computing. Stud. Health Technol. Inf. **289**, 465–468 (2021)

Internet of Things and Smart City/Smart Environment Applications

Smart City IoT On-Demand Monitoring System Using a Drone Fleet

Gordana Jotanovic[1]([✉]) [iD], Vladimir Brtka[2] [iD], Jelena Stojanov[2] [iD],
Zeljko Stojanov[2] [iD], Goran Jausevac[1] [iD], and Dalibor Dobrilovic[2] [iD]

[1] Faculty of Transport and Traffic Engineering, University of East Sarajevo,
Doboj, Bosnia and Herzegovina
{gordana.jotanovic,goran.jausevac}@sf.ues.rs.ba
[2] Technical Faculty "Mihajlo Pupin", University of Novi Sad, Zrenjanin, Serbia
vbrtka@tfzr.uns.ac.rs, {jelena.stojanov,zeljko.stojanov,
dalibor.dobrilovic}@uns.ac.rs

Abstract. This paper deals with the management of the Drone Fleet in the areas of Smart Cities that are not infrastructurally covered by continuous monitoring systems. The proposed IoT architecture of the system is based on the cloud and implies the existence of Vehicle Detection Sensors. The role of the drone navigation service is especially elaborated. The Smart City area is divided into sectors, and the value of the potential load of the sector (PSL) is proposed as a measure of the traffic load of the sector. The use of the n-neighborhood concept enables the selection of critical sectors and the implementation of an algorithm that controls the movement of drones. The performed simulation of drone movement, by varying the number of drones and the number of sectors, indicates a change in the length of the distance traveled and the time required to visit all critical sectors. Procedures based on the n-neighborhood concept tend to be general and insensitive to the dynamic nature of traffic, as the set of critical sectors changes.

Keywords: Smart city · IoT · On-demand monitoring · Drone fleets · Vehicle detection sensors · N-neighborhood · Cloud-based drone service

1 Introduction

The use of Unmanned Aerial Vehicles (UAV, a.k.a. drones) has increased in recent years in terms of the number of drones and the number of roles and tasks that drones perform. The application domains cover military, delivery, monitoring, control and recording, to name a few. Also, new fields of application are opening. At the same time, traffic-related problems are becoming significantly more complicated, especially motor vehicle traffic within urban areas. Traffic problems are solved by available methods, but the results of the solutions are not always satisfactory or good enough.

This paper deals with the use of drones in order to improve the quality of monitoring in the areas of Smart Cities, as well as the possibilities of managing and using the

D. Perakovic and L. Knapcikova (Eds.): FABULOUS 2022, LNICST 445, pp. 105–121, 2022.
https://doi.org/10.1007/978-3-031-15101-9_8

Drone Fleet for on-demand monitoring. The use of a Drone Fleet usually involves three or more drones engaged in the task, while fleet management is done from the control center by applying artificial intelligence methods, i.e., machine learning. This research relies on the results of previous research that has dealt with the movement of drones along predetermined routes, which cover part of the urban area, but here more general case of Drone Fleet management is considered, so that there are no predetermined routes [1, 2]. The approach shown here implies that the urban area is divided into sectors, as well as the existence of the possibility of vehicle detection. Also, there is a need for the existence of a Control Center. The problems of calculating total sector traffic load and directing drones to selected sectors (activation of the sector) are discussed. The functions of drones within the sector were discussed in the previous works, and they can be simply positioning the drone camera and recording the situation or touring the sector along a predetermined route. This would avoid several problems related to the need for constant "patrolling", although the need for the existence of vehicle detection sensors increases the cost of the proposed solution.

The rest of the paper is structured as follows: The second part describes the results of selected papers that are relevant to the presented research in terms of topic, subject and problem. Selected previous works mainly deal with the use of drones in urban areas, drone management problems and route calculations. The third part describes the proposed design of a cloud-based IoT layered architecture for on-demand monitoring. The fourth part deals with the analysis of the urban area from the point of view of the Drone Fleet operation in the urban environment. This section presents the theoretical basis for simulating the movement of a Drone Fleet. The fifth chapter presents the results of research (simulations) and discusses them. The results are analyzed, and some potential problems are considered. The concluding part summarizes the results and gives possible directions for future research and upgrades of the proposed solution.

2 Previous Work

Cloud based systems have been intensively used for integrating and managing various ubiquitous systems because they enable services availability for variety of users from anywhere. The use of unmanned aerial vehicles (UAVs), commonly named drones, has expansive growth recently, while estimations indicate that UAV market will surpass USD 28.27 Billion by 2022 [3]. Majority of commercial UAVS use point-to-point communication between the drone and ground stations by using WiFi and TCP protocols, which put limitations on communication range, especially in large scale environments such as cities or larger areas. Use of cloud-based systems for managing drones is recent solution that may help in overcoming communication problems and increase the efficiency and availability of these systems. Cloud based systems with variety of services for analytics, computation, storage, and visualization are well suited for this purpose [4].

Koubâa et al. [3] presented Dronemap Planner (DP), a service-oriented cloud-based system for managing drones. DP enables control, monitoring and communication with drones over the Internet. This solution aims in overcoming limitation of drones related to computation and energy resources, that prevent them to run heavy application onboard. Cloud system provides computing resources to drones, virtualizes access to drones through Web services, schedules drones' missions and support communications among them. DP software architecture contains the following layers or subsystems that contain loosely coupled software components: (1) Communication layer (network sockets and web sockets components), (2) Proxy layer (components for protocol-related operations for message parsing, dispatching, and processing), (3) Cloud layer (with software components Cloud Manager, Storage, Web Services, and Cognitive intelligence), (4) Drone layer (information related to drones), and (5) User layer (components that enable users to access cloud system through web services). Cognitive Engine (CE) is a software component based on artificial intelligence techniques for planning drone paths and solving problems. DP evaluation was performed using real drone for real-time tracking application DroneTrack for tracking moving objects through cloud [5].

Capello et al. [6] proposed a cloud-based supervision system for Remotely Piloted Aircraft Systems (RPAS) in urban environments. The system architecture contains five connected layers: (1) Map Generation Layer – reliable for creating a dynamical map that assists in assessing the risk in the navigation area, (2) Path Planning Layer – reliable for computing a path for RPAS by considering a risk map produced by Map Generation Layer, (3) Control System Layer – reliable for sending commands to hardware layer, performing diagnosis and detecting failures (4) On-board Control System Layer – reliable for flight safety in any condition (it is activated only if a bad connection to cloud is observed), and (5) Hardware Layer – reliable for receiving the control commands and actuating the control devices based on the received signals from the Control layers. Innovative elements in the proposed system are the definition of a dynamic risk-map, and on-board control system for performing emergency maneuvers when the communication with the cloud is critical.

Hu et al. [7] presented CloudStation, a cloud-based ground control station software that enables communication between pilots and drones through TCP and HTTP protocols. CloudStation software provides a graphical user interface for pilots that can control drones. CloudStation architecture contains three parts: (1) Web browser for accessing web application for controlling drones, (2) Linux server in the cloud, and (3) Linux companion computer and a flight controller running Ardupilot on the drone. The software at Linux cloud server is implemented by using with Django, a Model-View-Controller web framework.

Mehrooz et al. [8] proposed a cloud-based platform for open-source Internet of Drones (IoD) application. The platform is based on distributed cloud service data infrastructure, Service-Oriented Architecture (SOA), and Robot Operating System (ROS). The proposed solution has three layers: cloud services, drone computing unit, and drone flight simulator or real time drone flight controller depending on the use. Cloud services layer provides computing software application, storage and network infrastructure. Overall system architecture is modelled in UML and contains four packages related to cloud services, ROS internal communication, flight simulator and real flight control. Cloud services uses REST API to send navigation information relevant for flight (GPS coordinates, position of power towers, etc.) to drones. Test scenario for the proposed cloud-based infrastructure is generated and executed in simulation by using the AirSim/Gazebo simulator.

In [9], dynamic graph convolutional network was considered to predict traffic-flow. Reinforcement learning was used, and the illustration of the application is based on the use of real data on the movement of bicycles. Although the paper does not deal with the use of drones, it is very useful from the point of view of modeling dynamic traffic flows and the methods that were used. The paper contains a description of how to generate dynamic graphs in order to model traffic flows. Of particular interest is "the research of using Euclidean space to model traffic networks", where "the stations are often alone or aggregated in a two-dimensional grid structure, which obviously ignores the topology information between the stations". The above two statements give an idea of the possible way to generate a model of an urban environment or part of an urban environment, and the structure of the model has an impact on the definition of algorithms for drones belonging to the same fleet. The idea of transforming Euclidean space into a non-Euclidean (graph) form is especially considered.

In [10] a time-varying and price-sensitive drone fleet queueing model was formulated for delivery tasks. An approximation algorithm was designed to numerically tackle the problem of Quality of Service, and simulations were performed. The stochastic optimization model was constructed in order to maximize the overall profit, constrained by system performances. This research gives some insight to optimization problems regarding drone fleet performance, as well as the number of drones within the fleet.

Research presented in [11] is more specific and deals with the use of drones for medical item delivery from a logistical point of view. The timing of delivery is critical, and the problem is solved by selecting locations for charging stations, assigning clinics to providers, and scheduling and sequencing the trips. Experiments were conducted, and the number of drones was varied to gain insight into the performance of the solutions proposed. A timeslot trip scheduling formulation is proposed and evaluated. This research points out importance of choosing drone battery recharging station locations or selecting flight starting points for each of the drones. Also, a hint of the idea of an algorithm for drone movement can be gained.

In [12] is given a description of a research on a drone fleet management for providing connectivity to sensors and actuators in Industrial Internet of Things (IIoT) scenarios. The Reinforcement learning (RL) algorithm was applied in order to achieve optimal drone management, deciding the number of drones and taking care of bandwidth. However, it is assumed that it is possible to constantly charge drone batteries, which greatly simplifies the control problem.

Research presented in [13] deals with traffic optimization. It is stated that current Artificial Intelligence (AI) technologies have difficulty in adapting to the dynamic nature of traffic network. Graph Neural Network (GNN) is proposed in order to model and optimize traffic in datacenters. GNN can provide accurate estimation of never-seen network states, while the generalization enabled by GNN overcomes the difficulty of adapting to the dynamic nature of traffic network.

An overview of literature references enables gaining insight into the subject and highlights the characteristics of existing solutions and problems. Based on that, the architecture of the system and the way of managing the drone fleet is proposed in the following sections.

3 IoT Architecture for On-Demand Monitoring

In smart cities, the urban areas that need to be monitored are large. Therefore, it is necessary to provide infrastructure support or use many monitoring devices. The price and number of devices for continuous monitoring, as well as resources for data storage and processing are a significant expense in monitoring systems. The paper proposes an IoT system for monitoring only areas of interest. The system is designed to save data storage capacity and processing resources and optimize the number of drones required for monitoring. The Smart City IoT on-demand monitoring system operates so that Drone Fleet cover the areas that are not covered by infrastructure for continuous monitoring systems. The system is Cloud-Based IoT architecture. The proposed IoT architecture is defined through five layers: three horizontal layers and two vertical layers [4]. The horizontal layers are: Perception Layer, Network Layer, Service & Application Layer (Fig. 1).

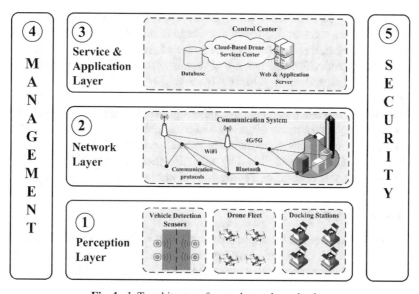

Fig. 1. IoT architecture for on-demand monitoring

The two vertical layers are Management and Security, which are responsible for the control and security of the entire proposed IoT system [14].

3.1 Perception Layer

The basic function of the Perception Layer is to collect data to identify specific parameters for each sector, such as location images, number of vehicles on roads in a defined time interval (traffic frequency), traffic noise, temperature, humidity and air pollution [15]. The perception layer of the IoT system presented in this paper contains Vehicle Identification Sensors, Drone Fleet, and Docking Stations that are necessary for data collection in a particular sector.

Vehicles Detecting Sensor are located along the length of roads in pre-determined urban areas that are of interest for observation and are not infrastructurally covered by monitoring systems. Such areas are named as sectors. Sectors can be of different sizes and shapes. Two adjacent sectors may or may not be interconnected. Depending on the road environment, sectors may have several entrances and exits. The sensors record the number of vehicles entering the observed sector and record the number of vehicles leaving the sector in a certain time interval. The number of vehicles in each sector may indicate the need for monitoring the sector. The images from drone cams are forwarded using the Communication System to the Control Center for processing. The Perception layer must contain a hub device that collects data from sensors and drone cams and allows them to communicate with each other, as well as sends data to the Network layer.

Drone Fleet in the case of the presented IoT system refers to a group of two or more drones that perform the task of supervision as needed and belong to the same Docking Station. Drone Fleet management is performed through the Drone Management Algorithm. The drones in the fleet communicate with the Control Center and with each other. The task of the drone fleet is to monitor a specific sector. The Control Center uses the Drone Management Algorithm to manage drones in the fleet and optimize the number of drones based on hardware performance of drones, maximum flight duration and sector parameters. Also, the number of drones in the fleet depends on the number of sectors and the capacity of the Docking Station.

Docking station contains an automated system that serves drones in terms of fast battery charging, servicing, garaging and other operations related to drones. It is also used for the take-off and landing of drones, and communication with the Control Center. The proposed IoT system envisages the use of static Docking Stations, and the connection with the Control Center is established by wire (Ethernet). The Docking Station is in a place that enables safe take-off or landing and uninterrupted communication of drones.

3.2 Network Layer

The Network Layer oversees the entire communication within the presented IoT system, and with the help of the Communication System it connects the entire system. The task of the Network layer is to achieve secure data transfer (Security Layer) between the drone fleet and the Control Center with the help of the Communication System and vice versa. The management of the entire IoT system is performed in the Control Center which is equipped with a Web & Application server and a database. The Web & Application server coordinates drones, receives data from drones, stores data in a database, performs analytics, and all types of processing. It also manages the data stored in the database and manages the fleet of drones based on the processed data. Internet of Drones (IoD) is also managed by the Control Center through the Cloud-Based Drone Service Center, see Fig. 2. Web and application servers can be low performance because pre-trained neural networks can be used to process and analyze data. Also, the reduction of IoT system costs can be achieved by a strictly controlled drone fleet management system.

Communication system provides two types of communication between drones. These two ways of networking are Drone-to-Drone (D2D) and Drone-to-Infrastructure (D2I). The IoT on-demand tracking system is oriented as Drone-to-Infrastructure (D2I) as communication is established between drones and Vehicles Detecting Sensors, and drones and Docking Stations. Communication is done by the Web & Application Server located in the Control Center. The Communication System uses Bluetooth and 4G/5G technologies. Bluetooth technology is needed to establish drone communication with the Docking Station. Base stations play a key role in maintaining the drone's connection with the Control Center. 4G/5G wireless technologies enable the establishment of drone communication with base stations. Given the location of the system setup and the terrain configuration, the network infrastructure should have support for roaming on Wi-Fi networks. The TCP/IP communication protocol is in the Network Layer.

3.3 Service and Application Layer

The Service & Application Layer is based on the concept of cloud computing and contains resources and elements of artificial intelligence (AI) for data processing. The Cloud-Based Drone Service architecture is presented in further lines.

Control Center enables the management of the entire IoT system and is equipped with a Web & Application server and a Database. Web & Application server, on which Web Services are executed, coordinates drones, receives data from drones, stores data in a database, performs analytics and all kinds of processing. It also manages the data stored in the Database and manages the Drone Fleet based on the processed data. The IoD is also managed by the Control Center through the Cloud-Based Drone Service Center (see Fig. 2).

The main idea of our approach is to integrate system parts implemented by using different technologies such as Internet of Things in sensing in urban area and Drone Fleet used for on-demand monitoring problems in Smart City urban area. The Cloud-based drone service architecture is used for the integration purpose, and it is presented in Fig. 2. For the cloud-based part of the system, a Service-Oriented Architecture (SOA) was accepted since it enables building software systems as a set of independent software services that communicate to achieve certain goals [16].

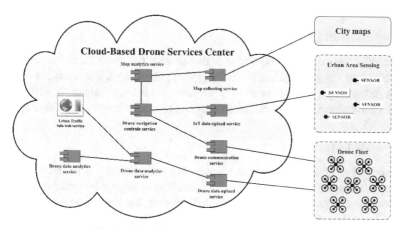

Fig. 2. Cloud-based drone service architecture

The central part is cloud-based system, named Cloud-Based Drone Services Center that is used for integration of different parts of the system. The cloud system is deployed at Linux server, while software services in the cloud are developed in JEE [17].

In the Urban Area Sensing part, sensors for counting the number of vehicles that moves between sectors in the urban area (Vehicle Detection Sensors) are deployed. These sensors send data to the cloud system, where IoT Data Upload Service collects data, do pre-processing (formatting of data) and sends data to Drone Navigation Control Service. All data necessary for further processing are stored in Database and Web & Application server.

Drone Navigation Control Service is a central software service in the cloud part of the IoT system that manages the Drone Fleet based on the Drone Management Algorithm, sending control messages via the Drone communication service. The control of drones is based on data collected from IoT sensors for counting vehicles by using IoT Data Upload Service, and data on sectors deployed on urban area map. The maps are collected by Map collecting service and delivered to Map analytics service for determining the sectors on the map.

The Service & Application Layer, with implemented Web Services, manages all applications and services in the IoT system (see Fig. 2). Drone Navigation Control Service is the central software service in the system and sends control messages via Drone communication service. The Drone Management Algorithm is executed on the Web & Application server.

Also, the Service & Application Layer has the task of integrating the data collected from drones that are uploaded with Drone data upload service, which sends data to Drone data analytics service. Based on the analysis of data obtained from drones, some info can be published by using Urban traffic info web service, while some urban emergency services can be called by using Emergency action service (police, ambulance or parking service). This part of the system will not be presented in detail in this paper. Since the focus is on controlling drone fleet, the following sections will provide details on Drone Navigation Control Service.

3.4   Management Layer

The vertical layer called Management is responsible for control and management of all the layers of the proposed IoT system (Fig. 1). Therefore, the Management Layer controls and manages the core systems in the proposed IoT architecture (Data Collection System, Communication System, Service and Application System and Security).

3.5   Security Layer

The Security Layer should cover all horizontally and vertically oriented layers in the proposed IoT concept. The IoT on-demand monitoring system includes a Drone Fleet with a low level of protection implemented. Therefore, the biggest problem in communication is the detection of anomalies in network traffic caused by DDoS (Distributed Denial of Service) attack. The security of the proposed IoT concept does not propose a new approach for the detection and elimination of network anomalies of DDoS traffic, but the use of already known security models [18].

4 Drone Fleet Operation in Urban Environment

Drone Fleet operation primarily depends on Vehicle Detector Sensors and Control Center. First, it is necessary to clearly define the concept of urban area and urban sectors within urban area (sectors in further text). The term urban area refers to a part of a Smart City or the whole Smart City in a special case. Second, sectors are defined as separate units of an urban area that do not have to be physically adjacent to each other (see Fig. 3).

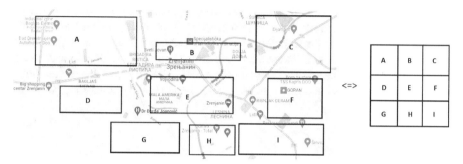

Fig. 3. Example of an urban area and sectors (3 by 3 grid)

Physical sectors are transformed to a Euclidean grid (Sector grid), and therefore the choice of sectors must enable this transformation. Also, sectors do not have to be of rectangular shape. Each of the sectors is defined by inputs (input roads) and outputs (output roads) where Vehicle Detection Sensors are located. For a time-interval [t_0, t_1] at moment t_1, it is possible to obtain the total number of vehicles that entered the sector, as well as the total number of vehicles that left the sector.

The parameters that affect the choice of urban area relate primarily to the available resources: Vehicle Detection Sensors that are pre-installed or there is a real possibility of implementing Vehicle Detection Sensors. Also, the architecture and layout (position) of Control Centers play a significant role in this. It is easy to see that the signal range (connection of the drone with the control center) is a significant parameter. In addition, the choice and size of this area, are directly related to the hardware performance of drones and maximum flight duration. The layout of battery replenishment stations (Docking Stations) also plays a significant role.

The representation of the urban area by sectors is suitable as a basis for drone management so that the sectors are further elaborated. The assumption is that sectors are accessible by air so that drones can reach them. There are several limiting factors for drone movement such as: obstacles (tall buildings…), weather conditions in general (rain, snow, wind direction and strength before all), restricted sectors, etc. Restrictive factors affect the length of the route, and thus prolong the length of the flight. Each of the sectors can contain:

- Road traffic infrastructure (intersections, roads, roundabouts, parking lots…).
- Residential infrastructure (buildings, green areas and parks…).

- Network infrastructure that allows drone operation within the sector. Possible drone functions were discussed in [1, 19] where the paths were predefined by a graph and Dijkstra [20, 21] and Floyd-Warshall [22–24] algorithms were used.

The next task of this research is to single-out the sectors that should be visited, so it is necessary to define the criteria for selecting the sector. As stated earlier, each sector is characterized by the total number of entering vehicles (summed data from all Vehicle Detection Sensors) in a certain time interval (in) and the total number of leaving vehicles (summed data from all Vehicle Detection Sensors) in the same time interval (out). The difference between inputs and outputs may be one of the indicators of the situation within the sector, but it should be borne in mind that the sectors are not the same size (area) and are different in structure. If this is considered, it would be necessary to define a threshold for each sector separately that determines whether the sector should potentially be processed. Instead, Potential Sector Load (PSL) as a criterion for sector selection is considered.

4.1 Potential Sector Load

Potential Sector Load (PSL) is a measure related to the worst-case scenario. In order to calculate PSL value, the immediate neighborhood of the sector S, 1-neighborhood, is considered, and in Fig. 4, 1-neighborhood and 2-neighborhood are shown to illustrate the concept of the n-neighborhood.

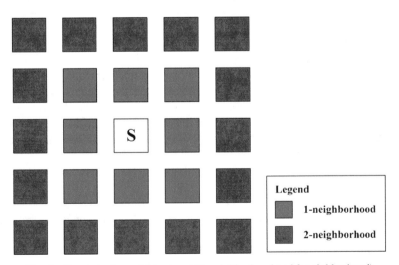

Fig. 4. Concept of n–neighborhood (1-neighborhood and 2-neighborhood)

For the sector S defined by coordinates (i, j), two values are calculated: Total entry into sector S at moment t (1) and total entry into sector S at moment t + 1 (2). Worst case scenario implies that at moment t all vehicles leaving the neighboring sectors (1-neighborhood) to S, move towards sector S, and at moment t + 1 all vehicles entering the neighboring sectors (1-neighborhood) to S, will also move towards sector S.

$$Input(t)_{i,j} = \sum_{\substack{m, n \in \{-1, 0, 1\} \\ m^2 + n^2 \neq 0}} out_{i+m,j+n}(t) \tag{1}$$

$$Input(t+1)_{i,j} = \sum_{\substack{m, n \in \{-1, 0, 1\} \\ m^2 + n^2 \neq 0}} in_{i+m,j+n}(t) \tag{2}$$

PSL value (3) for the sector S defined by coordinates (i, j) is calculated as difference between (2) and (1).

$$PSL_{i,j} = u_{i,j}(Input(t+1)_{i,j} - Input(t)_{i,j}) \tag{3}$$

In (3) $u\_(i, j)$ is sector coefficient that reflect sector features like: total number of parking spaces, usual traffic load, road quality, noise sensitivity, etc. In case when $Input(t+1)_{i,j} > Input(t)_{i,j}$ the value of $PSL_{i,j}$ is positive, meaning that there is a potential for sector overload. These calculations are executed in Control Center via *Drone navigation control service*.

4.2 Simulation

The drone management simulation was implemented in the Java programming language. Sectors are represented by a Sector grid (the obvious representation is a 2D matrix). For each sector the values of input (in) and output (out) are defined. These values consider the time of day, i.e., traffic peaks are simulated. For each sector in Sector grid the PSL value was calculated based on (3). Figure 5 shows the PSL values (Fig. 5a), and for a given threshold, the sectors in which the PSL value exceeds the specified threshold are selected (Fig. 5b).

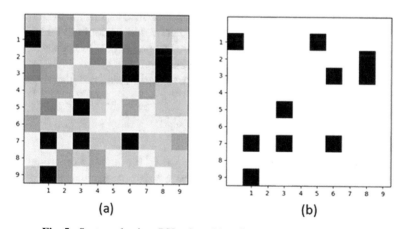

(a)   (b)

Fig. 5. Sector selection: PSLvalues (a) and complete graph nodes (b)

In this way Euclidean representation (Fig. 5a) is transformed to non-Euclidean (Fig. 5b): the selected sectors marked in black represent the nodes of the complete graph. This is a weighted complete graph where each two nodes are linearly connected by an edge having the weight equals the spatial distance. The edges of the graph are not shown for obvious reasons.

The parameters that determine the simulation are Sector grid size (Fig. 5 shows grid 10 by 10 for practical reasons only), the time of the day, the number of drones, the initial position of the drones and the threshold value.

4.3   Drone Management Procedure

The drone management procedure should determine the path for each drone. Given the low-cost variant of the system architecture, the Drone Management Algorithm must be memory and time undemanding.

The implemented procedure for drone management means that the n-neighborhood of each drone is examined, starting from 1-neigborhood. There are two obvious options for a drone current neighborhood:

1. there is not a single node whose PSL value exceeds a given threshold, and
2. there are several nodes (sectors) to visit.

In the first case, the neighborhood of the drone is expanded, after the 1-neighborhood a 2-neighborhud is considered, etc. In this way, the entire Sector grid is potentially tested. In the second case, the sector with the highest PSL value is selected. If drone priority is defined, there is no problem with two or more drones going into the same sector. The priority of drones is determined based on the remaining duration of the flight (depending on the battery) and drone location. The frequent occurrence of the drone neighborhood overlap problem also depends on the size of the Sector grid, number of drones and the initial positions of the drones.

For each drone, the n-neighborhood concept allows the application of multiple heuristic search strategies. In this case, the heuristic can be defined as follows: the most critical of the closest sectors has the advantage. In other words, sectors are ranked first by distance and then by criticality. Drone management procedure is executed in Web & Application server via Drone navigation control service.

A simulation of the proposed solutions was performed, and the discussion is presented in the following section.

5   Results and Discussion

The conducted simulation examines the influence of the number of drones and the dimensions of the Sector grid on the cost and the number of iterations required to visit all selected sectors. The cost value is calculated based on the total number of sectors that the drones visited (including those sectors that drones have just flown over), so it is only a rough indication of the total path cost that the drones would achieve in real-life circumstances. The number of iterations required for a Drone Fleet to visit all selected sectors is a rough indication of the time required. PSL values were calculated for each sector and normalized to [0, 255], while threshold was set to 150.

Two scenarios were simulated:

1. Sector grid size is constant while drone count variate.
2. Number of drones is constant while Sector grid size variate.

For each of the two scenarios, the simulation was repeated 1000 times, with the time during the day being constant (08:00 am), sector coefficient was set to 1 for all sectors and the displayed values of cost and number of iterations being mean values. Results are presented by tables and graphically. Table 1 shows the variation in cost and number of iterations depending on the number of drones in the fleet. Sector grid size is set to 50 for both dimensions.

Table 1. Cost and number of iterations depending on the number of drones.

Drones:	3	4	5	6	7	8	9	10
Cost	646	680	705	735	767	783	797	834
Iterations	38	29	23	20	17	15	13	12

Table 2 shows the variations in cost and number of iterations for a constant number of drones (five), with the Sector grid size varying in both dimensions.

Table 2. Cost and number of iterations depending on the sector grid size.

Sector grid size:	30	40	50	60	70	80	90	100
Cost	302	492	713	958	1243	1553	1891	2256
Iterations	12	17	24	30	38	46	55	64

Graphical representation is given in Fig. 6.

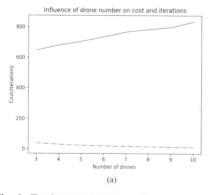 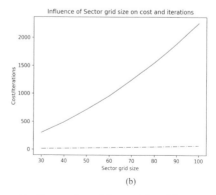

(a)   (b)

Fig. 6. Total cost and number of iterations influenced by the number of drones (a) and Sector grid size (b) (Color figure online)

The blue line indicates the cost, while the orange dashed line indicates the number of iterations. Both simulation scenarios confirm that the chosen heuristics for drone management work as expected. Table 1 and Fig. 6a show that increasing the number of drones in the fleet increases the total cost but decreases the number of iterations (time). On the other hand, the increase in the dimensions of the Sector Grid, with a constant number of drones, significantly affects the increase in cost, while the number of iterations is slightly growing (see Table 2 and Fig. 6b).

The problem that is becoming obvious is determining the optimal number of drones. This is a complex problem that depends on several parameters and is not considered in this paper.

In addition, two issues are interesting to consider. Namely, there is a possibility of changing the PSL value of the sector during the drone movement. In the case of a decrease in the PSL value below the preset threshold, the sector should not be selected, i.e., it is no longer active, which results in the removal of node and edges of the complete graph. The proposed method of drone management is not sensitive to these changes, which is certainly an advantage.

A problem that is also becoming apparent is the involvement of a Drone Fleet in the case of a small number of sectors whose PSL value exceeds the predefined threshold. This is the case of single sector with a PSL value greater than threshold, or there are several "scattered" sectors of this type. Such a situation corresponds to some night traffic regimes or special situations. Figure 7 shows examples of several situations. Figure 7a shows a common case of Sector grid to be processed. Figure 7b shows the case of a smaller number of active sectors but they are grouped, which may be the reason for drone fleet engagement. Figures 7d, 7e, and 7f show examples of the Sector grid that may not require Drone Fleet engagement.

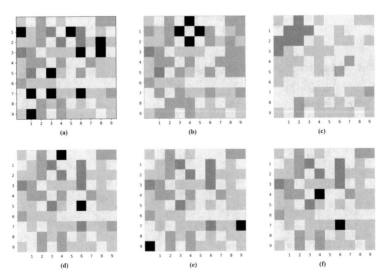

Fig. 7. Sector grids that need to be processed (a), (b), (c) and Sector grids that do not need to be processed (d), (e), (f)

The case that stands out is shown in Fig. 7c, there are no active sectors but there is a group of sectors that are congested with traffic, but no sector alone exceeds the PSL threshold. This situation may also be the reason for the drone fleet engagement. A situation with a small number of close sectors whose PSL values are higher or close to the threshold of $m \times n$ dimension Sector grid, is easily recognized by creating a frame (window) of dimensions $i \times j$ where $i < m$ and $j < n$ that would slide across the Sector grid and check the PSL of sectors it covers. However, it is possible to use Convolutional Neural Networks (CNN) to identify such potentially critical sectors. Based on previous experience, proposed CNN architecture is:

1. Convolution2D (kernel = 128, kernel_size = (3, 3), activation = 'relu')
2. MaxPooling2D (pool_size = (3, 3))
3. Dense (64, activation = 'relu')
4. Dense (1, activation = 'sigmoid')

A trained CNN can recognize a Sector grid that contains critical sectors, even if none of the sectors exceeds the PSL threshold. This solution enables generalization, i.e., identification of potentially critical situations that have not been seen before.

6 Conclusions

This paper deals with the management of the Drone Fleet in the areas of Smart Cities that are not infrastructural covered by continuous monitoring systems. Attention was primarily focused on the problem of drone control and management, with the aim of determining the locations that drones should visit. The proposed approach involves the use of a Drone Fleet working over sectors of the urban area.

First, the proposed IoT architecture is cloud-based and implies the existence of a Vehicle Detection Sensors. The basic idea was to integrate parts of the system implemented using different technologies such as the Internet of Things and a Drone Fleet. On-demand IoT monitoring system as well as drone management using Web Services are described.

Second, the sector grid generation procedure and the procedure for selection of critical sectors were proposed. These procedures are based on n-neighborhood concept and tend to be general and suitable for implementation. The Drone Management Algorithm also uses the concept of n-neighborhood and is not sensitive to the dynamic nature of traffic, given that the set of critical sectors is changing. The simulation conducted on two scenarios shows the impact of drone number and sector grid size on the path cost and the total time required to visit critical sectors. The criticality of the sector depends on the number of vehicles entering/leaving the sector. The results of the simulation indicate that increasing the number of drones increases the total path cost, but reduces the time required to visit all critical sectors. Increasing the size of the urban area also increases the total path cost and time required.

The possible roles of drones within the sector have not been considered. However, the role within the sector can be simple recording the situation, monitoring of traffic load, calculation and recalculation of routes presented by the graph, as well as monitoring of improperly parked vehicles. The number of possible roles within the sector is certainly higher.

It is useful to look at the prospects of real-life implementation. The research described in other papers provides insight into the problems of Drone Fleet management and parameters optimization. The possibility of using Graph Neural Networks (GNN), whose training requires significant resources, should be emphasized here, although the use of trained GNN is significantly less resource intensive. In addition, the choice of drone starting points and battery recharge station (Docking Station) positions is becoming clear, which is a separate study. Given that low-cost implementation in real-life conditions was anticipated, the assumption is that process power is limited. Also, the content of previous work provides a clear insight into the impact of weather conditions, which can be a limiting factor for implementation in real life. Therefore, the proposed solution allows the formation of nodes and an efficient and easy to implement Drone Management Algorithm.

The advantages of the IoT on-demand monitoring system are scalability and decentralization. The scalability of the IoT system can be achieved by developing Client Applications that are directed towards citizens and police, ambulance, and parking service. This is partially considered in the cloud-based architecture as Emergency action service, (see Fig. 2). Decentralization of the system can be done by each Docking Station taking the role of Control Center.

Future research may relate to the improvement of the Drone Management Algorithm as well as the further use of convolutional neural networks, primarily for the assessment of critical situations in Smart City traffic. The method of sector selection and the selection of significant sector parameters are also possible directions for future research.

Acknowledgments. Ministry of Education, Science and Technological Development, Republic of Serbia financially supported this research, under the project number TR32044: "The development of software tools for business process analysis and improvement", 2011–2021.

References

1. Jausevac, G., Dobrilovic, D., Brtka, V., Jotanovic, G., Perakovic, D., Stojanov, Z.: Smart UAV monitoring system for parking supervision. In: Perakovic, D., Knapcikova, L. (eds.) FABULOUS 2021. LNICSSITE, vol. 382, pp. 240–253. Springer, Cham (2021). https://doi.org/10.1007/978-3-030-78459-1_18

2. Dobrilović, D., Brtka, V., Jotanović, G., Stojanov, Ž, Jauševac, G., Malić, M.: Architecture of IoT system for smart monitoring and management of traffic noise. In: Knapčíková, L., Peraković, D., Behúnová, A., Periša, M. (eds.) 5th EAI International Conference on Management of Manufacturing Systems. EICC, pp. 251–266. Springer, Cham (2022). https://doi.org/10.1007/978-3-030-67241-6_21

3. Koubâa, A., et al.: Dronemap planner: a service-oriented cloud-based management system for the internet-of-drones. Ad Hoc Netw. **86**, 46–62 (2019)

4. Gubbi, J., Buyya, R., Marusic, S., Palaniswami, M.: Internet of Things (IoT): a vision, architectural elements, and future directions. Futur. Gener. Comput. Syst. **29**, 1645–1660 (2013). https://doi.org/10.1016/j.future.2013.01.010

5. Koubâa, A., Qureshi, B.: DroneTrack: cloud-based real-time object tracking using unmanned aerial vehicles over the internet. IEEE Access **6**, 13810–13824 (2018)
6. Capello, E., Dentis, M., Guglieri, G., Mascarello, L.N., Cuomo, L.S.: An innovative cloud-based supervision system for the integration of RPAS in urban environments. Transp. Res. Procedia **28**, 191–200 (2017)
7. Hu, L., et al.: "CloudStation:" a cloud-based ground control station for drones. IEEE J. Miniaturization Air Space Syst. **2**, 36–42 (2020)
8. Mehrooz, G., Ebeid, E., Schneider-Kamp, P.: System design of an open-source cloud-based framework for internet of drones application. Presented at the 2019 22nd Euromicro Conference on Digital System Design (DSD) (2019)
9. Peng, H., et al.: Dynamic graph convolutional network for long-term traffic flow prediction with reinforcement learning. Inf. Sci. **578**, 401–416 (2021)
10. Pei, Z., Dai, X., Yuan, Y., Du, R., Liu, C.: Managing price and fleet size for courier service with shared drones. Omega **104**, 102482 (2021)
11. Ghelichi, Z., Gentili, M., Mirchandani, P.B.: Logistics for a fleet of drones for medical item delivery: a case study for Louisville, KY. Comput. Oper. Res. **135**, 105443 (2021)
12. Faraci, G., Raciti, A., Rizzo, S.A., Schembra, G.: Green wireless power transfer system for a drone fleet managed by reinforcement learning in smart industry. Appl. Energy **259**, 114204 (2020)
13. Li, J., Sun, P., Hu, Y.: Traffic modeling and optimization in datacenters with graph neural network. Comput. Netw. **181**, 107528 (2020)
14. Kapoor, A.: Hands-On Artificial Intelligence for IoT: Expert Machine Learning and Deep Learning Techniques for Developing Smarter IoT Systems. Packt Publishing (2019)
15. Jotanovic, G., Brtka, V., Curguz, Z., Stojcic, M., Eremija, M.: Mobile applications for recording road traffic noise. In: Proceedings 8th International Conference on Applied Internet and Information Technologies, "St Kliment Ohridski" University-Bitola, Faculty of Information and Communication Technologies-Bitola, Bitola, Republic of Macedonia, pp. 94–98 (2018)
16. Rotem-Gal-Oz, A.: SOA Patterns. Simon and Schuster (2012)
17. Kumar, B.V.: Implementing SOA Using Java EE. Pearson Education India (2010)
18. Cvitić, I., Peraković, D., Periša, M., Botica, M.: Novel approach for detection of IoT generated DDoS traffic. Wirel. Netw. **27**(3), 1573–1586 (2019). https://doi.org/10.1007/s11276-019-020 43-1
19. Dobrilović, D., Brtka, V., Jotanović, G., Stojanov, Ž, Jauševac, G., Malić, M.: The urban traffic noise monitoring system based on LoRaWAN technology. Wirel. Netw. **28**(1), 441–458 (2021). https://doi.org/10.1007/s11276-021-02586-2
20. Dijkstra, E.W.: A note on two problems in connexion with graphs. Numer. Math. **1**, 269–271 (1959)
21. Junior, D.P., Wille, E.C.G.: FB-APSP: a new efficient algorithm for computing all-pairs shortest-paths. J. Netw. Comput. Appl. **121**, 33–43 (2018)
22. Floyd, R.W.: Algorithm 97: shortest path. Commun. ACM **5**, 345 (1962)
23. Anderson, J.: Discrete Mathematics with Combinatorics Pearson (2004)
24. Aini, A., Salehipour, A.: Speeding up the Floyd-Warshall algorithm for the cycled shortest path problem. Appl. Math. Lett. **25**, 1–5 (2012). https://doi.org/10.1016/j.aml.2011.06.008

An IoT Integrated Air Quality Monitoring Device Based on Microcomputer Technology and Leading Industry Low-Cost Sensor Solutions

Ioannis D. Apostolopoulos[1]([⊠]), George Fouskas[1], and Spyros N. Pandis[1,2]

[1] Foundation for Research and Technology Hellas – Institute of Chemical Engineering Sciences, Patras, Greece
`japostol@iceht.forth.gr`
[2] Department of Chemical Engineering, University of Patras, Patras, Greece

Abstract. Indoor and outdoor air quality monitoring is essential for the prevention of undesired exposure to air pollutants, especially for sensitive groups. Extensive exposure to particulate and gaseous pollutants can cause temporary and chronic respiratory and other diseases and even lead to premature death. The emergence of low-cost sensors enables the development of affordable devices that measure the concentrations of various pollutants and notify humans for the quality of the air that they breath. Current microcomputer technology and the advances in wireless communications, as well as data systems, provide space for Internet of Things devices that monitor, track, store and analyze pollutant concentration measurements enabling data analytics. In this work, we describe the development and testing of a compact, integrated air quality monitoring device that detects and reports fine particulate matter ($PM_{2.5}$), nitrogen dioxide (NO_2), and ozone (O_3) levels as well as temperature (T) and relative humidity (RH).

Keywords: Air quality monitoring · Internet of Things · Low-cost sensors · Calibration · Microcomputers · Raspberry PI

1 Introduction

In recent years, the monitoring and reporting of indoor and outdoor Air Quality (AQ) have become an urgent need [1]. Real-time monitoring can provide many benefits. For example, accurate knowledge of the level of air quality in a city can provide warnings for sensitive groups and also lead to mitigation actions to reduce the respiratory and other problems caused by the high air pollutant concentrations [2, 3].

Breathing particulate matter can cause premature death especially in people with heart or lung disease, aggravated asthma, decreased lung function, and increased respiratory symptoms, such as irritation of the airways, coughing or difficulty breathing [4]. Exposure to ozone has been found to trigger a variety of health problems, such as

D. Perakovic and L. Knapcikova (Eds.): FABULOUS 2022, LNICST 445, pp. 122–140, 2022.
https://doi.org/10.1007/978-3-031-15101-9_9

chest pain, coughing, throat irritation, and congestion [4, 5]. Nitrogen dioxide aggravates respiratory symptoms, increases hospital admissions, and emergency department visits, particularly in asthmatics, children, and older adults; increases susceptibility to respiratory infection [6].

Traditional monitoring and reporting the exact concentrations of pollutants require high costs. Accurate instruments are quite expensive and it is difficult to have tens of measurement stations even in a large city [7]. Precision air pollution measurement instruments can cost from a few tens of thousands of euro to hundreds for a complete measurement suite [1].

In recent years, several new micro-sensors for monitoring and recording the concentrations of particles and gaseous pollutants have been developed. These sensors have low-cost but they are less accurate than traditional air quality monitors. Low-cost sensors have attracted the interest of many institutes, scientific bodies and researchers, as well as companies [8–10]. Despite their disadvantages, such as measurement uncertainty, frequent errors, periods of instability, etc. [11], these sensors offer a new approach for high spatial resolution air quality monitoring (AQM) in urban areas in both the developed and the developing world.

A plethora of projects have employed various low-cost sensors to characterize air quality. For example, RAMP (SENSIT Technologies), is a device that can measure various gas pollutants, such as ozone, nitrogen dioxide, nitrogen monoxide, carbon monoxide, as well as particulate matter ($PM_{2.5}$ and PM_{10}) and carbon dioxide [12]. The RAMP has been evaluated in several research projects in urban, indoor, and industrial environments [12–14]. A low-cost device dedicated to particulate matter ($PM_{2.5}$ and PM_{10}) concentration measurement has been developed by PurpleAir and it intended for both indoor and outdoor use. Studies have shown that this particular device is an effective solution the measurements of fine particulate matter levels [15, 16]. AEROQUAL is another device developed for monitoring several gaseous pollutants and meteorological conditions [17].

In this work, we present an AQM solution, which offers stability, accuracy, and ease of use. Leveraging the capabilities of microcomputers and the Internet of Things (IoT), we propose a smart indoor and outdoor AQM device equipped with efficient, cutting-edge low-cost sensors, which are selected based-on recent research and evaluation campaigns. The device is based on the Raspberry PI microcomputer, which operates on top of the analog and digital sensors and is responsible for sensor data acquisition, storage and transmission. It also offers a variety of device monitoring services, such as network connectivity configuration. Low-cost sensors, such as Plantower PMS5003, Alphasense NO2-B43F and Alphasense OX-B431, are used to estimate the concentration of fine particulate matter ($PM_{2.5}$) and the two major gaseous pollutants (NO_2, O_3). Henceforth, this device is referred to as ENvironment SENSIng Appliance (ENSENSIA).

The overall contributions of the present work can be summarized as follows:

1. We present a low-cost AQM solution for indoor and outdoor environments
2. The proposed device is evaluated in real conditions against another well-established low cost device (RAMP)

3. ENSENSIA enables real-time parameter tuning for remote control and intelligent edge-computing implementation of linear corrections to the raw readings. The coefficients of the linear regression can also be tuned remotely
4. A functional and user-friendly platform is developed for visualizing the sensor's readings

2   Materials and Methods

2.1   Hardware

Raspberry PI Microcomputer. ENSENSIA relies on the newest Raspberry Pi Model 4B. Raspberry PI is a low-cost, credit-card sized computer that operates like a normal personal computer. Its small size enables its use in several environments and aids to its transferability. Raspberry PI Model 4B includes 4 USB ports, 2 mini-HDMI ports for screen display, as well as Ethernet port. Raspberry PI functionalities can be extended by leveraging the 40-pin headers, which allow for integrating several handcrafted or commercial Hardware Attached on Top (HAT). HATs are expansion boards that connect to the Raspberry Pi's set of 40 GPIO pins and add multiple functionalities, such as sensors, fans, 4G transmitters and more.

UPS. Falling voltages and long power outages can affect the operation of the device. Therefore, a UPS HAT was implemented to maintain the power supply. Waveshare UPS HAT uses I2C bus communication and offers real-time monitoring of battery voltage, current, power, and remaining capacity. This HAT integrates multi-battery protection circuits, such as discharge and over-charge protection.

2.2   PMS5003 Sensor

PMS5003 is a matchbox-sized particulate matter (PM) sensor that reports PM concentrations for various size ranges (including $PM_{2.5}$ and PM_{10}). It is based on laser technology under the light scattering principle to obtain its readings. PMS5003 has been examined and evaluated by several research studies [12, 18, 19] and stands out to be an excellent solution for low-cost AQM projects. Its characteristics are summarized in Table 1.

The PMS5003 performance for fine PM ($PM_{2.5}$) has been found to be very good under most conditions, while its ability to measure coarse particles (in the 2.5–10 μm diameter range) appears to be problematic [10]. Therefore, it will only be used for $PM_{2.5}$ measurements in the proposed device.

Table 1. PMS5003 sensor specifications

Specification	Value/description
Sensor type	Dust sensor – laser technology
Typical input voltage	4.5–5.5 V DC
Operating current	100 mA
Communication protocol	UART, TTL Serial
Power consumption in work mode	Below 100 mA
Sensitivity	50% – 0.3 µm, 98% – 0.5 µm and larger
Working temperature	−10 to 60 °C
Working relative humidity range	0–99%

2.3   Alphasense NO2-B43F Sensor

Alphasense sensors have been used in several AQM projects [20–22]. The US Environmental Protection Agency (EPA) is occasionally evaluating such sensors in ambient collocation setups, offering variety of reports that demonstrate reliability, accuracy, and precision. NO2-B43F is designed to measure nitrogen dioxide (NO_2) levels. The specifications of the sensor are summarized in Table 2.

Table 2. NO2-B43F sensor specifications

Specification	Value/description
Sensor type	Electrochemical NO_2 sensor
Typical input voltage	5 V DC
Communication protocol	Analog
Sensitivity	−220 to −650 nA/ppm at 2 ppm NO_2
Working temperature	−30 to 40 °C
Working relative humidity range	15–85%

2.4   Alphasense OX-B431 Sensor

Similar to the NO2-B43F sensor, OX-B431 is designed to measure ozone concentrations. It works in conjunction with NO2-B43F. The specifications of the sensor are summarized in Table 3.

The performance of OX-B431 has been also evaluated in several studies [23, 24] and has been found to be acceptable under specific environmental conditions.

Table 3. OX-B431 sensor specifications

Specification	Value/description
Sensor type	Electrochemical O_3 sensor
Typical input voltage	5 V DC
Communication protocol	Analog
Sensitivity	-225 to -750 nA/ppm at 2 ppm O_3
Working temperature	-30 to 40 °C
Working relative humidity range	15–85%

2.5 BME680 Sensor

BME680 (Bosch Sensortec) integrates temperature, humidity, and pressure sensors [25]. Its size and low-power consumption make it a good choice for portable devices and wearables. Its specifications are summarized in Table 4. BME680 has been evaluated in several studies and has been found to be one of the best options for the specific task [26, 27].

Table 4. BME 680 sensor specifications

Specification	Value/description
Sensor type	Meteorological
Typical input voltage	1.7–3.6 V DC
Communication protocol	I^2C and SPI
Working conditions	Temperature: -40 to 85 °C Humidity: 0 to 100% Pressure: 300 to 1100 hPa

2.6 PCB Development

All sensors operate via the SDA-SCL and RTX-TDX channels of the Raspberry PI, allowing for I^2C and SPI connectivity/communication protocols. The complete board is furnished with male and female pin-headers to host the sensor chips and ensure a stable card for their operation. To this end, a PCB has been developed and is illustrated in Fig. 1.

PCB is designed using the open-source software KICAD.

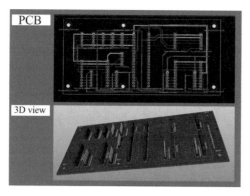

Fig. 1. PCB design.

2.7 Packaging of AQM Device

ENSENIA should operate without interruptions in various environmental conditions. Meanwhile, it is required to be of minimum size to increase its portability. Air pollutant sensors are exposed to ambient conditions and should be protected from wind gusts, rain, and dust. Therefore, we have designed a box for the device that meets these criteria (Fig. 2). The sensors are placed at the bottom of the box, in special holes that isolate the electronic parts of the sensor from the inlets from which the air to be measured enters.

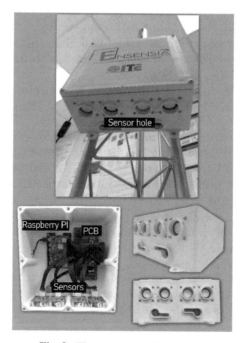

Fig. 2. The complete AQM device.

Around the edges of the sensor, and at a depth slightly greater than the depth of the exposed surface of the sensor, a plastic shield is placed. For further protection from living organisms, the surfaces of the sensors are protected by a special screen.

The box is designed to the specifications of a waterproof (IP65-66), durable and lightweight material and is manufactured via a 3D printer (Leapfrog – Bolt PRO). Figure 2 illustrates the inside and the outside of the ENSENSIA device.

2.8 Software

Raspberry PI Firmware, Internet and Functions. Raspberry PI's operational system is the official Raspberry PI OS. Raspberry PI consists of an integrated Wi-Fi-module and supports an Ethernet cable connection. For the specific project, the device is configured to use a Wi-Fi connection. ENSENIA operates within a Python Programming language framework (version 3.8). All configurable parameters are stored in a special file with an .ini extension. This file is read from the python scripts to adjust the corresponding tunable parameters in real-time.

MQTT Protocol. Data-centric communication is a new paradigm used in Wireless Sensor Networks (WSN). One form of data-centric communication examples is that of publish/subscribe messaging system that is dominant in distributed computing. MQTT is a topic-based protocol, based on publish/subscribe method [28]. MQTT uses character strings and enables the subscription to multiple topics. MQTT requires a client to setup a connection with a broker [28]. Both client and broker need to stay connected to a specific topic to exchange messages. Messages are not stored in any format with this communication protocol. Hence, a client publishing a message to a topic that a broker is not listening will be lost. The broker supervises the liveliness of the client/connection by a "keep-alive" timer, which defines the maximum time interval that may elapse between two messages received from that client.

We have used the Mosquitto [29] open-source implementation of MQTT protocol to enable such communication between the server and ENSENSIA.

Server-Side Data Processing and Storage (MariaDB). Messages published by the client (AQM device) are processed by a python script that operates on the server side and establishes an MQTT connection between the broker and the clients. The decoded messages are appropriately interpreted into useful measurements that are stored in a local database. We use MariaDB server for such operations, which is a popular and effective open-source relational database. MariaDB is furnished by the developer of MySQL and is the default database server for most Linux distribution systems. The sensor readings are organized into separate MySQL tables.

Alarms. Alarms play essential role in modern IoT applications [30]. They are designed to notify the user about a specific situation where a malfunction or an undesired event took place. ENSENSIA is configured to track and monitor its condition and inform the server about several critical factors that affect its AQM effectiveness. PCB and sensor I/O errors, abnormal sensor readings (such as peaks) and system-focused information, such as CPU temperature and available SD card memory space, are communicated with the server every 2 min. In this way, the user can have a complete overview of what is happening inside the device and can prevent potential malfunction.

Parameter Tuning and Real-Time Calibration. Remote parameter tuning is highly desirable in IoT devices and provides flexibility, transferability, and ease-of-use. The proposed AQM device supports remote parameter tuning in a secure way by leveraging the capabilities of MQTT.

ENSENSIA uses the MQTT protocol to mirror its current state in the server at a prefixed time interval (default is every 30 s). The server is listening to the MQTT messages from the device and is storing the device's current state in an SQL table. A second SQL table is utilised to store the desired state, which is defined by the remote user. A Python script operating on the server-side is responsible for comparing the two tables and generating the necessary messages back to the AQM device. Real time correction of the raw measurements is enabled by remotely tuning the coefficient a and the residual b of the linear correction formula based on the sensor calibration:

$$Measurement_{corrected} = a(Measurement_{raw}) + b \qquad (1)$$

In this way, the user can change if needed the calibration equation of the device effortlessly to correct for errors, such as over-time drift. The user can also manually place the device under zero air conditions and adjust the parameters to correct the sensor readings. Use of other more complex correction equations and algorithms is possible if needed.

2.9 Visualization

NetData Cloud. Inspection of ENSENSIA's real-time performance in terms of system operations is an essential feature of modern IoT devices. Netdata is a distributed platform that provides real-time performance and health monitoring of sensor devices, especially the ones operating with the Raspberry PI technology. The Netdata agent is free and open-source and comes with the Netdata cloud agent, which provides various visualizations for monitoring the system's activity.

Netdata collects thousands system, hardware and application metrics and utilizes approximately 1% of the CPU to offer this service. It is also endowed with hundreds of default alarms that are fully customizable.

Real-Time Air Quality Monitoring Visualizations. The ENSENSIA device comes with a specially designed web interface platform providing useful gauges, graphs, charts and forms to visualize the air quality and the device's functions. Those services are summarized in Table 5.

The web interface is developed using open-source software and is hosted by the Informatics and Communication Centre of the Institute of Chemical Engineering Sciences in Patras, Greece. Figure 3 illustrate some examples.

Table 5. Web interface utilities

Interface/page	Utilities
Gauges	Provides gauges for visualizing the sensor readings
Charts	Provides charts to illustrate historical sensor data
Status	Informs the user of the current status of the devices (online/offline)
Configuration	Enables remote parameter tuning
Alarms	Presents a set of pre-defined alarms
Map	Places each associated sensor on a map, where the user can inspect the locations of the sensors and access their current readings

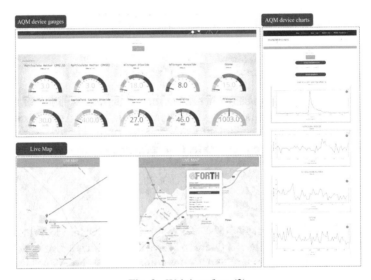

Fig. 3. Web interface (2)

2.10   Device Evaluation Co-location Setups

ENSENSIA has been tested in the field after co-location with established low-cost AQM systems (RAMP). In this way, the proposed AQM device is evaluated for its effectiveness compared to its counterpart, which is considered to be a stable and reliable low-cost AQM device. In this section, we provide descriptions of the measurement sites, the associated infrastructure and the experimental setups.

Measurement Sites. *FORTH/ICE-HT ambient*

The devices were placed on the roof of the institute's facilities, which is in a suburban area, about 5 km from the city of Patras, a city of approximately 300,000 inhabitants. The exact location of the site is at a latitude of 38.2979 and a longitude of 21.8090. The site is about 3 km from the coast.

FORTH/ICE-HT indoor

The AQM device was placed inside an office of the ICE-HT institute which contains three desks and several servers. During the campaign, there were on average two persons in the office during the working hours of 8 am to 4 pm.

Collocation Setups (CS). Preliminary evaluation setups are designed and performed to inspect the performance of the developed AQM device (Table 6). Indoor and outdoor performance was examined using other instrumentation next to RAMP. Inter-unit consistency tests were also conducted. Inter-unit consistency is an important test prior to evaluation with reference measurements. For the purposes of the campaign, a second identical ENSENSIA device was developed to inspect the response of both devices, when placed together under the same conditions.

Table 6. AQM device evaluation campaigns.

CS #	Starting date	End date	Measurement site	Devices
1	30/9/2021 12:00	5/10/2021 23:00	Indoor (office)	ENSENSIA, RAMP
2	14/10/2021 10:00	20/10/2021 10:00	Outdoor	ENSENSIA, RAMP
3	1/7/2021 10:00	13/7/2021 9:00	Outdoor	2 ENSENSIA devices

CS #1 refers to a 6-day evaluation of the device's performance in indoor conditions. The device was placed in the office, as explained earlier. A RAMP was also located inside the office next to our ENSENSIA device.

CS #2, an ambient collocation setup (CS #2) was used for seven days. A RAMP was located next to the ENSENSIA device.

CS #3 was used for 13 days in ambient conditions outdoors. During this campaign, two ENSENSIA devices were collocated to investigate the inter-unit consistency. No reference instrumentation was present in this setup.

Correction. The correction formulas for $PM_{2.5}$ proposed by [10] were used for the Plantower PMS5003 measurements. These have been developed for the same urban area. The corresponding correction equation is:

$$PM_{2.5\,|\,corrected} = 0.42 * PM_{2.5\,|\,measured} + 1.26\,\mu g\,m^{-3} \qquad (2)$$

where $PM_{2.5\,|\,measured}$ is the raw measurement reported by the sensor. More complex corrections are needed for the NO_2 and O_3 concentrations [12]. For the rest of the sensor readings of both RAMP and ENSENSIA, no further calibration formulas or methods were applied. RAMP sensors, as well, as ENSENSIA sensors come factory-calibrated. The user should note that field calibration is important for low-cost sensors and requires reliable reference instrumentation. The authors intend to perform such tasks in future studies.

Evaluation Metrics. A series of evaluation metrics can be used for the quantification of the performance of low-cost sensors. The Mean Error (ME) or Mean Error (ME) and

Root Mean Squared Error (RMSE) are absolute accuracy metrics and give the average errors with respect to the reference measurements. The Normalized Mean Error (nME) is a relative accuracy metric. Finally, the Mean Bias (MB) describes the bias of the sensor compared to the reference device.

Given a set of n values (O_i) from the reference instrument and a set of values (E_i) for the low-cost sensor the above metrics are calculated using the following equations:

$$ME = \frac{\sum_{i=1}^{n} |Ei - Oi|}{n} \tag{3}$$

$$RMSE = \sqrt{\frac{\sum_{i=1}^{n} (Ei - Oi)^2}{n}} \tag{4}$$

$$MB = \frac{\sum_{i=1}^{n} (Oi - Ei)}{n} \tag{5}$$

$$nME = \frac{\sum_{i=1}^{n} |Oi - Ei|}{\sum_{i=1}^{n} Ei} \tag{6}$$

R (correlation coefficient) and R^2 (coefficient of determination) are correlation metrics that describe the strength of relationship between the sensor readings and the reference measurements. Studies suggest that at least ME, RMSE, R, R^2, and nME [11] should be reported.

3 Results

3.1 Device Measurement Stability

We evaluated the stability of ENSENSIA with the following criteria: a) continuous, uninterrupted operation of the Raspberry PI device, and b) continuous, uninterrupted data flow at specific intervals (2 min). We monitored the device's battery level and data messages over a period of 30 days during July 2021. ENSENSIA is configured to transmit measurements ever two minutes. Hence, the total number of expected data packets was 21600. The received measurements were 21103 less than the expected, resulting in a data loss of 2.3%. This was mostly due to 3 power outages in the area and also to some Wi-Fi connectivity problems. There were no power outages of the Raspberry PI. The average battery charge (from 20% to 95%) time after a power outage was 4 h.

3.2 Indoor Assessment (CS #1)

The PM$_{2.5}$ concentrations during the measurement period varied from 3.75 to 10.9 $\mu g\,m^{-3}$ (average 6.5 $\mu g\,m^{-3}$). The corresponding range for NO$_2$ was 12–18 ppb (average 14.6 ppb) and O$_3$ from 2 to 18 ppb (average 9.6 ppb). The indoor evaluation metrics of ENSENIA against the RAMP measurements are summarized in Table 7. The metrics correspond to averages of the measurements over 60 min.

Table 7. Assessment metrics for CS #1 for hourly-averaged measurements

	PM$_{2.5}$ (μg m^{-3})	NO$_2$ (ppb)	O$_3$ (ppb)	Temperature ($^{\circ}$C)	Humidity (%)
R	0.96	0.76	0.56	0.95	0.90
R^2	0.92	0.58	0.38	0.91	0.81
ME	0.39	0.91	2.04	0.38	1.75
RMSE	0.49	1.12	2.58	0.48	2.1
MB	−0.02	−0.02	−0.17	−0.25	−1.42
nME	0.1	0.07	0.09	0.02	0.01

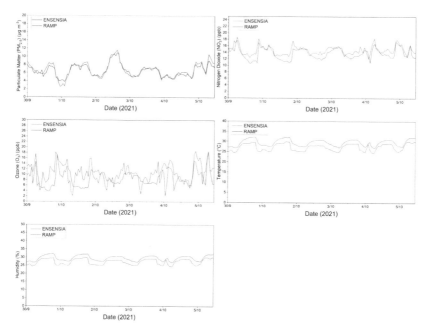

Fig. 4. Time-series for the measurements of PM$_{2.5}$, O$_3$, NO$_2$, T, and RH for CS #1 from the ENSENSIA device and the RAMP device.

The agreement of the ENSENSIA for PM$_{2.5}$ was encouraging with little bias (−0.02 μg m^{-3}), high correlation (R = 0.96) and a RMSE of only 0.39 μg m^{-3}. The normalized mean discrepancy (nME) is 1%. The two devices also gave similar NO$_2$ measurements with a nME of 7% and a RMSE of 1.1 ppb (Fig. 4).

The moderate correlation (R = 0.76) is due to a large extent to the narrow range of the concentrations during the measurements. Indoor ozone was quite low during the measurement period, but the two devices once more gave measurements consistent with each other (nME = 9%) and a RMSE of only 2.6 ppb. The meteorological sensors gave measurements with an average discrepancy of 1–2% (Fig. 5).

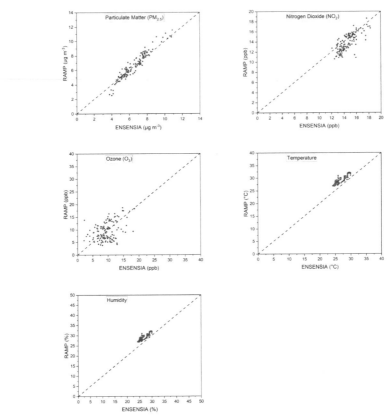

Fig. 5. Scatter plots for the measurements of $PM_{2.5}$, O_3, NO_2, T, and RH for CS #1.

3.3 Outdoor Assessment (CS #2)

The $PM_{2.5}$ concentrations during the measurement period varied from 2 to 23 $\mu g\ m^{-3}$ (average 7.24 $\mu g\ m^{-3}$). The corresponding range for NO_2 was 2–24 ppb (average 18.29 ppb) and O_3 from 2 to 60 ppb (average 29.9 ppb). The indoor evaluation metrics of ENSENIA against the RAMP measurements are summarized in Table 8. The metrics correspond to averages of the measurements over 60 min.

The agreement of ENSENSIA for $PM_{2.5}$ showed $-0.47\ \mu g\ m^{-3}$ bias, high correlation (R = 0.98) and little RMSE of 1.01 $\mu g\ m^{-3}$. nME is found to be 6%. The two devices also yielded similar NO_2 readings (R = 0.85) with a nME of 11%. Ozone levels were higher compared to the indoor experiments. Again, the two devices gave consistent measurements, with a nME of 10% and RMSE of 6.86 ppb. The moderate correlation (R = 0.71) is a result of discrepancy between the sensors in higher concentrations, as seen in Fig. 6.

The meteorological sensors gave measurements with an average discrepancy of 1–2% (Fig. 7).

Table 8. Assessment metrics for CS #2 for hourly-averaged measurements

	PM$_{2.5}$ (μg m^{-3})	NO$_2$ (ppb)	O$_3$ (ppb)	Temperature (°C)	Humidity (%)
R	0.98	0.85	0.71	0.95	0.97
R^2	0.96	0.72	0.50	0.92	0.94
ME	0.81	1.52	3.00	1.39	2.01
RMSE	1.01	2.38	6.86	2.04	2.56
MBE	−0.47	0.92	1.91	−1.33	−0.25
nMAE	0.06	0.11	0.10	0.01	0.01

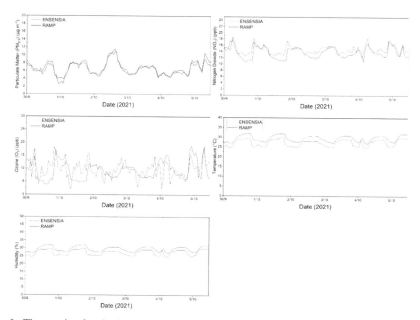

Fig. 6. Time-series for the hourly values of PM$_{2.5}$, O$_3$, NO$_2$, T, and RH for CS #2 from the ENSENSIA device and the RAMP device.

3.4 Inter-unit Consistency (CS #3)

Inter-unit consistency tests are conducted to validate measurement agreement between identical devices, in terms of hardware and software. Slight measurement variations are expected according to the manufacturers of the low-cost sensors. In Table 9, the evaluation metrics are presented. Assessment metrics are recorded from hourly-averaged values.

The two devices show high correlation factors among their readings. PM$_{2.5}$, PM$_{10}$, T, and RH yield a very high correlation (R = 0.99) and small RMSE and bias (Fig. 8).

The nME is found to be 1–2%. NO$_2$ and O$_3$ sensors show moderate correlation (R = 0.81 and R = 0.84 respectively) (Fig. 9).

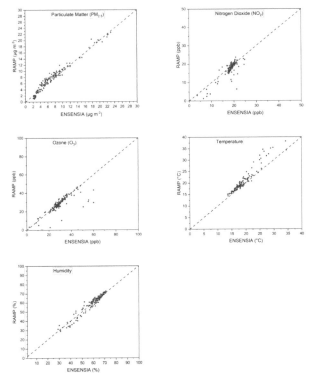

Fig. 7. Scatter-plots for the hourly values of $PM_{2.5}$, PM_{10}, O_3, NO_2, T, and RH for CS #2.

Table 9. Assessment metrics for CS #3 for hourly-averaged measurements

	$PM_{2.5}$ ($\mu g\ m^{-3}$)	NO_2 (ppb)	O_3 (ppb)	Temperature (°C)	Humidity (%)
R	0.99	0.81	0.84	0.99	0.99
R^2	0.98	0.62	0.71	0.97	0.98
ME	1.57	1.13	11.39	0.56	0.75
RMSE	1.77	1.80	15.21	0.56	0.91
MBE	1.53	0.76	−0.34	−0.24	−0.47
nMAE	0.02	0.16	0.03	0.02	0.01

4 Discussion and Conclusions

We presented the hardware and software components and the newly developed AQM device (ENSENSIA). The new device communicates with a user-friendly web interface that provides gauges, charts and real-time parameter tuning, as well as default alarms to monitor the device status. We evaluated ENSENSIA with respect to its operating stability, its agreement with a well-established AQM device counterpart (RAMP), and its agreement with an identical device (inter-unit consistency). Raspberry PI showed great stability during the assessment tests and proved to be a reliable low-cost solution

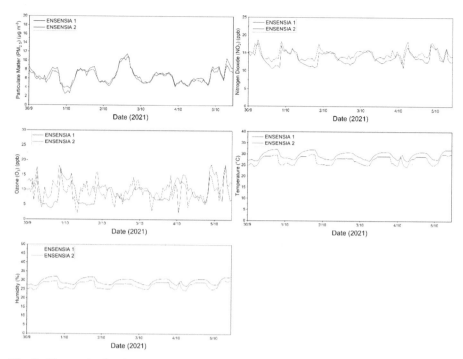

Fig. 8. Time-series for the measured and the reference hourly values of $PM_{2.5}$, PM_{10}, O_3, NO_2, T, and RH for CS #3.

for such AQM applications. The hourly measurements of the new device had normalized mean errors of less than 2% for $PM_{2.5}$, NO_2 and O_3 for both the indoor and outdoor tests compared to the established low-cost sensing RAMP system. Also, inter-unit consistency tests showed promising results. The discrepancy between the two identical units was little, as expected, and can be eliminated with the use of linear formulas that correct the bias. In the next steps of this work the new AQM device will be evaluated against reference instruments that are used for regulatory applications for much longer periods and for a much wider range of atmospheric concentrations and conditions. MQTT and web-interface security measures are already studied to limit security vulnerabilities.

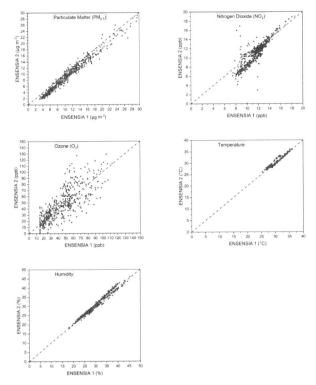

Fig. 9. Scatter-plots for the measured and the reference hourly values of $PM_{2.5}$, PM_{10}, O_3, NO_2, T, and RH for CS #3.

5 Conflicts of Interest

The authors declare that there are no conflicts of interest.

Funding. This work was partially supported by the "KRIPIS - Poiotita Zois II" project (MIS 5002464), which has received funding the General Secretariat for Research and Innovation, Greece.

References

1. Malings, C., et al.: Fine particle mass monitoring with low-cost sensors: corrections and long-term performance evaluation. Aerosol Sci. Technol. **54**, 160–174 (2020). https://doi.org/10.1080/02786826.2019.1623863
2. Lelieveld, J., Haines, A., Pozzer, A.: Age-dependent health risk from ambient air pollution: a modelling and data analysis of childhood mortality in middle-income and low-income countries. Lancet Planet. Health **2**, e292–e300 (2018). https://doi.org/10.1016/S2542-5196(18)30147-5
3. Goldemberg, J., Martinez-Gomez, J., Sagar, A., Smith, K.R.: Household air pollution, health, and climate change: cleaning the air. Environ. Res. Lett. **13**, 030201 (2018). https://doi.org/10.1088/1748-9326/aaa49d

4. Liu, X., et al.: Low-cost sensors as an alternative for long-term air quality monitoring. Environ. Res. **185**, 109438 (2020). https://doi.org/10.1016/j.envres.2020.109438

5. Nuvolone, D., Petri, D., Voller, F.: The effects of ozone on human health. Environ. Sci. Pollut. Res. **25**(9), 8074–8088 (2017). https://doi.org/10.1007/s11356-017-9239-3

6. Atkinson, R.W., Butland, B.K., Anderson, H.R., Maynard, R.L.: Long-term concentrations of nitrogen dioxide and mortality: a meta-analysis of cohort studies. Epidemiology (Cambridge, Mass.). **29**, 460 (2018)

7. Rai, A.C., et al.: End-user perspective of low-cost sensors for outdoor air pollution monitoring. Sci. Total Environ. **607–608**, 691–705 (2017). https://doi.org/10.1016/j.scitotenv.2017.06.266

8. European Commission Joint Research Centre: Evaluation of low-cost sensors for air pollution monitoring: effect of gaseous interfering compounds and meteorological conditions. Publications Office, LU (2017)

9. Schneider, P., Castell, N., Vogt, M., Dauge, F.R., Lahoz, W.A., Bartonova, A.: Mapping urban air quality in near real-time using observations from low-cost sensors and model information. Environ. Int. **106**, 234–247 (2017). https://doi.org/10.1016/j.envint.2017.05.005

10. Kosmopoulos, G., Salamalikis, V., Pandis, S.N., Yannopoulos, P., Bloutsos, A.A., Kazantzidis, A.: Low-cost sensors for measuring airborne particulate matter: field evaluation and calibration at a South-Eastern European site. Sci. Total Environ. **748**, 141396 (2020). https://doi.org/10.1016/j.scitotenv.2020.141396

11. Giordano, M.R., et al.: From low-cost sensors to high-quality data: a summary of challenges and best practices for effectively calibrating low-cost particulate matter mass sensors. J. Aerosol Sci. **158**, 105833 (2021). https://doi.org/10.1016/j.jaerosci.2021.105833

12. Zimmerman, N., et al.: A machine learning calibration model using random forests to improve sensor performance for lower-cost air quality monitoring. Atmos. Meas. Tech. **11**, 291–313 (2018). https://doi.org/10.5194/amt-11-291-2018

13. Jain, S., Presto, A.A., Zimmerman, N.: Spatial modeling of daily $PM_{2.5}$, NO_2, and CO concentrations measured by a low-cost sensor network: comparison of linear, machine learning, and hybrid land use models. Environ. Sci. Technol. **55**, 8631–8641 (2021). https://doi.org/10.1021/acs.est.1c02653

14. Landis, M.S., et al.: The U.S. EPA wildland fire sensor challenge: performance and evaluation of solver submitted multi-pollutant sensor systems. Atmos. Environ. **247**, 118165 (2021). https://doi.org/10.1016/j.atmosenv.2020.118165

15. Barkjohn, K.K., Gantt, B., Clements, A.L.: Development and application of a United States-wide correction for $PM_{2.5}$ data collected with the PurpleAir sensor. Atmos. Meas. Tech. **14**, 4617–4637 (2021). https://doi.org/10.5194/amt-14-4617-2021

16. Tryner, J., et al.: Laboratory evaluation of low-cost PurpleAir PM monitors and in-field correction using co-located portable filter samplers. Atmos. Environ. **220**, 117067 (2020)

17. Masey, N., et al.: Temporal changes in field calibration relationships for Aeroqual S500 O_3 and NO_2 sensor-based monitors. Sens. Actuators B Chem. **273**, 1800–1806 (2018). https://doi.org/10.1016/j.snb.2018.07.087

18. Malings, C., et al.: Development of a general calibration model and long-term performance evaluation of low-cost sensors for air pollutant gas monitoring. Atmos. Meas. Tech. **12**, 903–920 (2019). https://doi.org/10.5194/amt-12-903-2019

19. Feenstra, B., et al.: Performance evaluation of twelve low-cost PM2. 5 sensors at an ambient air monitoring site. Atmos. Environ. **216**, 116946 (2019)

20. Christakis, I., Hloupis, G., Stavrakas, I., Tsakiridis, O.: Low cost sensor implementation and evaluation for measuring NO_2 and O_3 pollutants. In: 2020 9th International Conference on Modern Circuits and Systems Technologies (MOCAST), pp. 1–4. IEEE (2020)

21. Mijling, B., Jiang, Q., de Jonge, D., Bocconi, S.: Field calibration of electrochemical NO_2 sensors in a citizen science context. Atmos. Meas. Tech. **11**, 1297–1312 (2018). https://doi.org/10.5194/amt-11-1297-2018

22. Spinelle, L., Gerboles, M., Aleixandre, M.: Performance evaluation of amperometric sensors for the monitoring of O_3 and NO_2 in ambient air at ppb level. Procedia Eng. **120**, 480–483 (2015). https://doi.org/10.1016/j.proeng.2015.08.676

23. Dallo, F., et al.: Laboratory calibration and field assessment of low-cost electrochemical Ozone sensors in Alpine and Arctic environments. In: Geophysical Research Abstracts (2019)

24. Zuidema, C., Afshar-Mohajer, N., Tatum, M., Thomas, G., Peters, T., Koehler, K.: Efficacy of paired electrochemical sensors for measuring ozone concentrations. J. Occup. Environ. Hyg. **16**, 179–190 (2019)

25. Yurko, G., et al.: Real-time sensor response characteristics of 3 commercial metal oxide sensors for detection of BTEX and chlorinated aliphatic hydrocarbon organic vapors. Chemosensors **7**, 40 (2019). https://doi.org/10.3390/chemosensors7030040

26. Catini, A., et al.: Development of a sensor node for remote monitoring of plants. Sensors **19**, 4865 (2019)

27. Marinov, M.B., Ganev, B.T., Nikolov, D.N.: Indoor air quality assessment using low-cost commercial off-the-shelf sensors. In: 2021 6th International Symposium on Environment-Friendly Energies and Applications (EFEA), pp. 1–4. IEEE, Sofia, Bulgaria (2021). https://doi.org/10.1109/EFEA49713.2021.9406260

28. Hunkeler, U., Truong, H.L., Stanford-Clark, A.: MQTT-S — A publish/subscribe protocol for Wireless Sensor Networks. In: 2008 3rd International Conference on Communication Systems Software and Middleware and Workshops (COMSWARE 2008), pp. 791–798. IEEE, Bangalore, India (2008). https://doi.org/10.1109/COMSWA.2008.4554519

29. Light, R.A.: Mosquitto: server and client implementation of the MQTT protocol. J. Open Source Softw. **2**, 265 (2017). https://doi.org/10.21105/joss.00265

30. Nguyen, T.D., Marchal, S., Miettinen, M., Fereidooni, H., Asokan, N., Sadeghi, A.-R.: DÏoT: a federated self-learning anomaly detection system for IoT. In: 2019 IEEE 39th International Conference on Distributed Computing Systems (ICDCS), pp. 756–767. IEEE, Dallas, TX, USA (2019). https://doi.org/10.1109/ICDCS.2019.00080

Information Service for the Visually Impaired Persons in Public Transport – MAppIN

Marko Periša⬤ , Petra Zorić(✉) ⬤ , and Valentina Anić

Faculty of Transport and Traffic Sciences, University of Zagreb, Vukelićeva 4, 10000 Zagreb, Croatia
{marko.perisa,petra.zoric}@fpz.unizg.hr

Abstract. Applying appropriate assistive technology makes it possible to ensure greater inclusion of persons with visual impairments in society. In this paper, research was conducted related to the attitudes and satisfaction of visually impaired persons with existing information services provided by public transport companies in the city of Zagreb. Functionalities of the information service for blind and partially sighted persons when using the public transport system are proposed based on the analysis of the collected and processed data. The conceptual architecture of the system for the delivery of information services of this group of users based on modern information and communication technologies has also been proposed. A test environment was created to check the operation of certain functionalities of the information service. The result of this is the proven operation of the proposed architecture of the information service delivery system. This solution can increase the degree of mobility and quality of life of this group of users, ensuring the implementation of the Society 5.0 concept.

Keywords: Assistive technology · Service delivery system · Society 5.0

1 Introduction

The development of new solutions in assistive technologies seeks to help persons with disability perform everyday activities more efficiently and safely. When using public transport services and moving part of the traffic network, visually impaired persons face several problems and challenges: waiting at the wrong stop, not being informed about the timetable, getting into the wrong vehicle, information in vehicles, and more.

This paper aims to investigate the needs of users (visually impaired) who use the public transport system and define the functionalities of the user information service. The purpose of using such a service is to raise users' quality of life to whom all relevant information is delivered in real-time via a mobile application solution.

Visually impaired persons differ in their characteristics and specific requirements that are considered when developing new innovative solutions and services. Therefore, users need to be provided with the availability and use of a reliable solution that will allow them to move quickly and safely from departure to destination. In this research, the conceptual architecture of the information service delivery system based on the technology and framework of the Society 5.0 environment was proposed.

D. Perakovic and L. Knapcikova (Eds.): FABULOUS 2022, LNICST 445, pp. 141–152, 2022.
https://doi.org/10.1007/978-3-031-15101-9_10

2   Previous Research

Currently available literature in the development of systems and services for informing users when moving the traffic network is focused on developing mobile application solutions for vehicle identification and user navigation services.

The proposed architecture of the Ariadna system allows users to be informed through Braille (a specific point of view and access to it) [1]. The system works on the principle of entering the found code, which is entered into the mobile application, after which the user receives the relevant information about the lines passing through this stop. The problem with this solution is that the user has to look for a label with a code every time, which is problematic for visually impaired users.

The OnBoard system has functionality for bus vehicle identification, where the user does not use his mobile device but a unique device integrated at the stop [2]. The user presses a button on the device, and with audio information, he receives information about the arrival of the bus and the line number and confirms the desired line. When the user confirms the desired line, the loudspeaker implemented inside the bus is activated, after which the user's sound signals indicate that he is entering the vehicle. The disadvantages of this solution are the dimensions of the device and its highly complex use.

Smart bus alert is a proposal for a bus identification service [3]. The service works on the principle of the implemented ZigBee module. The module provides the user with information about the arrival of an individual bus at the stop. Also, the user can enter their destination by voice, and the system will inform them of their arrival.

The GeoNotify mobile application, adapted to the degree of user damage, is used to navigate the user and detect unexpected temporary obstacles that could cause injuries [4]. The paper proposes using neural networks connected to data collection methodologies to define more accurate models capable of recognizing broad representations of obstacles in the real world.

The research showing the results of the Horizon 2020 project entitled "Sound of Vision: the natural sense of vision through acoustics and haptics" presented different models of designing user navigation systems and information in urban public transport [5].

The research results within the MOVIDIS project presented an alternative to help visually impaired users navigate the public transport system. The various modules of the MOVIDIS system communicate with each other via radio frequency (RF) and enable users to interact with buses and their stops. The first experimental results showed that RF communication is a viable option to help persons with visual impairments in public transport services [6].

The mentioned research describes previous research and challenges in developing navigation and information systems for the visually impaired [7]. Problems created by GPS technology in determining the exact location bring the user close to the destination, but not to the exact location, which causes challenges such as difficulties in locating the entrance to buildings or entering the public transport vehicle. Research [8] analyzed current solutions and user needs and the possibilities of applying a probing study using a new vision-based system called Landmark AI to understand how technology can better solve aspects of this problem.

In the Republic of Croatia, mobile applications are on the market of operators' providers of urban public passenger transport, ZET info, and HŽPP Planer.

The ZET Info mobile application informs users about emergencies, changes, and notifications about tram or bus traffic situations. Also, the user has an insight into the timetables of certain lines and is automatically shown the earliest time of arrival of the vehicle at the stop from the time when the application was launched [9]. HŽPP Planer mobile application provides the user with real-time information on train timetables, their location, ticket prices, changes in the time of train arrival at the station. Also, the symbol shows if the train is wheelchair accessible, which means it is insured access using lift ramps and that a vehicle seat is provided for such persons [10]. The disadvantages of advanced mobile applications are that there is no single solution for the user regardless of the traffic mode that needs to be used (bus, tram, train, taxi).

The introduction of sensor networks enabled real-time communication between devices and large amounts of data collection. In parallel, the concept of Society 5.0 was presented, which aims to enable the personalization of products and services according to the wishes of end-users. In doing so, it is necessary to balance social problems and economic growth with the development of information and communication systems, networks, technologies, and services. The Society 5.0 concept seeks to increase the quality of life of end-users. Thus, persons with various disabilities are allowed to actively participate in the community by applying assistive technologies tailored to their needs [11, 12].

3   User Needs Analysis

The World Health Organization (WHO) estimates that there are about 285 million persons with some form of visual impairment [13]. There are 19,132 users with visual impairments in the Republic of Croatia, while there are 2,498 users in Zagreb [14].

Visually impaired persons have different needs, and their way of moving is not equally pronounced in every user. Therefore, when defining the functionality of a new solution, it is necessary to consider the different needs and desires, and shortcomings in the function of user movement. Basic requirements may include information on the environment, navigation, arrival at the destination, location, and more.

Blind and partially sighted persons face various problems when using public transport services, such as:

- inability to identify a point of view due to lack of signs,
- inability to identify the vehicle at the stop,
- lack of timetable at stops that are legible to visually impaired persons.

In order to collect data on the satisfaction and attitude of visually impaired persons about the solutions and services implemented so far, a survey was conducted [15]. Based on the obtained results, the dissatisfaction of blind and partially sighted persons was noticed, indicating the need to improve existing solutions or develop and implement new solutions and services. In cooperation with the Up2Date association, the survey questionnaire collected 27 answers, i.e., 22 blind persons and 5 visually impaired persons participated. Persons using public transport services are of different age groups (Table 1).

Table 1. Age group of respondents

Age group of respondents	Percentage of persons belonging to an age group
15–20 years	15%
20–30 years	22%
30–40 years	30%
40–60 years	15%
60 years and over	18%

When asked about the type of public transport they use, the respondents with visual impairments answered that 46% travel by tram, 27% by bus, 4% by train, and 23% use taxi services. Therefore, it can be concluded that visually impaired persons mainly use trams and buses as a means of transport. Also, respondents stated that 48% travel daily, 48% several times a week, and only 4% travel several times a month on these modes of transport.

When asked what bothers them the most when using public transport services, visually impaired persons said that their biggest problems are external disturbances, such as noise and light (39%), a ban on introducing a guide dog to the vehicle (25%), incomprehension from others passengers (24%) and misunderstanding by the driver (12%). These problems and the associated data can be seen in Fig. 1.

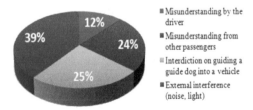

Fig. 1. Interference with the use of public transport services

Since mobile devices provide feedback in different ways, 77% of respondents want to receive audio information, 12% want information in the form of vibrations, and visually impaired persons or 11% want to increase the font.

Obtaining specific feedback for persons with visual impairments is of great importance in order to be able to orientate and create their image of traffic and the environment, which can be seen according to the results (Fig. 2). Thus, 23 respondents consider obtaining information about their location and their arrival at the point of view very important, and 4 of them consider it essential.

Navigation towards the vehicle door is very important for 22 respondents, while it is important for 5 persons. Furthermore, timetable information is very important for 19 persons and important for 7 respondents. 19 persons said that getting feedback on the location of the vehicle was very important to them, while 8 of them said it was important to them. Accident information and vehicle type information are very important for 14 respondents, important for 9 and neither important nor unimportant for 4 respondents.

15 respondents mentioned feedback on driving time as very important, 11 as important, and 1 respondent as neither important nor unimportant. Obtaining information on the number of persons within a particular vehicle is of great importance for 14 respondents, for 7 respondents it is important, for 5 it is neither important nor unimportant, and for 1 respondent it is very unimportant. Information on emergency transport is very important for 13 respondents and for 13 respondents it is important. For the possibility of an SOS call in case of danger, 13 persons stated that it would be very important to them, 10 persons would be important to them and for 4 persons the possibility would be neither important nor unimportant.

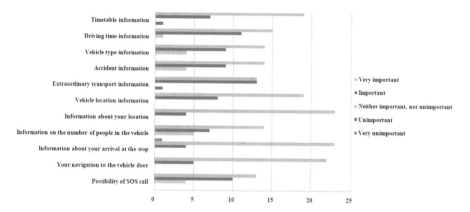

Fig. 2. The importance of getting feedback

Also, the majority of respondents (63%) expressed a desire for the possibility of buying tickets via the mobile application because they consider it safe to conduct money transactions via the Internet, and it would also facilitate the whole process of buying tickets.

It is necessary to enable users to receive feedback in a form that will be accessible to them. Therefore, blind persons need to be provided with information in the form of sound notifications or vibrations, while visually impaired persons can also use the ability to change the background color and change the font size. Respondents expressed the need for education that would enable them to get acquainted with how to use the solution, making it easier for them to navigate within the mobile application and navigate the traffic network. Given the data obtained, pointing to the fact that a large number of visually impaired and blind persons use public transport services every day, it can be concluded that it is necessary to present new opportunities for information services and develop a solution that satisfactorily meets the needs and requirements of users.

4   Functionalities of Mobile Application Solution MAppIN

Users' needs were identified based on the results obtained by implementing the survey method. Table 2 lists the functionalities of the mobile application solution for providing customer information services.

Table 2. Functionalities of the user information service in the public city transport system

Information service functionalities	
Registration (blind, visually impaired)	Proposing the choice of means of transport
Check-in/out	Education/user instructions
Informing about the timetable and driving duration	Account settings
Information on the type of transport	Travel and purchase history
Accident and emergency transport information	Navigation towards the vehicle door
Informing on arrival at the stop	Information on the number of persons in the vehicle
Buying tickets	SOS call
Ordering a taxi	Application for service provider and other stakeholders (data management)

User registration - depending on the degree of visual impairment and the possibilities of providing information, the user can choose the severity of the damage and the method of providing information (TTS - text to speech, font size, or contrast selection). The user also can enter information on the card method of ticket payment.

Check-in/out - the possibility of voice or written login/logout to the system to facilitate the launch of the user information service.

Informing about the timetable and driving duration - the possibility of providing information about lines, directions, stations, time of arrival at the stop, and the duration of the drive of each train line.

Information on the type of transport - shows the user information about the type of vehicle, whether it is a low-floor or a vehicle with stairs and a customized environment for persons with disabilities.

Accident and emergency transport information - in case of an incident situation, the information is provided to the user with instructions on getting out of the vehicle or calling the emergency services (firefighters, ambulance, police).

Informing on arrival at the stop - the stops must be equipped with Bluetooth Beacon technology which provides all the information on arriving at the stop/train line/place of entry into the vehicle. Upon the vehicle's arrival at a defined stop, the user receives information about the line and direction of movement. Based on this information, the user decides whether he wants to get into the vehicle or not. If the user has given an affirmative answer, navigating to the vehicle door begins by monitoring beeps or vibrations. If the user has decided not to enter the vehicle, he will receive information about the arrival of the following vehicle at the stop.

Buying tickets - the possibility of purchasing tickets for which the data entered during the registration of users in the system are required. The service informs the user about the successful or unsuccessful implementation of the purchase. Also, the user has forwarded an invoice about the completed purchase to his user email. If the purchase is unsuccessful, the user receives audio information about the reason for the canceled transaction.

Ordering a taxi - the possibility of choosing a taxi service provider and integration with the module of the taxi service provider selected by the user.

Proposing the choice of means of transport - depending on the different modes of transport and possible traffic jams, the user is provided with information on the mode of transport with the fastest and safest way to reach the destination.

Education/user instructions - the possibility of conducting user education on how to use the service and possible errors in how to manage the service.

Account settings - the ability to manage user information entered during user registration (name, surname, email, address, SOS numbers, card payment, type of damage, the ability to provide information, home, or work address).

Travel and purchase history – ability to view personal travel and ticket purchase history and saved invoices.

Navigation towards the vehicle door - user navigation to the vehicle entrance door using beacon technology.

Information on the number of persons in the vehicle – possibility to see the information of the number of passengers to easily avoid the crowd.

SOS call - when registering, the user enters the number for the SOS call in case of possible problems that may arise during the trip or when arriving at the starting point of the trip. The transport service provider can also make the call if this option is enabled.

Application for service provider and other stake-holders (data management) - possibility to apply for a service provider or other stakeholders interested in using the service. As one of the possible stakeholders, the taxi carrier logs into the system through the above functionality and thus can manage data for the provision of taxi services.

5 Proposal of the Conceptual Architecture of the Service Delivery System

In order to deliver the customer information service, a conceptual system architecture based on the Cloud Computing concept (CCfB) and Beacon technology has been proposed [16–18]. The CCfB architecture can connect with all stakeholders (stakeholders) of the system and manage and prepare data for different groups of persons with disabilities. In addition to the above, it is possible to integrate/connect with sensors from the environment using the IoT concept and collect them in real-time. Bluetooth beacon technology consists of small beacon devices that transmit a signal with a unique ID number identified by the user's mobile device and thus inform the user. The advantage of using Beacon devices is the reduced energy consumption enabled by Bluetooth Low

Energy (BLE) technology and the possibility of simultaneous data transfer to 20 devices within a range of up to 80 [m].

Figure 3 shows the proposed conceptual architecture of the system. The work of the proposed architecture is based on the IaaS model, where the service provider, users, and other participants are authorized to update and store new information. The information is distributed to end-users through the SaaS model via a mobile application or web browser and to other participants who develop applications through the PaaS model.

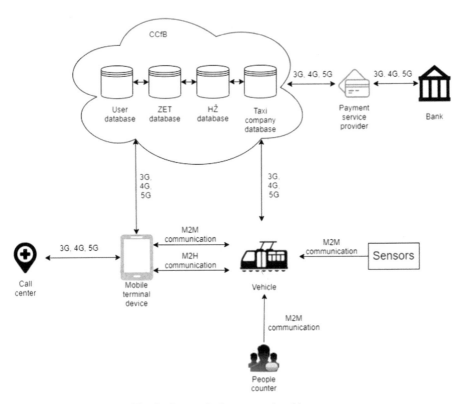

Fig. 3. Proposal of conceptual architecture

The cloud architecture consists of databases for managing information about users, public transport service providers (ZET, HŽPP, taxi transport). The user database stores data entered by the user during registration and login, during which authentication and authorization are performed. The ZET and HŽ database contains data on individual lines and timetables, emergencies, data collected from sensors, and more. The taxi company stores information about drivers, rented vehicles, transport orders, and more within the database.

A visually impaired person can access specific data stored in the cloud using a mobile application installed on a mobile terminal device. Blind users are provided with information via sound/vibrating notifications and signals, while visually impaired users can adjust the font size and background color, which improves the accessibility of the service.

Machine to Machine (M2M) communication occurs between the vehicle and the mobile terminal device, while Machine to Human (M2H) communication occurs between the mobile device and the user. The Bluetooth beacon is placed above the vehicle door so that audible signals towards the door can guide the user. In addition to the GPS module, tram, bus, or rail vehicles, implement a counter of persons according to whose data the user will decide whether to enter the vehicle or not. Information on the number of persons can be beneficial in today's Covid-19 situation that requires physical distance and a certain number of persons inside the vehicle.

The data collected by the sensors installed in the vehicle are sent to the cloud via the Internet, where they are stored and processed using M2M communication. Based on data from the cloud, the user is then provided with feedback in a customized form via M2H communication. Communication to the electronic/mobile service provider is performed via 3G/4G/5G mobile networks and communication to the CCfB environment. The user accesses the service using a mobile MAppIN (Mobile Application for Informing and Navigation) application and a mobile network.

6   Functionality Development of MAppIN Mobile Application

MAppIN is a mobile information and navigation application designed for blind and partially sighted users. In this paper, a test environment was created to check the operation of certain functionalities of the MAppIN application. MIT App Inventor is open-source software used to display and develop functionalities. It enables easy programming of mobile applications by drag and drop method for devices with the Android operating system.

The application colors used are defined in the test environment but selecting different sets may be offered in future development. The mobile application also uses a test database to store and distribute data. At startup, the user must register where the appropriate user data is entered. Different data entry conditions and restrictions are defined to alert the user. After the registration and login processes have been completed, the main menu opens for the user (Fig. 4).

The main menu consists of 4 links and, depending on the selection, data from a specific traffic area is displayed. Changes in traffic include information on accidents that have occurred, which interfere with the planned flow of traffic and include information on the organization of emergency transport. The user can view the above information in an additional menu but can also be informed at any time via a pop-up notification that appears on the screen.

By selecting tram traffic, information on tram lines, directions, and each vehicle's suitability for persons with disabilities are displayed. The list of all stops where the selected tram stops and the vehicles' arrival time at the stop is displayed after selecting a specific line. After activating the navigation button, the user confirms the start of navigation and routing to the defined location (Fig. 5).

When selecting rail traffic in the main menu, the user will be shown similar information for the tram, i.e., information on lines, timetables, directions, vehicle suitability, and

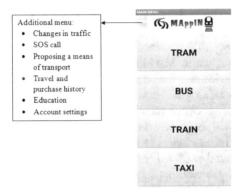

Fig. 4. Display the main menu

Fig. 5. Display of tram line stops and location navigation

like. Unlike tram traffic, rail can also include long-distance lines for which fair prices are defined. When the user selects the option to purchase a ticket, a new window opens (Fig. 6).

If all entered data are correct and funds are taken, the user is informed that the payment has been successfully made via a pop-up notification. Confirmation of the purchased ticket can later be found in the other menu if the ticket controller requires the person to show it.

7   Conclusion

Today's development of innovative solutions and services and their application in the Society 5.0 environment makes it possible to contribute to a sustainable social ecosystem. Assistive technologies that provide appropriate information to persons with disabilities play a significant role in the systems applied in the Society 5.0 environment.

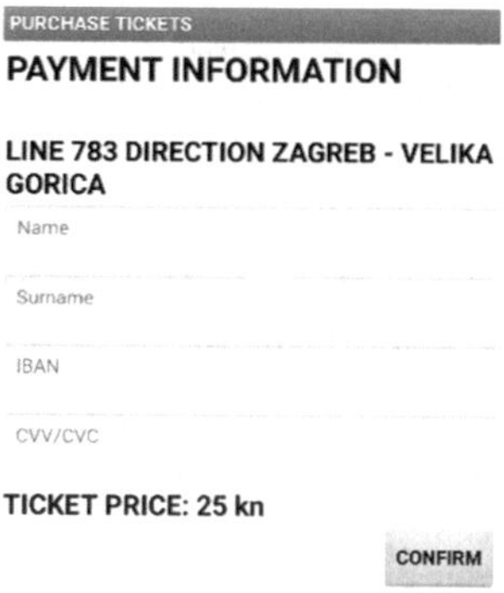

Fig. 6. Display the payment form

The proposed conceptual architecture of the system based on modern information and communication technologies aims to provide real-time information to users who move through the transport network and use the public transport system.

With accurate information, it is possible to raise the quality of life and equal integration in the society in which the user is located. Examining users' needs when using the public passenger transport system in the city of Zagreb is the starting point for defining the functionality of the information service. By applying the basic principles of universal design, the test layout of the application was proposed, as well as the verification of the operation of individual functionalities, which proved the operation of the proposed system architecture. Future research will focus on other technologies and frameworks of the Society 5.0 environment in different application scenarios to better integrate persons with disabilities into society.

Acknowledgement. This research was funded by the University of Zagreb through the Grants for core financing of scientific and artistic activities of the University of Zagreb in academic year 2020/2021 under the project (210219) "Challenges of information and communication networks, technologies, services and user equipment in establishing the Society 5.0 environment - phase 2".

References

1. Markiewicz, M., Skomorowski, M.: Public transport information system for visually impaired and blind people. In: Mikulski, J. (ed.) TST 2010. CCIS, vol. 104, pp. 271–277. Springer, Heidelberg (2010). https://doi.org/10.1007/978-3-642-16472-9_30
2. Mehra, D., et al.: Bus identification system for the visually impaired: evaluation and learning from pilot trials on public buses in Delhi. 16 (2015)
3. Sowmya Priya, V., Soundarya, M., Niketha, V., Thanuja, I.: Smart bus alert system for easy navigation of the blind. Int. J. Res. Appl. Sci. Eng. Technol. **6**, 1656–1659 (2018). https://doi.org/10.22214/ijraset.2018.5270
4. Kim, E., Sterner, J., Mashhadi, A.: A crowd-sourced obstacle detection and navigation app for visually impaired. In: Paiva, S., Lopes, S.I., Zitouni, R., Gupta, N., Lopes, S.F., Yonezawa, T. (eds.) SmartCity360° 2020. LNICSSITE, vol. 372, pp. 571–579. Springer, Cham (2021). https://doi.org/10.1007/978-3-030-76063-2_38

5. Strumillo, P., et al.: Different approaches to aiding blind persons in mobility and navigation in the "Naviton" and "Sound of Vision" projects. In: Pissaloux, E., Velázquez, R. (eds.) Mobility of Visually Impaired People, pp. 435–468. Springer, Cham (2018). https://doi.org/10.1007/978-3-319-54446-5_15

6. Sáez, Y., Muñoz, J., Canto, F., García, A., Montes, H.: Assisting visually impaired persons in the public transport system through RF-communication and embedded systems. Sensors **19**, 1282 (2019). https://doi.org/10.3390/s19061282

7. Real, S., Araujo, A.: Navigation systems for the blind and visually impaired: past work, challenges, and open problems. Sensors **19**, 3404 (2019). https://doi.org/10.3390/s19153404

8. Saha, M., Fiannaca, A.J., Kneisel, M., Cutrell, E., Morris, M.R.: Closing the gap: designing for the last-few-meters wayfinding problem for persons with visual impairments. In: The 21st International ACM SIGACCESS Conference on Computers and Accessibility, pp. 222–235. ACM, NY (2019). https://doi.org/10.1145/3308561.3353776

9. ZET: ZET Info. https://zet-info.com/. Accessed 15 Dec 2021

10. HŽPP: HŽPP PLANER. http://www.hzpp.hr/hzpp-planer-vas-suputnik-na-putovanju-vlakom. Accessed 15 Dec 2021

11. Peraković, D., Periša, M., Cvitić, I., Zorić, P.: Information and communication technologies for the Society 5.0 environment. In: Radojičić, V., Bojović, N., Marković, D., Marković, G. (eds.) PosTel 2020 – XXXVIII Simpozijum o novim tehnologijama u poštanskom i telekomunikacionom saobraćaju, pp. 203–212. University of Belgrade, Faculty of Transport and Traffic Engineering, Belgrade, Serbia (2020). https://doi.org/10.37528/FTTE/9788673954318/POSTEL.2020.020

12. Periša, M., Peraković, D., Zorić, P.: Challenges of assistive technologies implementation into Industry 4.0: a review. In: Janošević, D. (ed.) The Seventh International Conference Transport and Logistics, pp. 5–10. University of Niš, Faculty of Mechanical Engineering, Niš, Srbija (2019)

13. WHO: Disability and health. https://www.who.int/news-room/fact-sheets/detail/disability-and-health. Accessed 10 Dec 2021

14. Benjak, T.: Izvješće o stanju osoba s invaliditetom u Republici Hrvatskoj (2020)

15. Anić, V.: Razvoj funkcionalnosti mobilnog aplikativnog rješenja za pružanje usluge informiranja osoba oštećenog vida u prometu, University of Zagreb, Faculty of Transport and Traffic Sciences, Zagreb, Croatia (2021)

16. Periša, M., Marković, G., Kolarovszki, P., Madleňák, R.: Proposal of a conceptual architecture system for informing the user in the IoT environment. PROMET - Traffic Transp. **31**, 37–47 (2019). https://doi.org/10.7307/ptt.v31i1.2677

17. Periša, M., Cvitić, I., Peraković, D., Husnjak, S.: Beacon technology for real-time informing the traffic network users about the environment. Transport **34**, 373–382 (2019). https://doi.org/10.3846/transport.2019.10402

18. Periša, M., Cvitić, I., Sente, R.E.: IoT services for increasing user mobility in the smart city environment. In: 37. skup o prometnim sustavima s međunarodnim sudjelovanjem "Automatizacija u prometu 2017", pp. 147–151. Rijeka, Croatia (2017)

Data Collection and Processing Method in the Networks of Industrial IOT

Larysa Globa⬤, Vasyl Kurdecha$^{(\boxtimes)}$ ⬤, Demyd Popenko, Maksym Bezvuhliak, and Yevgeniy Porolo

National Technical University of Ukraine "Igor Sikorsky Kyiv Polytechnic Institute", Kyiv, Ukraine

lgloba@its.kpi.ua, kvv.vasyl@gmail.com

Abstract. The implementation of IIoT allows users to use data and analytics for predictive analysis, reduced equipment downtime, centralized storage and remote asset monitoring. With the introduction of reasonable production information obtained from the devices must be processed that requires significant time and memory to store the accumulated information. This poses the task of minimizing processing time and file size for network transmission.

The main purpose of this work is improving the efficiency of information collection and processing in the industrial Internet of Things through the use of the modified method.

The method of serialization and deserialization of data on the basis of the Protobuf method is offered in the work, which allows to increase the efficiency of information processing by time indicators and to reduce the volume of transmitted information. In the process of work achieved an increase in processing speed information received from IIoT equipment through use serialization mechanism, and reduce the file size of the information that transmitted over the network.

Keywords: IIoT · Collection of information · Processing of information · Serialization · Protobuf

1 Introduction

There are three existing methods [1] of data collection and processing, which were analyzed: "Method of collecting and processing information using a gateway", "Method of collecting and processing information using a smart hub", "Method of collecting and processing information based on industrial buses". The method of collecting and processing information using a smart hub has an advantage over other methods because it helps to modernize and achieve a high level of production in the manufacturing industry.

Devices and sensors generate and collect a huge amount of data, the total amount of data collected may be so large that it may be impossible to transmit them over the network for further analysis. Sensors can transmit this information every 30 s, and there may be several hundred such devices in stock. It can be just one of dozens of types of sensors that have different types of data, which together represent a massive inhomogeneous

© ICST Institute for Computer Sciences, Social Informatics and Telecommunications Engineering 2022
Published by Springer Nature Switzerland AG 2022. All Rights Reserved
D. Perakovic and L. Knapcikova (Eds.): FABULOUS 2022, LNICST 445, pp. 153–167, 2022.
https://doi.org/10.1007/978-3-031-15101-9_11

set of information from many sources. This leads to high costs for data collection and integration of equipment with the data processing system. Also a big problem is the lack of computing power and storage resources to perform complex tasks of analysis and machine learning.

In addition, large amounts of data are difficult to process because more time is required to respond. Thus, the transmission of confidential data over the Internet to perform important analysis often becomes a problem [2].

2   Background

A. *The method of collecting and processing information using a gateway*

This method contains three modules: the intelligent object module, the gateway module, and the control center (server) module. Each module is multilevel (including touch, network and application levels) and performs certain functions to support the monitoring of the interdependent environment [3].

The gateway module is a bridge between smart objects and the control center. On the other hand, in the case where intelligent objects do not have a direct connection available for direct communication with the control center via telecommunications technology, the gateways will connect these smart objects with the control center. Also, the gateway module will perform the duties of the application layer in the absence of the application layer in the module of the smart object.

B. *A method of collecting and processing information using a smart hub*

A method of collecting and processing information that allows the use of information and operational infrastructure to improve the management, monitoring and control of existing and new devices. It consists of three main components: a layer of devices, an intelligent hub, a microservice cloud platform. The presented method can also be implemented in existing intelligent enterprises to optimize the management of intelligent equipment and to increase production efficiency [4].

The intelligent hub can act as a gateway for existing IIoT devices. Functionally, the hub offers a simple and convenient way to pre-process data, exchange data and communicate between existing IIoT devices and the server platform, which means that using the intelligent hub can update or improve data exchange and communication channels.

C. *Method of collecting and processing information based on industrial tires*

This method is performed on four layers: the layer of devices, sensors and mechanisms, the layer of the data provider, the layer of cross-platform software and the application layer [5].

The data provider layer is designed to receive data from industrial buses and transfer them to the level of cross-platform software, which contains a software communication module for each industrial bus.

The purpose of this module is to implement an information collection cycle. The interface for receiving and transmitting data is used by the data provider, a separate software module, to receive data from industrial networks and to store them in the buffer cache. This memory is used to respond more quickly to requests from the middleware level.

The method of collecting and processing information using a smart hub has an advantage over other methods because it helps in modernizing and achieving a high level of production in the manufacturing industry. This is achieved due to the fact that the main element of this method is an intelligent hub, which provides convenient solutions for scaling the system with new devices, performs data collection and formatting using serialization processes, which reduces the amount of information needed to be transferred to the cloud platform for further analysis.

3   Modified Method of Collection and Processing Data

Based on the selected prototype, the modified method of collecting and processing information is as follows (Fig. 1).

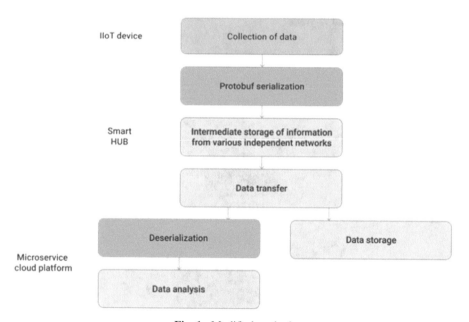

Fig. 1. Modified method

The basis of data collection are sensors, mechanisms, which are scattered in a certain geographical area. They exchange data over the network for autonomous data collection and transmission to a special node, which is considered an intermediate point for collecting information.

To store and transmit the information received from the devices, a serialization mechanism is used, which allows to reduce the size of the transmitted files, which in turn reduces the load on the network and reduces the time required to transmit information for further analysis.

The information received from sensors, mechanisms, devices is transferred to the intelligent hub, using the Internet of Things protocol CoAP or MQTT.

Analyzed on the IIoT microservice platform, the information can be transferred to other information or operating systems or stored in a database.

A. Collecting data

Depending on the requirements for information collection, the transfer of collected data may be carried out periodically or on an event basis. An intelligent hub is a node with two or more network interfaces, it collects and performs intermediate processing of data received from information collection devices.

Sensorsand mechanisms are small electronic devices capable of measuring physical quantities (eg, temperature, light, pressure) and transmit it to the information processing unit. Given the achievements in the field of microelectronics, technology and software for wireless data transmission allow to produce microsensors with a volume of several cubic millimeters [5].

The general process of collecting information and transmitting it to an intelligent hub is shown in Fig. 2. Devices can have their own communication methods, such as Wi-Fi, BLE, ZigBee and Z-Wave.

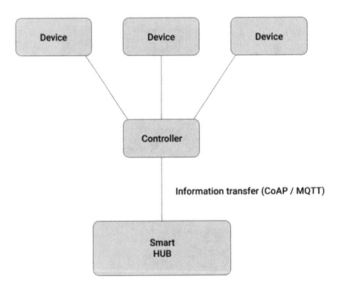

Fig. 2. The general process of collecting information

B. Technologies transmition data to HUB

Sensor networks are spatially distributed sensors that monitor physical or environmental conditions, such as temperature, sound, pressure, etc., and jointly transmit their data over the network. Such networks can be used in a large number of different applications: industrial automation, microclimate control systems, security and fire alarm systems, energy consumption accounting and optimization, etc. [6]. The coverage area of such networks can be from several meters to several kilometers. One of the main standards for the implementation of these networks are Wi-Fi, BLE, ZigBee, Z-Wave.

C. Protocols for information data

In the modified method, the CoAP protocol is intended for transmission between devices in one limited network, for example, with low power consumption, in lossy networks, as well as between devices in different networks connected to the Internet. CoAP can be integrated with data formats such as XML, JSON, Protobuf for effective communication with other platforms.

In the modified method, the MQTT protocol provides minimum resource requirements and is used to transmit information. The protocol does not impose restrictions on the data format.

D. Serialization

Figure 3 shows the general process of serialization-deserialization.

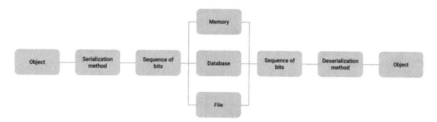

Fig. 3. The general process of serialization-deserialization

In the proposed method of creating a distributed service, parts of which must exchange information with a complex structure, in this case, for the data to be transmitted, a code is created that performs the processes of serialization and deserialization. For the object filled with the necessary data, the created serialization code is called, as a result on an output we receive, for example, an XML file.

The resulting sequence of bits is written to a database, memory or file, which is then sent to the receiving party. For deserialization, the recipient service creates an object of the same type and calls the required code, resulting in an object with the same data as the sender service object.

Comparison of serialization methods

Table 1 presents a description of the main characteristics of serialization methods using XML, JSON, Protobuf.

For a modified method of collecting and processing information, it is proposed to use the method of serialization Protobuf.

Compared to Protobuf, JSON and XML pass metadata details, which adds a payload to the payload. Using Protobuf for serialization and deserialization will consume less CPU time and memory, so processing time is faster compared to JSON and XML.

Protobuf compresses data and generates dense data. When compared to XML, it is almost 1/3 of the size, and when compared to JSON, then 1/2 [7].

JSON and XML are readable by humans and are not secure for data transmission over the network. If it is necessary that the answer is not read by the user, then it is necessary to use Protobuf. The user also needs an proto file to deserialize the object stream.

E. Microservice platform

In the modified method, the microservice platform structures the application as a set of services. Microservices are usually based on business functions.

Deployment using containers provides portability. Containerization reduces deployment time, as it requires only the inclusion of the required container, without affecting other containers running on the same host [8].

Table 1. Description of the main characteristics of serialization methods

Features	JSON	XML	ProtoBuf
Standardization	Yes	Yes	Yes
Specification	STD 90/RFC 8259	Recommendations W3C: 1.0 and 1.1	Developer Guide: Encoding
Binary	No	Partly	Yes
Available for human reading	Yes	Yes	No
Link support	Yes	Yes	No
Standard APIs	JSONQuery, JSONPath, JSON-LD	DOM, SAX, XQuery, XPath	C++, Java, C#, Python, and other

The microservice platform may transmit useful statistics or information to other information or operating systems, such as a production management system, an automated storage and retrieval system, and an enterprise asset management system using Protobuf using the CoAP or MQTT protocol.

4   Comparative Evaluation of the Proposed Method

The simulation process serializes the files before sending them over the Internet, as this can significantly reduce the time required to do so. Also serialized files reduce the amount of space required for data storage [9, 10].

To obtain a comparative assessment of the proposed solution, three methods of serialization using XML, JSON, Protobuf were studied according to the following criteria (Fig. 4):

– the time required to serialize the input data;
– time required to deserialize serialized data;
– time required for serialization and deserialization of input data;
– the size of the serialized file.

According to the selected criteria, it is possible to determine how much the time and speed of information processing required to send information will be reduced, using the proposed method.

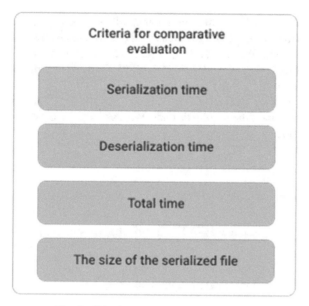

Fig. 4. Criteria for comparative evaluation

Figure 5 shows a full-scale model. The information generated by the device is transmitted to the controller. The process of serialization is called on the controller, as a result of which we get a serialized file that can be transmitted over the network. The deserialization process is called on the receiver side and the initial information is restored.

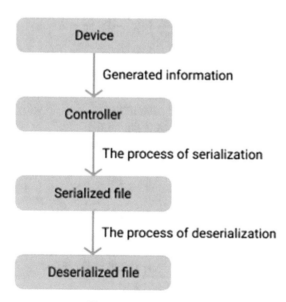

Fig. 5. Full-scale model

The tests are repeated for different amounts of input data (Table 2). Initialize the experiment to write to the file by different methods of serialization of 50, 500, 5000, 5000 lines of the input file. In each test, write the appropriate number of rows of generated data to a file. For each method (XML, JSON, Protobuf) we perform serialization and deserialization operations 9 times and calculate the average value for each method. In each of the 9 iterations for each method, we measure the time of serialization, deserialization, and the total time in milliseconds. We also measure the size of the serialized file for each method. Figure 6 shows the process of modeling.

Using the method of finding intermediate values for a known discrete set of values, we determine:

1. For serialization time, deserialization time and total time

$$t = b + \left(\frac{n - n_0}{n_1 - n_0} \right) * (a - b), \; n_0 \leq n < n_1 \tag{1}$$

    where
        t is the serialization/deserialization/total time,
        n is the number of lines of the input file,
        n_0 is the initial number of lines of the input file,
        n_1 is the maximum number of lines of the input file,
        a is the time of serialization/deserialization/total time with the maximum number of lines of the input file,
        b is the serialization/deserialization/total time at the initial number of lines of the input file.
2. For the size of the serialized file

$$s = d + \left(\frac{n - n_0}{n_1 - n_0} \right) * (c - d), \; n_0 \leq n < n_1 \tag{2}$$

where
    s is the size of the serialized file,
    n is the number of lines of the input file,
    n_0 is the initial number of lines of the input file,
    n_1 is the maximum number of lines of the input file,
    c is the size of the serialized file with the maximum number of lines of the input file,
    d is the size of the serialized file lines of the input file. For the size of the serialized file.

Table 2. Input parameters for simulation

Data types	int, double, string, list of objects
Number of input data (lines)	50, 500, 5000, 50000
Number of tests	4
Number of iterations for each test	9

The obtained mathematical expressions will allow you to quickly calculate the time of serialization, deserialization and total time, as well as the size of the serialized file depending on the amount of input data.

For serialization in tests the class Object which consists of types int, double, string, and also the list of objects is used. The test results are stored in text files.

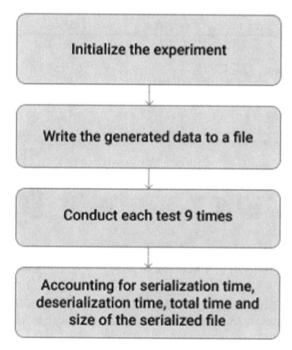

Fig. 6. Modeling process

The results will always be different for different hardware, operating systems, but there is one thing that remains the same - the relative difference between the methods of serialization.

Evaluation of the proposed method of serialization

To conduct a comparative assessment, we will build graphs according to certain criteria (the time required to serialize the input data).

According to the results of four tests, Table 3 shows the generalized results of the serialization time for the three methods. Figure 7 shows a graph of serialization time depending on the number of lines of the input file.

According to the simulation results, the following mathematical expression for the serialization time using Protobuf was obtained:

$$t = \begin{cases} 0{,}508*n, 0 \le n <50 \\ 25, 4 - 1, 91 * 10^{-2}*(n - 50), 50 \le n <500 \\ 16, 8 + 4, 467 * 10^{-3}*(n - 500), 500 \le n <5000 \\ 36, 9 + 4, 311 * 10^{-3}*(n - 5000), 5000 \le n <50000 \end{cases}$$

Table 3. Input serialization time

The number of lines of the input file	Protobuf (ms)	JSON (ms)	XML (ms)
50	25,4	37,1	25,6
500	16,8	24,7	33,2
5000	36,9	100,3	285,7
50000	230,9	753,4	2594,2

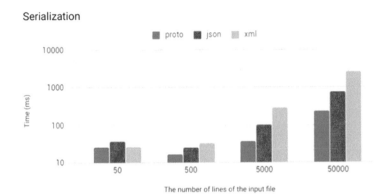

Fig. 7. Serialization time depending on the number of lines of the input file

As can be seen from the graph, in different tests the serialization time using Protobuf is the lowest compared to JSON and XML. XML serialization time is longer than JSON, except for the first test.

According to the results of four tests, Table 4 shows the generalized results of the deserialization time for the three methods. Figure 8 shows a graph of deserialization time depending on the number of lines of the input file.

Table 4. Time of deserialization of input data

The number of lines of the input file	Protobuf (ms)	JSON (ms)	XML (ms)
50	0,7	6,4	2,7
500	4,1	11,9	14,2
5000	41,1	91,4	111,6
50000	294,6	1071,4	1050,1

According to the simulation results, the following mathematical expression for the deserialization time using Protobuf was obtained:

$$t = \begin{cases} 0{,}014*n, \ 0 \ \le n < 50 \\ 0,7+7,556 * 10^{-3}*(n-50), \ 50 \le n < 500 \\ 4,1+8,222 * 10^{-3}*(n-500), \ 500 \le n < 5000 \\ 41,1+5,633 * 10^{-3}*(n-5000), \ 5000 \le n < 50000 \end{cases}$$

Deserialization

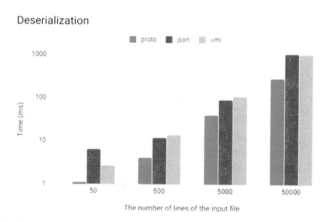

Fig. 8. Deserialization time depending on the number of lines of the input file

As can be seen from the graph, in the four trials, the deserialization time using Protobuf was the lowest compared to JSON and XML. In the first test, the XML deserialization time is much shorter than JSON, in other cases it is almost the same.

According to the results of four tests, Table 5 shows the generalized results of serialization and deserialization time for the three methods. Figure 9 shows a graph of serialization and deserialization time depending on the number of lines of the input file.

Table 5. Time of serialization and deserialization of input data

The number of lines of the input file	Protobuf (ms)	JSON (ms)	XML (ms)
50	27,1	44,3	28,5
500	21,3	37	48
5000	78,6	192,3	397,9
50000	526,2	1825,3	3645

According to the simulation results, the following mathematical expression for the total time of serialization and deserialization using Protobuf:

$$t = \begin{cases} 0{,}542*n, & 0 \le n < 50 \\ 27,1 - 1,289*10^{-2}*(n-50), & 50 \le n < 500 \\ 21,3 + 1,273*10^{-2}*(n-500), & 500 \le n < 5000 \\ 78,6 + 9,947*10^{-3}*(n-5000), & 5000 \le n < 50000 \end{cases}$$

As can be seen from the Fig. 9, in different tests the total serialization and deserialization time using Protobuf is the lowest compared to JSON and XML. However, in the first test, Protobuf is almost indistinguishable from XML, although in other tests, as the number of lines of input increases, the difference increases.

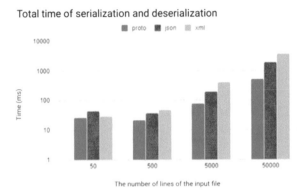

Fig. 9. Serialization and deserialization time depending on the number of lines of the input file

According to the results of four tests, Table 6 shows the generalized results of the sizes of serialized files for the three methods. Figure 10 shows a graph of the sizes of serialized files depending on the number of lines of the input file.

Table 6. Sizes of serialized files

The number of lines of the input file	Protobuf (kbit)	JSON (kbit)	XML (kbit)
50	41,6	52	71,4
500	402	501,6	688,8
5000	4005,5	4997,2	6862,1
50000	40040,7	49953,2	68606,3

According to the simulation results, the following mathematical expression is obtained for the size of the realized files using Protobuf:

$$s = \begin{cases} 0{,}832{*}n,\ 0 \leq n < 50 \\ 41,6 + 0,8{*}(n - 50),\ 50 \leq n < 500 \\ 402 + 0,801{*}(n - 500),\ 500 \leq n < 5000 \\ 4005{,}5 + 0{,}801{*}(n - 5000),\ 5000 \leq n < 50000 \end{cases}$$

As can be seen from the graph, in all four tests the size of the serialized file using Protobuf is the smallest compared to JSON and XML. On the other hand, using XML, the largest serialized file sizes were obtained in all tests compared to Protobuf and JSON.

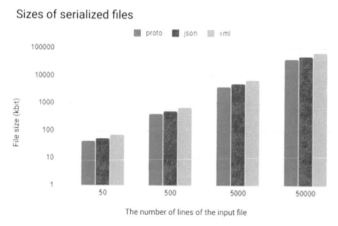

Fig. 10. The size of serialized files depending on the number of lines of the input file

As can be seen from the results of all four tests, the best results for all criteria were obtained using the Protobuf serialization method. It can be seen that as the volume of incoming data increases, the difference between serialization methods using XML, JSON, and Protobuf increases.

This is due to the fact that data with Protobuf is transmitted without metadata details, and this, in turn, does not add load to the payload. Also, Protobuf tightly compresses data, due to which the size of the serialized file is reduced in comparison with XML, JSON.

5 Conclusions

In this paper, the analysis of existing methods of information collection and processing in the IIoT network were analyzed, based on the prototype of the information collection and processing method was chosen.

The technique of collecting and processing informationhas been modified, which differs in the use of serialization based on the Protobuf method, which allows to increase the efficiency of information processing over time and reduce the amount of transmitted information.

Full-scale modeling of the proposed solution due to the implementation of software based on a modified method. A feature of the method is the fixation of parameters- time and size of the serialized file. This simulation confirmed the efficiency of the proposed solution. Mathematical expressions were formed on the basis of the generalized results obtained in each test, which allow to determine the time and size of the serialized file for a given number of lines of the input file.

According to the simulation results, the proposed solution was evaluated - in comparison with JSON, Protobuf serialization time is 3.27 times less, deserialization time is 3.64 times less, total time is 3.5 times less, and file size is 1.25 times smaller.

References

1. Ven, R.: Three Industrial IoT Implementation Challenges (2018). https://dzone.com/articles/3-iiot-industrial-internet-of-things-implementatio
2. Khare, S., Totaro, M.: Big Data in IoT (2019). https://www.researchgate.net/publication/338365769_Big_Data_in_IoT
3. Khan, W.Z., Aalsalem, M.Y., Khan, M.K., Hossain, M.S., Atiquzzaman, M.: A reliable Internet of Things based architecture for oil and gas industry. In: 2017 19th International Conference on Advanced Communication Technology (ICACT), pp. 705–710. IEEE (2017). https://doi.org/10.23919/ICACT.2017.7890184
4. Lee, C.K.M., Zhang, S.Z., Ng, K.K.H.: Development of an industrial Internet of things suite for smart factory towards re-industrialization. Adv. Manuf. 5(4), 335–343 (2017). https://doi.org/10.1007/s40436-017-0197-2
5. Ungurean, I., Gaitan, N.C., Gaitan, V.G.: A middleware based architecture for the industrial internet of things. KSII Trans. Internet Inf. Syst. 10(7), 2874–2891 (2016). https://doi.org/10.3837/tiis.2016.07.001
6. Al Hadidi, M., Al-Azzeh, J.S., Tkalich, O.P., Odarchenko, R.S., Gnatyuk, S.O., Khokhlachova, Y.Y.: Zigbee, bluetooth and Wi-Fi complex wireless networks performance increasing. Int. J. Commun. Antenna Propag. 1(48), 1–48 (2017). https://doi.org/10.15866/irecap.v7i1.10911
7. Shinde, Y.: Protobuf Performance Comparison (2016). https://dzone.com/articles/protobuf-performance-comparison-and-points-to-make
8. Babaria, U.: IoT Development Needs Microservices and Containerization (2018). https://www.einfochips.com/blog/why-iot-development-needs-microservices-and-containerization
9. Popenko, D., Kurdecha, V.: Analysis of object serialization methods for building a platform of big industrial data. Modern challenges in telecommunications, Kyiv, p. 222 (2020)
10. Demyd, P.: Protobuf application on industrialinternet of things. Prospects for development of information-telecommunication technologies and systems. Kyiv, p. 369 (2020)
11. Globa, L., Kurdecha, V., Ishchenko, I., Zakharchuk, A.: An approach to the Internet of Things system with nomadic units developing. In: 14th International Conference the Experience of Designing and Application of CAD Systems in Microelectronics (CADSM), Lviv, pp. 248–250 (2017). https://doi.org/10.1109/CADSM.2017.7916127
12. Globa, L., Kurdecha, V., Ishchenko, I., Zakharchuk, A., Kunieva, N.: The intellectual IoT-system for monitoring the base station quality of service. In: 2018 IEEE International Black Sea Conference on Communications and Networking (BlackSeaCom), Batumi, pp. 1–5 (2018). https://doi.org/10.1109/BlackSeaCom.2018.8433715

13. Globa, L.S., Skulish, M.A.: The model of multithread routing for broadband digital networks with integral service. In: 2008 18th International Crimean Conference - Microwave & Telecommunication Technology, Sevastopol, Crimea, pp. 376–377 (2008). https://doi.org/10.1109/CRMICO.2008.4676420
14. Senchenko, V.R., Koval, O.V., Globa, L.S., Novogrudska, R.L.: Intelligent modeling system based on cloud-technology. In: 2016 International Conference Radio Electronics & Info Communications (UkrMiCo), Kiev, pp. 1–4 (2016). https://doi.org/10.1109/UkrMiCo.2016.7739646

Information and Communications Technology

QoE Assessment Aspects for Virtual Reality and Holographic Telepresence Applications

Georgios Kougioumtzidis[1]([✉]), Vladimir Poulkov[1], Zaharias Zaharis[2], and Pavlos Lazaridis[3]

[1] Technical University of Sofia, Sofia, Bulgaria
{gkougioumtzidis,vkp}@tu-sofia.bg
[2] Aristotle University of Thessaloniki, Thessaloniki, Greece
zaharis@auth.gr
[3] University of Huddersfield, Huddersfield, UK
p.lazaridis@hud.ac.uk

Abstract. The cutting-edge evolution of mobile communication systems and Internet technologies in nowadays transitional period from the information age to the experience age has brought attention to the evolving virtual reality (VR) and augmented reality (AR) applications and moves towards the development of holographic telepresence systems. Since these applications are devoted in creating immersive and interactive experiences, the quality of experience (QoE) as it is perceived by the end-users will become fundamental constituent in their performance evaluation process. In this paper, the significance of QoE in the development and implementation of the emerging technologies of VR and holographic telepresence systems is analyzed. Moreover, the QoE influencing factors for VR applications and the distinction among this evolving technology and the conventional 2D video content are outlined. Furthermore, a classification of the QoE assessment methods, together with an analysis of the more significant metrics with regard to VR applications is presented.

Keywords: Quality of experience (QoE) · Virtual reality · Augmented reality · Holographic telepresence

1 Introduction

The interest in video streaming services is ever-increasing and the mobile video traffic has seen an exponential growth in recent years, accounting for the bulk of the mobile data traffic. As video resolution competency along with the capabilities of terminal equipment is upsurging at a fast pace and the ultra-high channel bandwidths and novel physical layer practices of the forthcoming beyond 5G (B5G) and sixth generation (6G) of mobile communication systems are underway, the research attention is being drawn towards the virtual reality (VR) and augmented reality (AR) applications.

The interest in such technologies is envisioned to grow exponentially in the years to come, which will lead forward to the next step of the extended reality (XR) implementations that will be focused on holographic telepresence applications. Holograms

D. Perakovic and L. Knapcikova (Eds.): FABULOUS 2022, LNICST 445, pp. 171–180, 2022.
https://doi.org/10.1007/978-3-031-15101-9_12

constitute the evolution of video communications, offering a significantly more complete experience to the users. Holographic telepresence will allow remote users to be rendered as a local presence, enabling a substantial number of innovating interactive usage scenarios, including tele-conferencing, tele-surgery and tele-education.

The fact that these technologies rely on interactivity and immersiveness, renders the users' quality of experience (QoE) a particularly crucial parameter during their development. In the course of implementing VR and holographic applications and designing future usage scenarios, it is very significant to comprehend the experiences and expectations of users as they are expressed and conveyed through QoE. QoE is a multidisciplinary measure affected by a wide range of factors belonging to various fields. It has become an essential element in the assessment of network services and operations in recent years, enabling for a greater understanding of how network technical aspects influence the quality of service as it is perceived by end-users.

In this paper, we discuss and analyze the significance of QoE in the development and implementation of the emerging technologies of VR and holographic telepresence systems. Moreover, we examine the QoE influencing factors for VR applications and underline the distinction among this evolving technology and the conventional 2D video content. Furthermore, we classify the QoE assessment methods with regard to VR applications and provide analysis of the more significant metrics both subjective and objective. Last, we examine the parameters of holographic telepresence systems that effect QoE, as embedding QoE-awareness in their design is still an open research issue.

2   QoE Influencing Factors

QoE influencing factors (IFs) can be characterized as the true state or adaptation of any attribute of a user, system, service, application or context that might impact the user's perceived quality [1]. The IFs contain attributes such as the form and properties of an application or service, the utilization context, the fulfillment of the user's expectations, the user's cultural background, socioeconomic status and psychological portrait, and ultimately, the user's emotional state [2]. QoE IFs can be classified as human-related, system-related and context-related [3] (Table 1).

2.1   Human-Related Factors

Any variant or invariant attribute or trait of a user is referred to as a human IF. Human IFs may have an impact on the development of a particular experience, as well as its overall quality. Because of their subjectivity and connection to internal processes of the human, they are extremely complicated [4]. Human IFs in VR applications include the physiological features of the user such as age and gender, anomalies in the human visual system (HVS) [5], as well as impairments in the human auditory system (HAS) [6], the simulator sickness which is caused by visual stimuli and can induce symptoms like fatigue, perspiration, vertigo or nausea [7], the level of user's immersion and also the user's expectations and expertise with VR applications [3].

Table 1. QoE influencing factors.

Influence factor	Feature	Description
Human factors	Physiological features	User's age & gender
	HVS & HAS	Impairments in human vision and hearing system
	Simulator sickness	Symptoms like fatigue, perspiration, vertigo & nausea
	Immersion	The user's propensity in experiencing immersion
	Expectations & expertise	The level of user's experience with VR systems
System factors	Content-related	Spatial audio, spatial depth & spatiotemporal complexity
	Media/codec-related	Compression, video codecs, audio, storage & transport, bitrate, resolution, frame rate, audio sample rate & coding delay
	Network/transmission-related	Delay, bandwidth & packet loss
	Hardware-related	HMD, headphones, decoder performance, head-tracking, FoV, display resolution & refresh rate
Context factors	Physical context	The environment in which a user interacts with a VR system
	Temporal context	The frequency & duration of utilizing a VR service
	Social context	Interaction with other users & consideration on popularity of a VR content & the way a VR service is accessed
	Task context	The purpose of using a VR service

2.2 System-Related Factors

System IFs are qualities and features that have an impact on the overall performance of a VR application or service with regard to technical parameters. VR system IFs can be further classified into four categories, which are as follows: content-related, media/codec-related, network/transmission-related and hardware-related [3, 4]:

- Since different content properties may need distinct system features, the content and its nature have a significant impact on the overall QoE of the system. The content-related IFs include parameters such as spatial audio, spatial depth and spatiotemporal complexity.

- The media/codec-related IFs refer to media configuration features such as compression, video codecs, audio, storage and transport, bitrate, resolution, frame rate, audio sample rate and coding delay.
- The network/transmission-related IFs are influenced by errors that occur during network transmission and are inextricably linked to network quality of service (QoS). The network/transmission-related IFs include parameters such as delay, bandwidth and packet loss.
- Hardware-related IFs pertain to terminal systems and equipment of the transmission channel and refer to components such as head-mounted display (HMD), headphones, decoder performance, head-tracking, field of view (FoV), display resolution and refresh rate.

2.3 Context-Related Factors

Context IFs encompass any situational feature to define the user's surroundings. Context IFs may arise at various degrees of magnitude, behavior, and occurrence patterns, both individually and in combinations, and they can be classified as physical context factors, temporal context factors, social context factors and task context factors.

3 QoE Assessment

There are two approaches for assessing QoE: the subjective and objective assessment. In subjective models human assessors are subjected to a range of tests or stimuli in order to provide information about quality [8]. Objective models on the other hand are regarded as a way for assessing subjective quality using solely objective quality metrics [9].

3.1 Subjective Methods

Quantitative methodologies from adjacent fields such like psychophysics and psychometrics are used in the subjective methods, by employing ratings that represent the assessors' perception of the level of quality they experienced. Additionally, qualitative methods including focus groups, interviews and profile surveys are also utilized to discover which IFs contribute to QoE and in what extent [8]. Ordinarily, assessors rank a series of perceived quality characteristics on a mean opinion score (MOS) scale, which ranges from 1 to 5 (i.e., bad to excellent) and indicate their degree of satisfaction with a particular service [10]. Owing to direct data obtainment from end-users, the subjective assessment approach offers the most accurate outcomes. These outcomes are used as reference in model training and affirmation. The fundamental drawbacks of the subjective methods on the other hand, stem from the fact that they are expensive, time-consuming, incapable for use in real time and unrepeatable [11].

In the case of VR applications, the subjective QoE assessments should be carried out with use of HMDs to preserve the immersive traits and ensure exact perception of the quality of panoramic videos [12]. Moreover, the spatial and temporal perceptual information of the test sequence are vital factors, since they determine the feasible amount of video compression and, as a result, the degree of impairment that is afflicted when the test sequence is broadcasted over a fixed-rate communication channel [13]. The subjective VR QoE assessment methods should value the assessors' ratings on a series of perceptual scales, including audiovisual quality, simulator sickness symptoms and exploration behavior [14] (Table 2):

- The most frequently used metrics to evaluate the audiovisual quality include the absolute category rating (ACR) and the degradation category rating (DCR). The ACR metric is a single stimulus approach that can be utilized in case testing time is critical, because it generates a large number of ratings in a short amount of time. The DCR metric, also known as the double stimulus impairment scale (DSIS), is a double stimulus approach that generates smaller number of ratings in the same amount of time in comparison with ACR, but is statically more reliable [15].
- Simulator sickness is an unpleasant condition induced by a sensory imbalance among the visual and vestibular systems. For measuring simulator sickness symptoms, the simulator sickness questionnaire (SSQ) is indicated [7]. The virtual reality sickness questionnaire (VRSQ) is a condensed version of the SSQ that only examines the subsequent symptoms: overall discomfort, tiredness, eyestrain, poor concentration, headache, head heaviness, blurred vision, dizziness with eye closed and vertigo [16]. When simulator sickness requires to be examined often and due to the objective of the testing quick self-reporting from the assessors is essential, it is advised to utilize the vertigo score rating (VSR) [17].
- The participant's exploration behavior is measured by tracking the position of the head rotation throughout the active viewing session. Head rotation position is required to be monitored at regular intervals and timed to the beginning of each test sequence, such that exploration behavior can be linked to the content of the test sequence. Likewise, eye movements can be captured utilizing eye trackers embedded in the HMDs [18].

Table 2. Subjective assessment metrics.

Perceptual feature	Metric	Description
Audiovisual quality	ACR	Single stimulus ratings of test sequence on a five-level class scale
	DCR/DSIS	Double stimulus ratings of test & reference sequence on a five-level class scale
Simulator sickness	SSQ	Questionnaire method for simulator sickness evaluation
	VRSQ	Compacted version of SSQ
	VSR	Rapid self-reporting method
Exploration behavior	Head rotation	Head position tracking
	Eye movement	Eye trackers embedded in HMDs

3.2 Objective Methods

Due to the constraints of subjective methods, there has been a considerable push to implement objective models that predict the subjective perceived quality based solely on physical traits. The objective methods are projected to generate a prediction of the QoE value that approximates the ratings of the subjective assessment methods. The objective approach has the advantage of being simple to apply and modify, as the assessment process has only to account on the observable QoS parameters and corresponding correlation mathematical models. The objective assessment's drawback is its inaccuracy, as the computed QoE is only an approximation instead of an exact value of the quality as perceived by the end-users [19].

Objective quality assessment methods can be classified in five categories [20]: 1) media-layer models, which take actual media audiovisual signals as input and incorporate codec compression and channel features; 2) packet-layer models, which calculate QoE only based on packet header data; 3) bitstream models, which handle encoded bitstream data as well as packet header data as input; 4) hybrid models, which are a fusion of the aforementioned models that use as much information and data as feasible to evaluate QoE; and 5) planning models, which use network or terminal quality planning features to calculate their input.

Table 3. Objective assessment metrics.

Source information	Metric	Description
Full reference	SSIM	Still image sequence quality metric based on luminance, contrast & structure
	VQM	Video quality metric based on structural & temporal features
	VIF	Still image quality metric based on the ratio of the distorted image to reference image
	PSNR	Image & video quality metric that assesses the variance between source & distorted signals
	VMAF	Video quality metric that evaluates the influence of compression & rescaling
Reduced reference	STRRED	Calculation of the impairment among a distorted & a reference video sequence
	SpEED-QA	Mean-subtracted pixel values of frames and frame variances in video sequences
No reference	NR-P	Video quality metric based on the decoded representation to compute the quality of a received stream
	NR-B	Video quality metric based on parameters extracted from the encoded bitstream

The objective metrics employ audio, image and video attributes to assess quality and they are classed as full reference, reduced reference or no-reference, depending on the amount of source information available [21] (Table 3):

- The reference and result video sequences are both supplied in the full reference (FR) metrics, allowing for thorough comparison of the videos [22]. Paradigms of such metrics include the structural similarities (SSIM), video quality model (VQM), visual information fidelity (VIF), peak signal to noise ratio (PSNR) and video multimethod assessment fusion (VMAF).
- The reference and result video sequences are generated by employing the same selection of attributes in reduced reference (RR) metrics. Just a selection of partial features from the source input sequence are necessary for the quality assessment [23]. Examples of RR metrics include the spatio-temporal reduced-reference entropic differencing (STRRED) and spatial efficient entropic differencing for quality assessment (SpEED-QA).
- No reference (NR) metrics have access only in the outcome video sequence and the quality evaluation is achieved by employing information comprised in a related image or video media stream. The computing demands of NR techniques are the lowest when compared to the other methods and they also have the fastest temporal response, but they are unable to provide an accurate evaluation across a wide range of video states [24]. NR metrics include the pixel-based methods (NR-P) and bitstream methods (NR-B).

Recent works focusing on the VR QoE assessment have provided enhanced variants of objective metrics [25], including PSNR of spheres (S-PSNR) and perceptual PSNR (P-PSNR) [26], weighted PSNR (W-PSNR) [27] and spherical SSIM (S-SSIM) [28].

4 Holographic Telepresence Applications

Holographic telepresence communications will allow users from remote locations to interact with holographic data over a communication channel. Consequently, hologram-based applications will impose considerable demands on network capacity, including the ability to provide ultra-low latency, very high bandwidth, and the coordination, synchronization and dynamic adaptation of numerous data streams. The addition of parallax in a holographic material denotes that the viewer may interact with the images in a way that depends on the viewer's location. This shifts the user's participation from being passive in 2D and 3D video to become active and engaged in holograms, significantly boosting the network's requirements. As a result, it necessitates solutions for data capture, transmission and interactivity [29].

The network parameters that are critical in the development of holographic communications and impact significantly QoE include the following [30]: 1) data rates, which are contingent on the hologram's structure, the type of the display and the amount of images to be synchronized; 2) latency, which needs to be ultra-low for truly immersive experiences and avoidance of simulator sickness; 3) synchronization, which is essential for the coordinated provision of data streams from multiple sources; 4) security, which is contingent on how critical is the type of application; 5) resilience, which decreases packet loss, jitter and latency at the system level, whereas the corresponding QoE metrics at the service level would be availability and reliability; and 6) computation, which is contingent on the real-time requirements for hologram generation and reception.

The next breakthrough in XR communications include holograms and multisense communications. While the senses of sight and hearing are already included in audio, video and VR applications, holographic communications integrating all five senses is gaining significant research interest. In principle, holograms may be used to combine a range of sensory experiences and digital encounters can be enhanced with scents and tastes. The emotion-sensing wearable equipment adept of monitoring mental health, enabling social connections and enhancing the user's experience will become the foundations of future mobile networks, employing the holograms as the means of communication [31].

Since the perceived quality of a hologram is determined by a variety of factors such as frame resolution and rate, as well as degree resolution, a comprehension of the implications of each parameter on user perception is critical for reducing bandwidth utilization while preserving QoE. In holograms, the spatial resolution gives an additional dimension for trade-offs that can be used to maximize QoE, similar to how quality of individual images can be sacrificed for frame rates in conventional video. This, nevertheless, necessitates the capacity to adapt parameters in a dynamic manner [29].

5 Conclusions

QoE has a crucial role in the development of the emerging VR and holographic telepresence systems, as these technologies are committed in providing immersive and interactive experiences to their users, thus the quality as it is perceived by the end-users is of outmost importance. In this paper we presented and analyzed the QoE influencing factors and examined the aspects of QoE assessment with regard to VR applications. Moreover, we outlined the elements in the holographic telepresence systems architecture that have an impact on QoE of the end-users.

Acknowledgement. This work was supported by the European Union, through the Horizon 2020 Marie Skodowska-Curie Innovative Training Networks Programme "Mobility and Training for beyond 5G Ecosystems (MOTOR5G)" under grant agreement no. 861219.

References

1. Brunnström, K., et al.: Qualinet white paper on definitions of quality of experience. In: Fifth Qualinet Meeting, Novi Sad (2013)
2. ITU-T, Rec. ITU-T P.10/G.100: Vocabulary for performance, quality of service and quality of experience (2017)
3. ITU-T. Rec. ITU-T G.1035: Influencing factors on quality of experience for virtual reality services (2020)
4. Reiter, U., et al.: Factors influencing quality of experience. In: Möller, S., Raake, A. (eds.) Quality of Experience. TSTS, pp. 55–72. Springer, Cham (2014). https://doi.org/10.1007/978-3-319-02681-7_4

5. Burbeck, C.A., Kelly, D.H.: Spatiotemporal characteristics of visual mechanisms: excitatory-inhibitory model. J. Opt. Soc. Am. **70**(9), 1121–1126 (1980)
6. Greenberg, S., Ainsworth, W.A.: Speech processing in the auditory system: an overview. In: Speech Processing in the Auditory System. Springer Handbook of Auditory Research, vol. 18. Springer, NY (2004). https://doi.org/10.1007/0-387-21575-1_1
7. Kennedy, R.S., Lane, N.E., Berbaum, K.S., Lilienthal, M.G.: Simulator sickness questionnaire: an enhanced method for quantifying simulator sickness. Int. J. Aviat. Psychol. **3**(3), 203–220 (1993)
8. Schatz, R., Hoßfeld, T., Janowski, L., Egger, S.: From packets to people: quality of experience as a new measurement challenge. In: Biersack, E., Callegari, C., Matijasevic, M. (eds.) Data Traffic Monitoring and Analysis. LNCS, vol. 7754, pp. 219–263. Springer, Heidelberg (2013). https://doi.org/10.1007/978-3-642-36784-7_10
9. Takahash, A.: Framework and standardization of quality of experience (QoE) design and management for audiovisual communication services. NTT Tech. Rev. **7**(4), 1–5 (2009)
10. ITU-T, Rec. ITU-T P.800.1: Mean Opinion Score (MOS) Terminology (2006)
11. Alreshoodi, M.A., Woods, J.C.: Survey on QoE/QoS correlation models for multimedia services. Int. J. Distrib. Parallel Syst. **4**(3) (2013)
12. Zhang, Y., et al.: Subjective panoramic video quality assessment database for coding applications. IEEE Trans. Broadcast. **64**(2), 461–473 (2018)
13. ITU-T, Rec. ITU-T P.910: Subjective video quality assessment methods for multimedia applications (2008)
14. ITU-T, Rec. ITU-T P.919: Subjective test methodologies for 360° video on head-mounted displays (2020)
15. Singla, A., Robitza, W., Raake, A.: Comparison of subjective quality test methods for omnidirectional video quality evaluation. In: Proceedings of the MMSP 2019, Kuala Lumpur (2019)
16. Kim, H.K., Park, J., Choi, Y., Choe, M.: Virtual reality sickness questionnaire (VRSQ): motion sickness measurement index in a virtual reality environment. Appl. Ergon. **69**, 66–73 (2018)
17. Perez, P., Oyaga, N., Ruiz, J.J., Villegas, A.: Towards systematic analysis of cybersickness in high motion omnidirectional video. In: Proceedings of the QoMEX 2018, Cagliari (2018)
18. David, E.J., Gutiérrez, J., Coutrot, A., Da Silva, M.P., Le Callet, P.: A dataset of head and eye movements for 360° videos. In: Proceedings of the MMSys 2018, Amsterdam (2018)
19. Wang, Y., Zhang, P.: QoE Management in Wireless Networks, Springer, NY (2016). https://doi.org/10.1007/978-3-319-42454-5
20. ITU-T, Rec. ITU-T G.1011: Reference guide to quality of experience assessment methodologies (2016)
21. Fiedler, M., Hossfeld, T., Tran-Gia, P.: A generic quantitative relationship between quality of experience and quality of service. IEEE Netw. **24**(2), 36–41 (2010)
22. Juluri, P., Tamarapalli, V., Medhi, D.: Measurement of quality of experience of video-on-demand services: a survey. IEEE Commun. Surv. Tutor. **18**(1), 401–418 (2015)
23. Song, W., Tjondronegoro, D.W., Docherty, M.J.: Understanding user experience of mobile video: framework, measurement, and optimization. In: Mobile Multimedia - User and Technology Perspectives, InTech, Rijeka, pp. 3–30 (2012)
24. Vega, M.T., Perra, C., De Turck, F., Liotta, A.: A review of predictive quality of experience management in video streaming services. IEEE Trans. Broadcast. **64**(2), 432–445 (2018)
25. Ruan, J., Xie, D.: A survey on QoE-oriented VR video streaming: some research issues and challenges. Electronics **10**(17), 2155 (2021)
26. Liu, Y., Yang, L., Xu, M., Wang, Z.: Rate control schemes for panoramic video coding. J. Vis. Commun. Image Represent. **53**, 76–85 (2018)
27. Zakharchenko, V., Choi, K.P., Park, J.H.: Quality metric for spherical panoramic video. In: Proceedings of the SPIE Optics + Photonics 2016, San Diego, CA (2016)

28. Chen, S., Zhang, Y., Li, Y., Chen, Z., Wang, Z.: Spherical structural similarity index for objective omnidirectional video quality assessment. In: Proceedings of the IEEE ICME 2018, San Diego, CA (2018)
29. Tataria, H., Shafi, M., Molisch, A.F., Dohler, M., Sjöland, H., Tufvesson, F.: 6G wireless systems: vision, requirements, challenges, insights, and opportunities. Proc. IEEE **109**(7), 1166–1199 (2021)
30. Clemm, A., Vega, M.T., Ravuri, H.K., Wauters, T., De Turck, F.: Toward truly immersive holographic-type communication: challenges and solutions. IEEE Commun. Mag. **58**(1), 93–99 (2020)
31. Shu, J., Chiu, M., Hui, P.: Emotion sensing for mobile computing. IEEE Commun. Mag. **57**(11), 84–90 (2019)

Selected Application Tools for Creating Models in the Matlab Environment

Stella Hrehova$^{(\boxtimes)}$ (ID) and Jozef Husár (ID)

Faculty of Manufacturing Technologies with a Seat in Prešov, Department of Industrial Engineering and Informatics, The Technical University of Košice, Bayerova 1, 080 01 Prešov, Slovak Republic
{stella.hrehova,jozef.husar}@tuke.sk

Abstract. The issue of analysis, data evaluation and prediction has resonated in every area for several years. With the introduction of the Industry 4.0 philosophy, data is becoming the centre of attention. The constant development of new measurement technologies and applications, as well as the possibilities of data storage and sharing, also contribute to the constant increase in the amount of data. Application developers who are already firmly established in the company are trying to develop new, user-friendly tools. These application are focused on advanced data evaluation and modelling capabilities. Matlab is one such application. Its advantage is the constant development of individual advanced tools - toolboxes specialized in various areas. The presented paper will describe selected data visualization options. We will also focus on the description of selected tools using machine learning techniques to find and design the best model for data prediction. The data is obtained through the SCADA user interface and relates to the issue of building heating. In the presented paper, we will point out the advanced data display and compare models created using the Regression Learner and Neural Net Fitting tools.

Keywords: Data · Visualisation · Neural network · Matlab · Heating process

1 Introduction

Data and methods of their acquisition, processing and evaluation have long been the subject of intense interest. By implementing current information and communication technologies in the spirit of Industry 4.0 principles in several areas, we gain much greater opportunities to obtain the required data [1, 2]. Thanks to increasingly advanced data acquisition technologies, we are able to capture large amounts of data. It is therefore understandable that new, advanced methodologies, procedures and applications are emerging in many areas that focus on data management. Undoubtedly, computer application programs have an important place in this area of interest, which makes it much easier for users to work with data management. During the current development in the field of data processing, the individual stages that are necessary for the interpretation of the data we obtained were correct. The following figure represents one of the many schemes of the individual stages of data processing [3] (Fig. 1).

© ICST Institute for Computer Sciences, Social Informatics and Telecommunications Engineering 2022
Published by Springer Nature Switzerland AG 2022. All Rights Reserved
D. Perakovic and L. Knapcikova (Eds.): FABULOUS 2022, LNICST 445, pp. 181–192, 2022.
https://doi.org/10.1007/978-3-031-15101-9_13

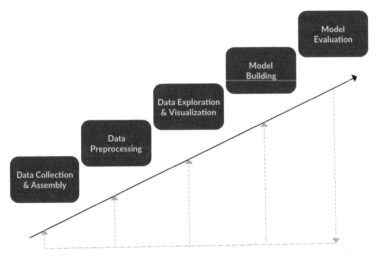

Fig. 1. Simple textual data task framework

a) Data collection & Assambley - this part is already largely ensured by the application of the Industry 4.0 philosophy in practice. Various measuring units, sensors and other elements of advanced measuring technology are introduced, which are able to collect and store data.

b) Data pre-processing - data pre-processing is generally required to correct for variance, baseline changes, peak shifts, noise, missing values, duplications, and several other features so that the "true" relevant basic structure or property of the data can be highlighted. The purpose of these adjustments is to prepare the source data so that they can be interpreted correctly [4].

c) Data Exploration & Visualisation - data visualization is an efficient process for presenting data and information graphically or using pictures. It emerges as a powerful and widely applicable and acceptable tool for interpreting and analyzing large and complex data [5]. Visualisation is useful in cleaning data, examining data structure, detecting outliers and unusual groups, identifying trends and clusters, identifying local patterns, evaluating modeling outputs, and presenting results [6].

d) Model building – the choice of a suitable model depends on the requirements. Currently, there are many applications that are able to create a model. However, we need to know the goal, what information we want to obtain from the source data, what method and tools we will use for their analysis and other information [7, 8]. Model creation is thus a complex activity where close cooperation with experts in several areas is required.

e) Model Evaluation – many publications describe several options for evaluating the proposed model. However, we should remember that it is also important to examine the quality of the proposed model [9].

In the presented paper we will focus on the areas of visualization and model creation in the Matlab software application. The presented data were obtained via a user interface created through the system Supervisory Control and Data Acquisition (SCADA). It is basically industrial control system, witch processing data in real time. It helps to control and monitor the operations in the many industrial areas [10]. The source data were obtained through user interface, which is displayed on the next figure (Fig. 2).

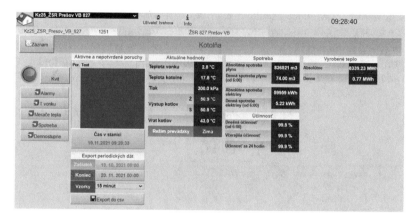

Fig. 2. SCADA user interface

The user is able to export data in different time periods through this interface. For the submitted paper, we used data from the year 2019, in the scheme once an hour for each day of the month (see Fig. 3).

	A	B	C	D	E	F	G	H	I	J	K	L
1	Datum a cas	K1TSPALIN	K1TVRAT	K1TVYSTU	K1VYKON	K2TSPALIN	K2TVRAT	K2TVYSTU	K2VYKON	K3TSPALIN	K3TVRAT	K3TVYSTU
2	1.1.2019 0:00	41	-3276,8	49,5	49	21	-3276,8	39	0	21	-3276,8	42
3	1.1.2019 1:00	46	-3276,8	55,5	64	21	-3276,8	38	0	21	-3276,8	40,5
4	1.1.2019 2:00	44	-3276,8	55	64	36	-3276,8	51	99	22	-3276,8	39,5
5	1.1.2019 3:00	43	-3276,8	52,5	48	24	-3276,8	44	0	22	-3276,8	38,5
6	1.1.2019 4:00	35	-3276,8	66	0	47	-3276,8	45,5	18	39	-3276,8	64,5
7	1.1.2019 5:00	49	-3276,8	57	64	48	-3276,8	57	64	48	-3276,8	47
8	1.1.2019 6:00	55	-3276,8	66	64	45	-3276,8	64	64	32	-3276,8	58,5
9	1.1.2019 7:00	50	-3276,8	64,5	0	50	-3276,8	59,5	39	49	-3276,8	56
10	1.1.2019 8:00	53	-3276,8	62,5	64	50	-3276,8	59,5	64	29	-3276,8	51

Fig. 3. Part of source data

As part of the presentation of the Matlab application, only certain variables were selected from the given data, which have a high informative value - gas consumption per day SPZPLYNDEN, electricity consumption per day SPELDEN, outdoor temperature TVONKU and required heating temperatures for the given circuits UKTVODZ. The table is extracted in.csv format, which is suitable for Matlab application. However, be aware that the decimal separator must be a dot so that Matlab does not have problems identifying data. To import data to Matlab environment we used the Import option.

2   Chosen Methods and Matlab Tools

2.1   Machine and Deep Learning

Advanced machine learning analysis is becoming increasingly popular as it can be applied in almost any field. Machine learning is a sub-area of artificial intelligence (AI) in which computers derive new information or decisions by learning data using algorithms and programs [11]. The goal of machine learning is to model machine learning algorithms based on input data in a defined solution space. The following figure shows an overview of the learning types for machine learning [12] (Fig. 4).

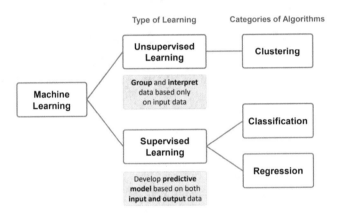

Fig. 4. Overview – Machine learning

In this paper, we have focused on the Supervised Learning section, in which input and output data are marked for classification so as to provide a basis for future data processing learning [13].

Deep learning - deep learning is a subset of machine learning in artificial intelligence that is able to learn from data that is not marked or unstructured [14]. It is machine learning technique that learns features and tasks directly from data. The term "deep" is related to the depth of neural network architecture, which is used when-ever the network contains at least two hidden layers [15].

The next table compares these techniques in some areas [16] (Table 1).

Table 1. Comparison

	Machine learning	Deep learning
Training dataset	Small	Large
Choose your own features	Yes	No
# of classifiers available	Many	Few
Training time	Short	Long

2.2 Matlab and Description of Chosen Tools

The Matlab system is a tool both for comfortable interactive work and for the development of a wide range of application programs. Its possibilities are constantly expanding into several areas by developing new extensions - toolboxes. These extensions allow users who do not need to be IT experts to use a wide range of application, software and analytics tools. In the form of guides, they make it possible to intuitively create process models and thus obtain the necessary information. The data flow in the Matlab environment is shown in the following figure [17] (Fig. 5).

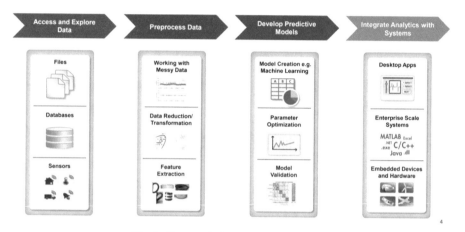

Fig. 5. Data analytics workflow in Matlab

The descriptions of used tools will present the real data that were presented in the introductory chapter.

1. Visualisation – in the field of data visualization, Matlab offers a really wide range of possibilities. It offers suitable graphs when marking the required variables. The representation of the graphical form can be changed both programmatically (using commands) and through a graphical interface (Property Editor), where the user selects the individual properties of the graphical display. When plotting a simple dependence, it also offers the possibility of displaying basic statistical characteristics in a clear table.
2. Regression Learner basically allows us to create regression models interactively without writing code and measuring the accuracy and performance of the models. It allows fast experimentation with multiple regression algorithms and quickly compares the performance of different regression models and functions [18].
3. Neural Net Fitting – it is application which allows create, visualize, and train a two-layer feed-forward network to solve data fitting problems. It is possible to choose from three different algorithms for updating weights. They are Levenberg–Marquardt, Bayesian regularization, and scaled conjugate gradient. Levenberg–Marquardt backpropagation algorithm is one of the most popular algorithms in the MATLAB toolbox [19]. It is one of the fast algorithms which has reasonable performance

and it is used more than the other ones. This algorithm has better regression (curve fitting).

2.3 Used Methods to Evaluate of Created Models

Toolbox Machine and deep learning offers several methods for creating models. The MSE characteristics and the correlation coefficient R are mainly used to assess the suitability of the resulting models [20].

- MSE is used to determine how close the regression line is to the measured data. An MSE value close to 0 means that the model complies with the data.

$$MSE = (1/\text{Number of sample}) \times \sum \text{Square errors} \tag{1}$$

- R is a statistical measurement of the relationship between variables and their interconnection.

$$R = \frac{\sum (x_i - \bar{x})(y_i - \bar{y})}{\sqrt{\sum (x_i - \bar{x})^2 \sum (y_i - \bar{y})^2}} \tag{2}$$

where R is the correlation coefficient, x_i values of the x-variable in a sample, $\bar{x}$ mean the values of the x-variables, y_i values of the y-variable in a sample, $\bar{y}$ mean of the values of the y-variables.

3   Model Design

When presenting the described tools, we assume that the data is pre-processed and cleaned up. For using chosen applications within Machine a Deep Learning Toolbox we work with average values of gained data.

3.1   Visualisation

During visualization, we are interested in the course of the monitored parameters, especially if they are dependent on the same variable. From the point of view of our data, these are, for example, the required values of the water temperature in the individual circuits of the heating system. Here are effective tools *parallelplot*, respectively *stackedplot*, when you just need to mark the data imported in the table or matrix (Fig. 6).

Similarly, you can easily use the *stackedplot* option, which allows display individual columns of imported data as separate rows in the graphics window, which are also interconnected. In this case, outdoor temperature, energy and gas consumption for the selected date (Fig. 7).

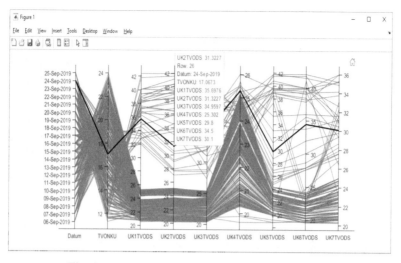

Fig. 6. Representation of chosen data using *parallelplot*

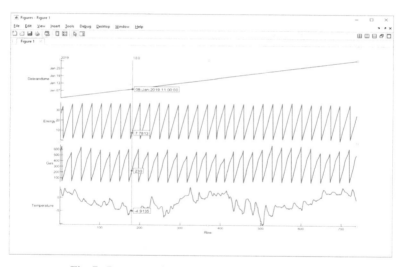

Fig. 7. Representation of chosen data using *stackedplot*

3.2   Model Design Using Machine and Deep Learning

Regression Learner

The average values of the outdoor temperature (predictor) and the corresponding average value of electricity consumption (response) were used to present the creation of the model using Regression Learner. After setting the required parameters, training was started using all options. We used this option so that the system itself found the most optimal variant (see Fig. 8).

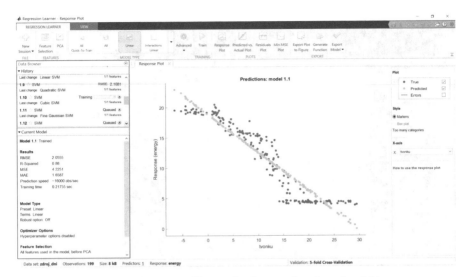

Fig. 8. Environment of Regression Learner for selected variables

From the picture it is possible to observe the course when the data are gradually trained and the optimal variant is sought. At the end of the training, the best option is automatically marked. The MSE and R values show how the model is "good". The resulting dependence is shown in the following figure (Fig. 9).

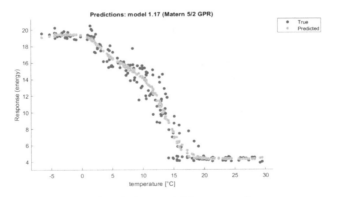

Fig. 9. The best model from regression

Neural Net Fitting

To use this tool, we will generate the variables needed to train the model *xtrain* - there will be an average outdoor temperature and *ytrain* - will be an average energy consumption. This tool is created in the form of a guide, where we proceed step by step and use built-in algorithms to design our model. We have a choice of three training algorithms, we used the possibility of the Levenberg-Marguard algorithm, the principle of which was described, for example, in the literature [21]. If the resulting values of

MSE and correlation coefficient do not correspond to our ideas, respectively they are unacceptable, we can retrain the training data set. We can repeat this process several times. Another option is to increase the number of inner layers or increase the number of training data. The *plotregression* output is displayed on the Fig. 10.

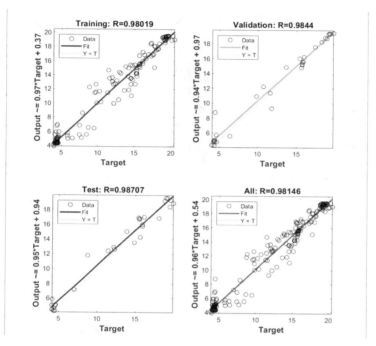

Fig. 10. The output from interface - Regression

Both described tools have the ability to generate functions that are then used for new data. The Neural Net Fitting tool also has the option of creating a schema in the Simulink environment (Fig. 11).

4   Result

To select the best model, we compared the individual qualitative indicators (Table 2).

The model created by Neural Net Fitting shows slightly better values. In order to compare the created individual models, the real values from 2020 were exported via the user interface. The following figure presents a graphical comparison of the predicted data obtained from both models with the real measured values (Fig. 12).

It can be seen from the figure that both models copy the real data quite well except for the area between months 4 and 5. This situation could have arisen due to various influences that will need to be defined and incorporated when implementing the models.

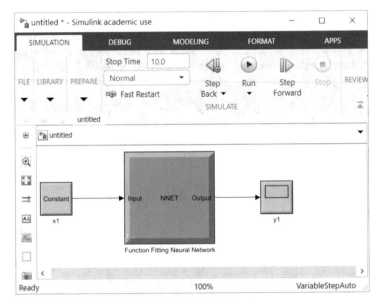

Fig. 11. Scheme in Simulink environment

Table 2. Model comparison

Coefficient	Regression learner	Neural net fitting
MSE	1,4196	1,3394
R	0,96	0,980,192

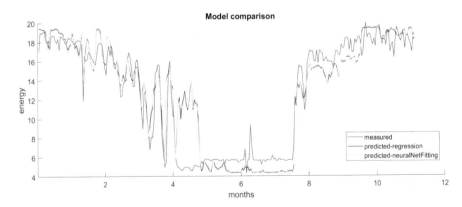

Fig. 12. Model comparison

5 Conclusion

Data can be a source of a lot of useful information if we can process it properly. They do not only tell about the state of the past, but provide opportunities for forecasting in the future. This potential only allows them to rapidly develop application environments that focus on data management. However, compared to others, MATLAB is easier and faster for many users to apply modern tools for learning. In this paper, we pointed out the use of the Machine and Deep Learning toolbox in creating two prediction models. These models are based on the use of historical data to predict the consumption of electricity when heating a selected building. The quality of the models was compared using the MSE and R indicators, where there are only small deviations. The next goal will be to create a user interface through Matlab tools so that the results are more accessible to a wider range of users.

Acknowledgements. This work was supported by the Slovak Research and Development Agency under the contracts No. APVV-19-0590 and also by the projects VEGA 1/0700/20, KEGA 055TUKE-4/2020 granted by the Ministry of Education of the Slovak Republic.

References

1. Peraković, D., Periša, M., Sente, R.E.: Information and communication technologies within Industry 4.0 concept. In: Advances in Design, Simulation and Manufacturing. DSMIE 2018. LNME. Springer, Cham (2019). https://doi.org/10.1007/978-3-319-93587-4_14
2. Trojanowska, J., Kolinski, A., Galusik, D., Varela, M.L.R., Machado, J.: A methodology of improvement of manufacturing productivity through increasing operational efficiency of the production process. In: Hamrol, A., Ciszak, O., Legutko, S., Jurczyk, M. (eds) Advances in Manufacturing. LNME. Springer, Cham (2018). https://doi.org/10.1007/978-3-319-686 19-6_3
3. Mayo, M.: Data a general approach to preprocessing text data. https://www.kdnuggets.com/2017/12/general-approach-preprocessing-text-data.html. Accessed 21 Oct 2021
4. Mishra, P., Biancolillo, A., Roger, J.M., Marini, F., Rutledge, D.N.: New data preprocessing trends based on ensemble of multiple preprocessing techniques. TrAC - Trends Anal. Chem. **132**, 116045 (2020). https://doi.org/10.1016/j.trac.2020.116045
5. Gandhi, P., Pruthi, J.: Data visualization techniques: traditional data to big data. In: Anouncia, S., Gohel, H., Vairamuthu, S. (eds) Data Visualization. Springer, Singapore (2020). https://doi.org/10.1007/978-981-15-2282-6_4
6. Unwin, A.: Why is data visualization important? What is important in data visualization? Harvard Data Sci. Rev. **2**(1) (2020). https://doi.org/10.1162/99608f92.8ae4d525
7. Husar, J., Knapcikova, L., Balog, M.: Implementation of material flow simulation as a learning tool. In: Advances in Design, Simulation and Manufacturing. DSMIE 2018. LNME. Springer, Cham (2019). https://doi.org/10.1007/978-3-319-93587-4_4
8. Kliment, M., et al.: Production efficiency evaluation and products' quality improvement using simulation. Int. J. Simul. Model. **19**(3), 470–481 (2020)
9. Hicks, S.C., Peng, R.D.: Evaluating the success of a data analysis. arXiv:1904.11907 (2019)
10. Manda, V.K., Poosapati, V., Katneni, V.: Super SCADA systems: a prototype for next gen SCADA system. IAETSD J. Adv. Res. Appl. Sci. (2018)

11. Chen, Q., Lee, S.: A machine learning approach to predict customer usage of a home workout platform. Appl. Sci. **11**, 9927 (2021). https://doi.org/10.3390/app11219927
12. Diether, A.: Machine learning for financial applications, mathworks. https://www2.humusoft.cz/www/papers/finkonf-2017/diethert.pdf. Accessed 21 Nov 2021
13. Bitna, K., Young, H.P.: Beginer's guide to neural networks for the MNIST dataset using MATLAB. Korean J. Math. **26**(2), 337–348 (2018). https://doi.org/10.11568/kjm.2018.26.2.337
14. Al Zamily, J.Y., Abu Naser, S.S.: Lemon classification using deep learning. Int. J. Acad. Pedagog. Res. (IJAPR) **3**(12) (2019)
15. Hošovský, A., Piteľ, J., Trojanová, M., Židek, K.: Computational intelligence in the context of Industry 4.0. Implementing Industry 4.0 in SMEs. Palgrave Macmillan, Cham (2021). https://doi.org/10.1007/978-3-030-70516-9_2
16. Phitchayanon, P.: Machine learning & deep learning with Matlab. https://muit.mahidol.ac.th/muit_training/matlab2019/Machine-Learning-and-classification-App.pdf. Accessed 22 Nov 2021
17. Mathworks: Matlab for Data analytics. http://lib.itpcas.ac.cn/documents/18/0/Data+Analytics+MATLAB.pdf. Accessed 21 Nov 2021
18. Siirtola, P., Röning, J.: Comparison of regression and classification models for user-independent and personal stress detection. Sensors **20**, 4402 (2020). https://doi.org/10.3390/s20164402
19. BKA, M.A.R., Ngamkhanong, C., Wu, Y., Kaewunruen, S.: Recycled aggregates concrete compressive strength prediction using artificial neural networks (ANNs). Infrastructures **6**(2), 17 (2021). https://doi.org/10.3390/infrastructures6020017
20. Ocampo, I., López, R.R., Camacho-León, S., Nerguizian, V., Stiharu, I.: Comparative evaluation of artificial neural networks and data analysis in predicting liposome size in a periodic disturbance micromixer. Micromachines **12**, 1164 (2021). https://doi.org/10.3390/mi12101164
21. Vagaská, A., Gombár, M.: Comparison of usage of different neural structures to predict AAO layer thickness. Tehnicki Vjesnik **24**(2) (2017). https://doi.org/10.17559/TV-20140423164817

Intelligent Monitoring of Loading and Unloading Process in Enterprise Transport System

Lucia Knapčíková[1]([⊠])[ID], Matúš Martiček[1], Jozef Husár[1][ID], and Jakub Kaščak[2][ID]

[1] Faculty of Manufacturing Technologies with a Seat in Prešov, Department of Industrial Engineering and Informatics, The Technical University of Košice, Bayerova 1, 080 01 Prešov, Slovak Republic
{lucia.knapcikova,jozef.husar}@tuke.sk,
matus.marticek@student.tuke.sk
[2] Faculty of Manufacturing Technologies with a Seat in Prešov, Department of Computer Aided Manufacturing Technologies, The Technical University of Košice, Štúrova 31, 080 01 Prešov, Slovak Republic
jakub.kascak@tuke.sk

Abstract. Organizations and businesses need an information infrastructure that will enable them to cope with the enormously rapid development, i.e. the process of globalization and integration of the world economy. It allows you to make accurate decisions in real-time, focus on customer dissatisfaction while maintaining competitiveness and profitability. The result is optimising the supply chain to integrate processes, approaches, systems, databases, strategies between different business partners. The consequence of e-technology is the reorganization of the enterprise's current information base, the calculation of implementation costs, and the consideration of the marketing approach as a source of information advantage. For logistics, it means a significant reduction in delivery times, increasing receipt and order processing automation. High flexibility and reliability are expected, costs do not show an increase, and the importance of planning in the chain is growing, which must be faster and more accurate. The paper aims to monitor the loading and unloading of goods from rail transport using a simulation program regarding protecting employees' health, minimizing the time required for unloading and loading pallets with goods.

Keywords: Monitoring · Simulation · Efficiency · Loading-unloading · Industry

1 Introduction

Under the term logistics system, we understand a system of transport, production and information activities that follow each other and serve to meet customers' needs in a certain place and at a certain time [1]. It is done with the help of sources of raw materials, information and workforce. By using and transforming them, we can satisfy these

© ICST Institute for Computer Sciences, Social Informatics and Telecommunications Engineering 2022
Published by Springer Nature Switzerland AG 2022. All Rights Reserved
D. Perakovic and L. Knapcikova (Eds.): FABULOUS 2022, LNICST 445, pp. 193–203, 2022.
https://doi.org/10.1007/978-3-031-15101-9_14

needs [2]. We can also understand the logistics system as a system of tools, constructions and organizations that implement supply chain flows between suppliers of material inputs and customers of material outputs [3]. The logistics system includes all logistics chains of the enterprise created for individual products or customers (supply, production, distribution and trade links are a subsystem), works with logistics resources (goods, people, information), which optimally deploys, focusing on customer needs. Also pursues the main goal and sub-goals of the enterprise's logistics [4, 5].

The logistics system in metallurgical enterprise can be characterized as a technical–technological system (technical means and various equipment, buildings, transport routes with personnel equipment), management system (control elements), information system (collection, processing, transmission and storage of information for the control system), communication system (technical means and transmission equipment, automation and computer technology), financial system (financial resources, transactions and financial flows) [6].

Transport is an important element of the logistics system. Transport costs make up a large part of the logistics costs. Transport logistics deals with solving logistics tasks and measures that need to be implemented to prepare and implement transport [7]. These are activities that are related to material flow, storage of finished products up to the sale. We also include information related to these activities. The transport function is irreplaceable [8]. The logistics chain from the material supplier, through the manufacturer to the customer, consists of a large part of the transport chain's transport links.

The following attributes accompany the application of logistics in transport [9]:

- the ability of transport to form networks,
- ability to transport theoretically any quantity,
- degree of transport speed,
- degree of time certainty of transport performance,
- level of comfort,
- degree of traffic safety,
- degree of provision of other services,
- the amount of rising costs.

Shipment affinity is characterized by the following features [10]:

- the place of origin and termination of the transport, or the transport route if he wants to choose it the transport user himself - the carrier,
- the usual quantity of goods transported in one consignment, expressed in weight units or number of pieces,
- speed requirements, requirements for time security of delivery of the consignment, which can be determined in time, an indication of when the consignment must be delivered concerning the exact renewal period stocks based on the optimized mode of operation of the warehouse system, for entry shipments to the next phase of production in the Just-in-Time system,
- the resilience of the consignment to the effects of traffic, including the protection of the shipment by transport cover,

- requirements for additional services,
- limits on transport costs concerning the system of circulatory processes, price goods.

Table 1 presents intelligent transport system solutions, mostly used in manufacturing enterprises.

Table 1. Intelligent transport system solutions [11].

Intelligent transport system		
Government	Enterprise	Public user
Traffic management and Guidance	Vehicle schedule/Decision support	Elaborated Geo-info service
Road planning/Law enforcement	Accidents Real-time alarming	Accurate traffic info service
Road prewarning/Emergency response	Commercial data analysis	Real-time vehicle info service
Bus supervision and Management		Parking guidance service

When we start from the generally acceptable function of logistics as a cross-cutting function, it is necessary to consider the company's cost elements [12].

These are:

- capital tied up in stocks and goods in the working process,
- space and area costs (warehouse, transhipment areas, transport routes),
- transport (internal, customer deliveries, express surcharges),
- trade (personnel costs, equipment),
- administration (order processing, information base),
- packaging, transport and storage units,
- consequential costs (unclear agreements, quality deficiencies, losses,
- damages, etc.) [13].

From the point of view of reducing costs, it is clear that knowledge of the factors of its impact must be manifested in such a logistical understanding of the service [14]:

- product characteristics (diversity of components, climate, packaging, disposal),
- procurement (ordered quantity, procurement time),
- sales (sales forecast, frequency of deliveries, delivery dates, special services),
- organization of flows (information flows, responsibilities),
- circulation times, dwell time,
- spatial distribution of undertakings, transport routes,
- habitats, company, individual areas,
- environment, regulations, competition, customer wishes, disposal of packaging, etc.

Companies force economic constraints, limited resources, competitive pressures and requirements customers to make the most efficient and productive decisions possible about the choice of mode of transport and the choice of carriers [15–18]. Considering that transport affects customer service, time of the transportation of goods, reliability of service, stocks, packaging, storage, energy consumption, pollution levels and other factors must traffic management to create the best possible strategy of the method of transport or selection carriers [19].

2   Work Methodology

Intelligent monitoring of individual work activities over time is used in companies where there has been a radical change in corporate policy. The metallurgical industry is one of the most successful and competitive industries, supplying key intermediates and end products and the solutions themselves to virtually all other sectors. It is made possible by high production standards, comprehensive infrastructure and tailor-made logistics with a clear emphasis on reliability, quality and safety. The paper uses the monitoring method of loading and unloading goods in metallurgical enterprise transport logistic supply chain railway conditions concerning the ergonomic aspect using the Static strength prediction method.

2.1   Static Strength Prediction by Loading and Unloading System

The concept consists of two basic alternatives of ergonomic and time evaluation. The first alternative combines human labour and machine loading [20]. This alternative assesses the worker's load and the total time required to load the total load containing 15 pallets. The second alternative is focused on the evaluation of pallet loading in terms of time. The following Table 2 shows the input data for the simulations.

Table 2. Input parameters.

Employer specification	
Gender	Male
Height [cm]	178
Weight [kg]	81
Material specification	
Size [mm]	590 × 490 × 650
Weight [kg]	10

The static force prediction method provides an approximate strength prediction for the subsequent use of appropriate simulation tools (Fig. 1). We will use this method to evaluate the physical work of loading and unloading goods.

Further monitoring consists (Fig. 2) of evaluating the time required to load a predefined load. Loading was simulated in a combination of manual work (loading the rear row - 5 pallets) and loading via forklift (loading the middle and front row - 10 pallets).

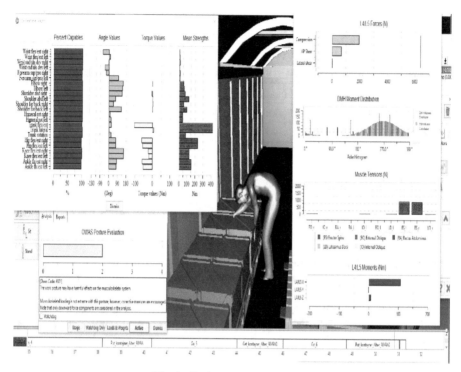

Fig. 1. Static strength prediction.

The values are given in the following Table 3.

With a combination of manual loading and forklift loading, a total time of 357.05 s was achieved, 6.79 min. This time exceeds the set loading/unloading limit of up to 5 min.

Fig. 2. Simulation of loading and unloading process

Table 3. Input parameters by SSP method.

	Operation	Time [s]
Rear row	Forklift - 5 pallets	50.15
	Manual work - 5 pallets	256.85
Middle + front row	Forklift - 10 pallets	100.20
Total time		407.20

3   Results and Discussion

Transport performance has the special character of activities to ensure the optimization of the logistics chain:

- increasing demand for transport performance,
- transport performance is many times linked to the performance of different modes of transport or services,
- transport provides decisive development impulses to economic and social entities,
- high intensity the facilities of many transport operators result in a constant supply and a significant fixed cost structure.

The way to reduce logistics costs leads through the most reliable transport [21]. Restructuring of corporate logistics systems or concentration and centralization of the warehouse network by a logistics distribution centre can also be performed [22]. Another possibility is the reorientation of goods from road transport to rail or the relocation of production plants closer to the focus of consumption. The results after simulation of human/workers activity by loading and unloading process is presented in Fig. 3.

Because the evaluated work position is - the employee's orientation in the forward bend, the evaluation was supplemented by a fourth analysis - Lower Back Analysis. This analysis estimates the spinal compression and shear forces acting on the worker's lower back. Transport logistics is of great importance within the entire logistics system.

It takes place in three basic stages of the reproductive process [23–25].

- in production: satisfying the needs caused by production technology, division of activities, cooperation of individual phases, etc.
- in circulation: relocation necessary for the implementation of economic circulation.
- in consumption: relocation of products that have already entered the consumption of tangible goods.

Transport logistics is a transport system that is suitable for the logistics management of circulation processes [26]. It is a control system which, in addition to managing the technological operations of individual activities of the circulatory process, optimizes the overall effect of the circulatory process with the help of all related information.

The technological capacity of transport logistics is affected by:

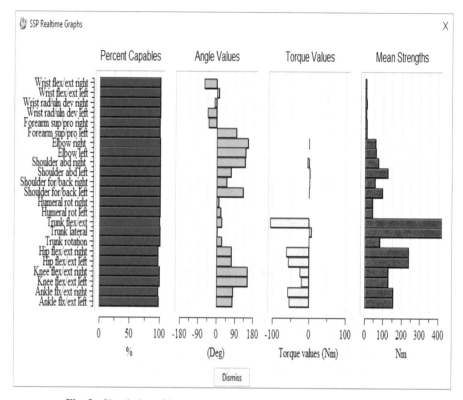

Fig. 3. Simulation of human activity by loading and unloading process.

- the capacity of stable means used by transport logistics: transport routes, transport nodes of the transport system, transport nodes in connection with the user, transport nodes in contact with different types of transport or transport systems,
- the capacity of means of transport,
- capacity compliance transport routes, transport hubs and means of transportation,
- optimal transport process technologies using a certain technical basis [27–29].

The moment distribution, muscle tensions and human forces are presented in the Fig. 4.

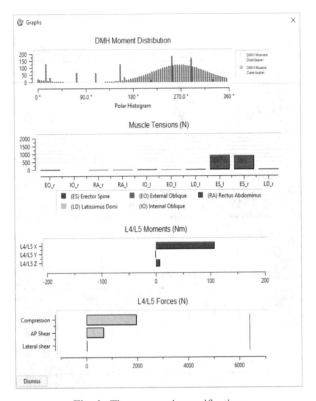

Fig. 4. The ergonomic specification.

The low back compression force of 1969.00 is below the Back Compression Action Limit of 3400 N, representing a nominal risk of low back injury for most health workers. The following Table 4 shows the overall evaluation of the loading time.

Table 4. Final operation time.

Operation	Time [s]
The arrival of the forklift to the carriage - 5 pallets	50.15
Loading with a manual forklift - 5 pallets	208.37
Loading with forklift - 10 pallets	110.40
Total time	368.92

As can be seen from the scoreboard for the second alternative, the time required to load 10 pallets with a combination of manual forklift and forklift also exceeded the required value.

Supply chain management integrates business processes from the end-user to the primary suppliers, who provide products, services and information that add value [30].

Key strategies include customer relationship management, customer service management, demand management, order fulfilment, production management, procurement, product development and commercialization, return channels [31]. Therefore, supply chain management represents a systemic approach that is interactive and complex and simultaneously requires a simultaneous assessment of a set of different links [32]. It crosses the boundaries of one company, includes links within the organization and links between organizations, where stocks are maintained and where it is necessary to perform individual parts.

4 Conclusion

The monitoring of transport logistics processes raises mainly these transport requirements, maximum flexibility in capacity and specialization, the greatest possible combination possibilities and a smooth transition of transport packaging, means of loading between different transport systems, versatile usability of means of transport, the shortest possible availability or immediate access to vehicles and objects of transport. Transportation needs to be managed in the logistics system in terms of the optimal division of labour between the various modes of transport in the logistics chain, the optimal quality of transportation and the minimization of costs for the actual relocation process and overall circulation processes. In addition to minimizing costs and increasing or optimizing the enterprise's performance, the most important goal of logistics is the maximum satisfaction of customer requirements. It is reflected in the quality of the product, the price of the product and the delivery service. The customer is the most important link in the whole chain. It provides information on the requirements for securing the supply of goods and related other services. The customer also ends the logistics chain, ensuring the movement of material and goods. Strengthening the enterprise's market position is the main objective to which the sub-objectives are subject. These are powerful, that is, delivering the right goods, to the right place, at the right time, in quantity and quality, and economical, that is, doing it at the right cost. The future direction of our research is focused on the monitoring and evaluation of automatic loading and unloading systems by which will be minimized human errors. We can improve working time with the impact of health and environmental protection.

Acknowledgements. This paper is part of a project that has received funding from the European Union's Horizon 2020 research and innovation programme under grant agreement No.723274.

http://www.lessthanwagonload.eu

References

1. Periša, M., Cvitić, I., Peraković, D., Husnjak, S.: Beacon technology for real-time in forming the traffic network users about the environment. Transport **34**, 373–382 (2019). https://doi.org/10.3846/transport.2019.10402
2. Davis, J.: 3D modeling CAD software. https://www.3dhubs.com/knowledge-base/3d-modeling-cad-software/. Accessed 15 Oct 2020
3. Matulić, I., Msa, M., Peraković, D.: Information and communication infrastructure for the organisation of railway passenger transport. In: Čokorilo, O. (ed.) Proceedings of the Second International Conference on Traffic and Transport Engineering ICTTE. City Net Scientific Research Center Ltd., Belgrade, Serbia, pp 410–419 (2014)
4. Optimizing Target Detection and Tracking Stability. https://library.vuforia.com/features/images/image-targets/best-practices-for-designing-and-developing-image-based-targets.html. Accessed 21 Oct 2021
5. Cvitić, I., Peraković, D., Periša, M., Husnjak, S.: An overview of distributed denial of service traffic detection approaches. Promet - Traffic Transp. **31**, 453–464 (2019). https://doi.org/10.7307/ptt.v31i4.3082
6. European Commission: Directive 2008/57/EC of the European Parliament and of the Council of 17 June 2008 on the interoperability of the rail system within the Community (2008)
7. Lyons, G., Jain, J., Weir, I.: Changing times – a decade of empirical insight into the experience of rail passengers in Great Britain. J. Transp. Geogr. **57**, 94–104 (2016). https://doi.org/10.1016/j.jtrangeo.2016.10.003
8. Transport Focus: Rail passengers' priorities for improvements (2014). https://www.transportfocus.org.uk/publication/rail-passengers-priorities-for-improvements-october-2014/. Accessed 17 Sep 2021
9. Peña Miñano, S., et al.: A review of digital way finding technologies in the transportation industry. In: Advances in Trans disciplinary Engineering. IOS Press BV, pp 207–212 (2017)
10. Camacho, T.D., Foth, M., Rakotonirainy, A.: Pervasive technology and public transport: opportunities beyond telematics. IEEE Pervasive Comput. **12**, 18–25 (2013). https://doi.org/10.1109/MPRV.2012.61
11. Nagyova, A., Pacaiova, H., Markulik, S., et al.: Design of a model for risk reduction in project management in small and medium-sized enterprises. Symetry-Basel **13**(5), 763 (2021). https://doi.org/10.3390/sym13050763
12. Shao, X., Liu, J.J., Gao, Z.M., Wang, P.: A study on intelligent onboard rail passenger service systems. In: Ni, Y.Q., Ye, X. (eds.) Proceedings of the 1st International Workshop on High-Speed and Intercity Railways. Springer, Heidelberg, pp 69–82 (2012). https://doi.org/10.1007/978-3-642-27960-7_7
13. Straka, M., Khouri, S., et al.: Utilization of computer simulation for waste separation design as a logistics system. Int. J. Simul. Model. **17**(4), 83–596 (2018). https://doi.org/10.2507/IJSIMM17(4)444
14. Kornaszewski, M., Pniewski, R.: The impact of new telematics solutions on the safety of railway traffic on the example of modern simulators railway traffic control devices. In: Mikulski, J. (ed.) Development of Transport by Telematics, pp. 32–43. Springer, Cham (2019). https://doi.org/10.1007/978-3-030-27547-1_3
15. European Commission: COMMISSION REGULATION (EU) No 454/2011 of 5 May 2011 on the technical specification for interoperability relating to the subsystem 'telematics applications for passenger services' of the trans-European rail system (Text with EEA relevance) (2011)

16. Zorić, P., Mikulčić, M., Musa, M., Kuljanić, T.M.: Analysis of available information and communication solutions and services for railway passenger information in the EU. In: Knapčíková, L., Peraković, D., Behúnová, A., Perisa, M. (eds.) 5th EAI International Conference on Management of Manufacturing Systems. Springer, Cham (2021). https://doi.org/10.1007/978-3-030-67241-6_29

17. Peraković, D., Periša, M., Petrović, M., Cvitić, I., Zorić, P.: Studija implementacije sustava informiranja putnika na željezničkoj mreži. Zagreb, Croatia (2020)

18. Peraković, D., Periša, M., Cvitić, I., Brletić, L.: Innovative services for informing visually impaired persons in indoor environments. EAI Endorsed Trans. Internet Things **4**, e4 (2018). https://doi.org/10.4108/eai.5-3-2019.156720

19. Pacaiova, H., Sinay, J., Markulik, S., et al.: Measuring the qualitative actors on copper wire surface. Measurement **109**, 359–365 (2017). https://doi.org/10.1016/j.measurement.2017.06.002

20. Periša, M., Kuljanić, T.M., Cvitić, I., Kolarovszki, P.: Conceptual model for informing user with innovative smart wearable device in industry 4.0. Wireless Netw. **27**(3), 1615–1626 (2019). https://doi.org/10.1007/s11276-019-02057-9

21. Meinig, M., Sukmana, M.I., Torkura, K.A., Meinel, C.: Holistic strategy-based threat model for organizations. Proc. Comput. Sci. **151**, 100–107 (2019)

22. Islam, M.A., Vrbsky, S.V.: Transaction management with tree-based consistency in cloud databases. Int. J. Cloud Comput. **6**(1), 58–78 (2017)

23. Gou, Z., Yamaguchi, S., et al.: Analysis of various security issues and challenges in cloud computing environment: a survey. Identity Theft: Breakthroughs in Research and Practice, pp. 221–247. IGI global (2017)

24. Olakanmi, O.O., Dada, A.: An efficient privacy-preserving approach for secure verifiable outsourced computing on untrusted platforms. Int. J. Cloud Appl. Comput. (IJCAC) **9**(2), 79–98 (2019)

25. Song, D., Shi, E., Fischer, I., Shankar, U.: Cloud data protection for the masses. Computer **45**(1), 39–45 (2012)

26. Tran, H.-Y., Jiankun, H.: Privacy-preserving big data analytics a comprehensive survey. Parallel Distrib. Comput. **134**, 207–218 (2019)

27. Hugos, M.H., Hulitzky, D.: Business in the Cloud: What Every Business Needs to Know About Cloud Computing. John Wiley & Sons, Hoboken, p. 139 (2010)

28. Mehmood, U., Moser, I., Jayaraman, P.P., Banerjee, A.: Occupancy estimation using Wi-Fi: a case study for counting passengers on busses. In: IEEE 5th World Forum on Internet of Things, pp 165–170 (2019)

29. Prandi, C., Nunes, N., Ribeiro, M., Nisi, V.: Enhancing sustainable mobility awareness by exploiting multi-sourced data: the case study of the Madeira Islands. In: Sustainable Internet and ICT for Sustainability (SustainIT), Funchal, pp. 1–5 (2017)

30. Oransirikul, T., Nishide, R., Piumarta, I., Takada, H.: Measuring bus passenger load by monitoring Wi-Fi transmissions from mobile devices. Procedia Technol. **18**, 120–125 (2014)

31. Le, T.V., Song, B., Wynter, L.: Real-time prediction of length of stay using passive Wi-Fi sensing. In: 2017 IEEE International Conference on Communications (ICC), Paris, pp. 1–6 (2017)

32. Grgurević, I., Juršić, K., Rajič, I.: Review of automatic passenger counting systems in public urban transport. In: Proceedings of 5th EAI International Conference on Management of Manufacturing Systems, EAI MMS 2020, Cyberspace (2020)

Optimalization of Business Logistics Processes Through Implementation of Business Information Systems

Lucia Zemanová[1], Marcel Behún[2] ⓘ, and Annamária Behúnová[2(✉)] ⓘ

[1] Faculty of Civil Engineering, Technical University of Košice, Vysokoškolska 4, 042 00 Košice, Slovakia
lucia.zemanova@tuke.sk

[2] Faculty of Mining, Ecology, Process Control and Geotechnology, Institute of Earth Resources, Technical University of Košice, Letna 9, 042 00 Košice, Slovakia
{marcel.behun,annamaria.behunova}@tuke.sk

Abstract. The basic goal of logistics activities is the complete satisfaction of specific customer wishes at the optimal time. The customer is the central link in the whole chain because the initial impulse comes from him, and at the same time, the whole chain ensures the movement of means of tangible and intangible nature. On the other hand, the internal goals of logistics are focused on the gradual reduction of costs while meeting the external goals. These are mainly the costs of stocks, production, transport, handling, management, etc. This paper aims to analyze and design the operation of the partial logistics process and monitor the wheelsets' entire life cycle in the conditions of a particular company. The proposal also includes a request from the director of the production department to eliminate the shortcomings of the current process of monitoring the registration of wheelsets, restocking, production and consumption in the assembly of chassis. This design ensures traceability of the components used, streamlining the technical documentation, simplifying the handling of the wheelsets, and removing paper labels.

Keywords: SAP · Intelligent transport system · Industry 4.0

1 Introduction

The basis of the entire logistics communication of the company is logistics information systems, which ensure not only effective inventory management, transport or warehouse management, but also effective communication with the customer in the field of receiving and processing orders, where the emphasis is placed on quality and speed of information flow [1]. The flexibility and quality of the company's response to rapid changes in the market are primarily a reflection that the right information is available to the right user in the right place and at the right time. Only enough quality information is a source of more informed decisions [2, 3]. Information is the key to integrated logistics management, and it is inconceivable that any movement of a material or product can occur

D. Perakovic and L. Knapcikova (Eds.): FABULOUS 2022, LNICST 445, pp. 204–217, 2022.
https://doi.org/10.1007/978-3-031-15101-9_15

without it. Information drives innovative change, encourages creativity and is considered a renewable and inexhaustible resource [4, 5].

Information increases the value of products and becomes part of them. They have value over time, which they gradually lose, so companies must always consider information systems' time factors [3].

The value of the information lies in its basic characteristics [6]:

- consistency with other findings;
- timeliness;
- reliability;
- processability;
- media portability.

Information technology has been used in logistics for several years and is considered an essential element of competition. Their constant innovation enables companies to increase the economy and efficiency of their activities in many areas. For this reason, their importance continues to grow. Information technologies for information sharing include EDI (Electronic Data Interchange), POS (Electronic Sales Information Collection), EFT (Electronic Money Transfer) or a barcode system. The development of information technology allows companies to work with large databases and adjust the offer according to the wishes and needs of target segments. Without these technologies, it is impossible to manage any inventory or rapid response systems [4–8].

1.1 Information System SAP

SAP is currently the largest provider of enterprise applications and one of the largest software companies in the world. SAP stands for "Systems, Applications and Products in Data Processing." The company is headquartered in Walldorf, Germany. SAP software was developed in 1972 by five former IBM employees in Mannheim, Germany, who had one vision: to develop a software package containing all possible business functions. The first version of SAP enterprise software was the R/one financial accounting system. The R/1 version was replaced by the R/two versions in the 1970s. The idea was to help different companies replace ten or even 15 different business applications. To fulfil its initial vision, SAP has developed a multilingual and multinational platform that makes it easy to incorporate new standard business processes. SAP has revolutionized the monolithic foundations of enterprise applications. They deliberately said goodbye to the monolithic model for mainframe computers that prevailed in the enterprise application market in the 1970s. SAP has developed its system to run on various hardware platforms, operating systems, and databases. In less than 20 years of its existence, SAP has become the largest software vendor in Europe and has begun to play a strong role in the international market for both IBM and other companies. During the 1990s, new players also appeared on the enterprise applications market, including, e.g. Oracle Corporation, PeopleSoft, Baan, JD Edwards. In general, at the same time as new enterprise software companies began to gain market share, new database vendors emerged, such as Oracle, Sybase, and Informix [9–11].

SAP often confuses the term component with enterprise applications, usually abbreviated to applications. On the other hand, SAP modules offer some functionality within some components. The basic SAP modules can be seen in Fig. 1.

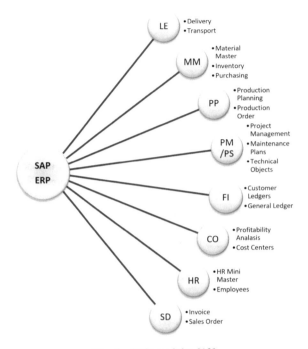

Fig. 1. SAP modules [12]

The basic SAP modules include [9]:

Financial Accounting (FI) - this financial accounting module assists the employees of the finance department in the management of data involved in financial transactions in this unified system. The FI module fulfils the requirements reporting function well, is very flexible and works well in any economic situation. SAP implementation helps consolidate data for various business transactions and legal requirements. The FI module helps the company gain a financial position in the market in real-time. SAP FI combines with modules such as SAP SD, SAP MM, SAP PP for better work results.

Controlling (CO) - The controlling module supports planning, reporting and monitoring operations in the company. These are ways of viewing and organizing the costs necessary for financial statements. The CO module allows you to monitor, plan, implement and report costs. Includes master data management and configuration, covering cost centres, order items, and functional areas.

Sales and Distribution (SD) - The SAP SD module performs all transactions ranging from requests, quotations to quotations and more. The sales and distribution module assists in inventory management and control. SAP SD consists of master data, system configuration and transactions. Some of the sub-components of this module are master data, sales support, sales, invoicing, shipping and transportation costs, sales information system, credit policy and the like.

Logistics Execution (LE) - logistics operations.

Production Planning (PP) - The SAP PP module is another important module that contains software designed specifically for production planning and management. The module consists of master data, system configuration, and transactions to meet the production process plan. The production planning module cooperates with the main data such as business and operational planning, KANBAN, material requirements planning, distribution planning, cost planning and the like, while working on production management in companies.

Materials Management (MM) - As the name suggests, this module manages the company's material requirements, processes and production. This module controls different types of process procurement. The more well-known sub-components of this module are delivery data, consumption based on planning, purchasing, billing verifications, inventory management and the like. It starts with a quotation, a tender, the issuance of a purchase order, an invoice and the issue of material.

Quality Management (QM) - The SAP QM Module assists in managing the quality of production across the entire process in the organization. This quality management module helps companies accelerate their business by adopting quality management structures and organizational direction in various processes. The QM module cooperates in the field of purchasing and sales, production planning, inspection, control, audit management.

Plant Maintenance (PM) - maintenance management;
Project System (PS) - product module;
Human Resources (HR) - human resources.

SAP offers a range of tailor-made products according to the customer's requirements and the industry in which it operates and provides easy collaboration via the Internet. These solutions can be used as a whole in SAP Business Suite and separately. Some of the most used products [9, 10]:

- SAP CRM - Customer Relationship Management is a unique solution that connects employees, partners, processes and technologies into a comprehensive system. SAP CRM provides functionality for the entire business cycle, providing the tools needed for services, sales, specific centres, analysis, e-commerce, and collaboration with partners.
- SAP ERP - Enterprise Resource Planning - provides human resource management, analysts, operations, corporate services and financiers. Provides support for system administration such as user management, centralized information management, configuration, web services management. The SAP ERP solution is extended with industry-specific functions and workflows. It is a comprehensive solution designed to support international business.
- SAP SRM - Supplier Relationship Management automates processes between resources and intermediaries. SAP SRM controls the entire supply cycle from strategy to its operation within the company and the supply area, optimizing the supplier selection, shortening the cycle duration, and building lasting relationships with suppliers.

- SAP SCM - Supplier Chain Management is the only comprehensive supply chain management solution that improves an organization's ability to adapt deliveries to an ever-changing competitive environment. SAP SCM creates scalable supply networks by building the planning and decision-making capabilities needed to manage business operations and coordinate and collaborate to expand activities beyond the organization.
- SAP BW - Business Warehouse provides data warehouse functionality and a Business Intelligence interface. It provides flexible reporting and analytical tools for data evaluation, interpretation, and distribution. Businesses can thus make important decisions based on these analyzes.
- SAP PI - Process Integration (successor to SAP XI) thanks to this module, business processes can be shared globally and integrated with applications from other vendors. Provides communication and information exchange between internal and external software.
- SAP EP - Enterprise Portal is a single access point for employees, customers, partners and suppliers to access corporate applications, services and information needed for daily work. The portal offers the ability to easily create and edit pages as needed and create their content.
- SAP SMP - Solution Manager Platform for comprehensive lifecycle management of SAP applications. It provides SAP system functions and integrates other tools to ensure a comprehensive approach. It allows central access to all necessary functions and access to the necessary information. In addition, it ensures effective customer cooperation with SAP support.
- SAP BO - Business Objects is a solution that simplifies data manipulation. It allows users to navigate, access, analyze, format, and share information across the enterprise. SAP BO provides a wide range of processes from simple navigation through search to advanced analysis, reporting, business queries and dashboards to visualize and manage infrastructure information.
- SAP Netweaver - currently, the SAP Netweaver platform is used on a technical basis. This platform brings a range of enterprise technologies that allow you to extend the applications used, change business processes quickly and in a controlled manner, make them accessible to more people and introduce new processes. Helps improve team productivity and business integration.

2 Methodology

The company in which the research was carried out implemented the integrated information system SAP as the main ERP system of the company, which provides monitoring of processes in the economic area, logistics, production and human resources using all modules contained in the core of the SAP system. SAP is connected to the WINDCHILL system, which supports the activities of the company's design and semi-technology department. The production planning and control (PP) module also has an extensive functional deployment. In addition to standard functionality, it is complemented by user applications that the company needs for production planning and management processes and monitoring of logistics operations in the company.

The presented paper focuses on optimising the process of procurement, handling and production processing of wheelsets that enter the final assembly of chassis. Wheelsets (Fig. 2) represent a purchased item for the company, supplemented by bearings in further processing in the production process (unless it is procured in the purchase as born wheelsets).

Fig. 2. Wheelsets

As a semi-finished product of its production or purchased bearing wheelsets, it is consumed in chassis assembly. The purchased wheelset has a raw material type assigned in the SAP system. The assignment of the wheelset material type defines its definition in terms of purchasing, layout data, storage data, wheelset posting and their calculation. For the possibility of filtering wheelsets according to certain specific properties, it is defined in the SAP system as a group of materials that is part of the parametric settings of the system. Each wheelset type is defined using a material master record in the SAP system. For further detailed identification and monitoring of the movement of an individual wheelset within the production process processing, the batch system's functionality is used, where the rule applies: each wheelset is assigned a unique number - batch. The batch content of the purchased wheelset currently contains the wheelset number under which the supplier manufactures it.

The supplier provides a certificate with precise technical parameters of the wheelset and measurement protocol. Options for suppliers). For the monitoring and management of each business case, a project team is assembled consisting of employees of individual departments that participate in the project: responsible salesman, designer, technologist, buyer, planner, BU manager. A description of the actual operation of the wheelset operations is shown in Fig. 3.

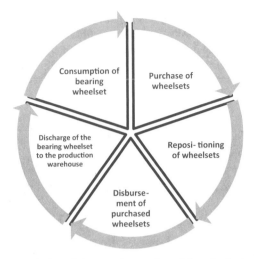

Fig. 3. A description of the actual operation of the wheelset operations

3 Results

The following sub-processes define the new life cycle of wheelsets:

- Issuing an order to purchase wheelsets.
- Receipt of wheels at the warehouse to order.
- Relocation of the wheelset from the wheelset warehouse to the production warehouse (to the depository, only applies to unloaded wheelsets).
- Consumption of wheelsets to production order (bearings).
- Drainage the bearing wheels from the production order directly to the chassis assembly production warehouse.
- Consumption of the wheelset to the production order of the chassis assembly.

The purchasing department provides the process of procuring wheelsets by issuing an order in the SAP system and attaching to it in the appendix a request with a code list for stamping customer numbers of wheelsets. The wheelset itself contains the customer number of the wheelset, which is stamped directly on it. Thus the wheelset is directly intended for a specific business case (in SAP, the business case defined in the project system). Procurement takes place in freely usable stocks and is not blocked for the project. We do not propose any change in this step of the process.

The warehouseman takes over the delivery of the wheelsets. He performs the storage of each piece of the wheelset separately based on the delivery note and the identification label with bar codes affixed directly to the wheelsets. The actual warehousing process in the system will be carried out using a new terminal application, which will ensure that the customer number of the wheelset, which is identical to the stamped number on the wheelset, will be stored in the batch number in the SAP system. At the same time, when receiving, attaching a tag that has an assigned constant number (unchanged during its lifetime, and is also displayed on the tag in bar code), which will be installed on the bike for the entire life of the bike from receipt at the warehouse. Up to consumption in the chassis. The tag number will be firmly linked to the batch number in the system. The batch will be constant as the tag number will be constant throughout the life of the wheelset, and the connection to the tag will be stored in the batch classification in the system. The terminal application for the reception will require inputs (Fig. 4): order number (from the delivery note in the bar code), delivery number (from the delivery note in the bar code), material number (from the identification plate on the wheelset in the bar code), batch (customer from the identification wheelbarrow in barcode), supplier's wheelset number (from the identification wheelbarrow in barcode), assigned tag number (from the identification tag on the tag).

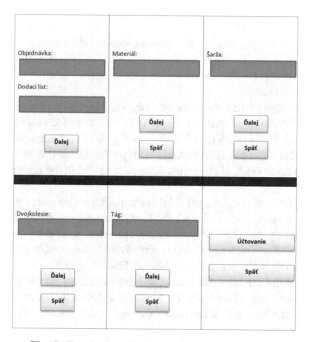

Fig. 4. Terminal application design - material receipt

It is necessary to ensure at the supplier: change the prefix of the barcodes on the label so that they correctly indicate the content of data in the SAP system in the company (Fig. 5) and add the delivery note number in the barcode on the Delivery note.

Fig. 5. Wheelset identification plate

Proposed prefix designation on the wheelset identification plate:

- Order (N) - no change.
- Material (P) - no change.
- Batch (H) - change to (B), the content changes. This identification represents the supplier's batch number, stored in the batch attribute after the new one.
- Customer Batch Number (B) - Changing to (H) will represent the batch number (specified by the customer or company). The prefix before the barcode defines the field in the SAP system, and the prefix designation is set in the company by the user.

After storing the scanned data, the SAP system will receive a receipt at the wheelset warehouse, where each piece of the wheelset will have an assigned batch corresponding to the customer's wheelset number. Further processing of the process is different for bearing wheelsets, which are brought directly to the assembly of the chassis and unprocessed proceed to the production process of the bearing.

Bearing wheelsets, the life cycle after admission to the company is realized under the following processes: relocation from the wheelset warehouse (purchasing warehouse) to the production warehouse (chassis assembly) and consumption of the wheelset to the chassis assembly.

Non-bearing wheelsets, the life cycle is realized under the following processes: relocation from the wheelset warehouse to the wheelset bearing warehouse, expenditure of the wheelset on the bearing production order, removal of the bearing wheels from the bearing production order to the chassis assembly warehouse and consumption of the wheelset to chassis assembly.

Transferring wheelsets to the depository will continue to be triggered by issuing a transfer reservation (referred to in the company as the Transfer Request), which includes a two-wheel external procurement warehouse, re-storage two-wheel assembly warehouse.

The transfer will be performed by a modified terminal application, which will require (Fig. 6): reservation number (from the printed reservation in paper form, where the reservation number is also printed in the barcode), material (input type wheelset, identification in the reservation barcode), expense warehouse (preset from the reservation, confirmation will be required), receipt warehouse (preset from the reservation, confirmation will be required), tag number (scanned directly from wheelset), the batch of wheelset (automatically preset and derived from tag number), wherein the new the operation of the process will no longer store the wheelset number of the supplier. Still, the customer will be identical to the stamped wheelset number for visual inspection.

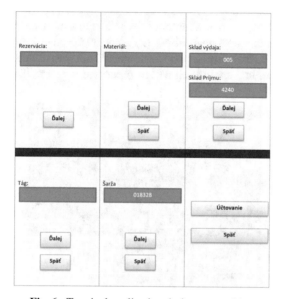

Fig. 6. Terminal application design - restocking

The picking plan (Restocking Reservation), which provides bringing material into production in the SAP system, will continue to be compiled manually in the SAP system environment, using a modified user transaction. The basis for the reservation establishment will continue to be the chassis assembly plan, where the mounted wheelsets are delivered directly to the assembly line in real-time at assembly time (Just in Time). This terminal application will also transfer loaded wheelsets from the shopping warehouse to the chassis assembly warehouse. A Transfer Transfer will be established in the SAP system for this logistics movement. The transfer reserve remains unchanged in the new process design and will continue to be compiled by the technical staff of the deposit centre.

The process is activated if it is required to change the stamped wheelset number. This occurs when the relevant wheelset (identified by the customer number) needs to be used to assemble the chassis of another business case (in an SAP project). The process requires a change of the wheelset number specified by the supplier in the new operation (a change of the batch). This happens in cases where the supplier did not deliver the wheelset or wheelset within the required deadline, the identified error during the entry inspection or the wheelset was damaged during handling in the company. When changing the customer batch number (physical breakdown of the number on the wheelset), the transfer system must be moved in the SAP system from the original batch to the new batch to ensure that the batch is identified for the wheelset in SAP with the number stamped on it. In the current operation of the process, this change is not identified. The attribute is not overwritten - the customer number in the batch classification, and in the visual inspection, the numbers on the wheelset plate are different from the stamped number.

The terminal application will require inputs (Fig. 7): tag number (number acquisition), wheelset number (derived from the tag number, preset on the terminal application), the new batch of wheelset (manual entry of the batch number using the terminal keypad according to the number on the wheelset), tag number (reload of the tag, which remains physically attached to the wheelset). If the number is not interrupted, the process is not activated. A new terminal application will be processed to record the transfer.

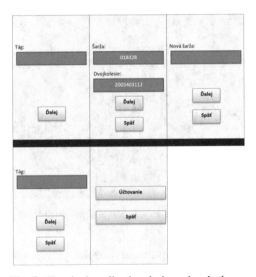

Fig. 7. Terminal application design – batch change

The method of consuming the wheelsets in the production order of the bearing remains the same, i.e. that the expenditure on the contract will be realized by retrograde collection. Retrograde material picking on a production order is a method of material consumption performed against the background of feedback on the operation to which the material is attracted. The wheelsets are brought to the line before bearing. The order is determined by the so-called bearing change plan, which determines the bearing sequence according to the projects to ensure the smooth assembly of the chassis line on which the projects alternate. The assembly of bogies must ensure the production of different types of bogies for the parallel production of assembly lines of railway wagons.

Consumption expenditure on order will be realized by a modified terminal application with the following inputs: bearing operation number from the production order (identification from the production change plan, which contains operations of individual orders), the order number fields and project, tag number (the bar code of the tag is scanned by the terminal directly from the wheelset), the material number (displayed by deriving from the tag number) and the batch number (displayed by deriving from the tag number).

By displaying the batch number on the terminal application, it is possible to visually check the customer batch number with the embossed number on the wheelset, which must be identical. After the wheelset has been posted for consumption to the production order, the tag, which is used to derive the batch of the wheelset (in which the customer number of the wheelset is stored), remains on the wheelset, and the bearing process for surface treatment continues.

The method of removing the bearing wheelset from the production order of bearings to the warehouse remains and will be realized by automatic warehousing of production with feedback of the last production operation of surface treatment. The definition of the automatic discharge of semi-finished or final products from production to the warehouse is performed parametrically in the SAP system by the control key of the operation in the workflow. A terminal application was designed to remove the production of the bearing wheels to the warehouse as follows: workplace number (scanning of the barcode of the surface treatment workplace) *, tag number (scanning of the barcode from the tag of the wheelset), production order (automatically derived from tag numbers), batch (automatically derived from tag number), wheelset (derived from tag number, preset on terminal application). * Each workplace identified in SAP is marked with a bar code for production feedback and material handling in production on site.

The bearing wheelsets are stored directly at the chassis assembly warehouse and are physically ready for assembly. At present, the addition represents the physical relocation of the bearing wheelset to the chassis assembly line. In reality, the pre-sun handling technique is implemented for several tens of meters. Finally, the bearing will be moved to the chassis assembly line. The bearing wheelsets will be moved along the rails for assembly, thus eliminating damage to the wheelsets during handling and transport outside the rails.

The method of consuming the wheelsets in the production assembly order will be maintained by retrograde consumption. The wheelsets are brought to the assembly line. Their consumption will be performed in the background when feedback of the chassis assembly operation to which the wheelsets are attached. Because two wheelsets enter the assembly of one bogie, we propose elaborating a new variant of the terminal application, which will be used to consume wheelsets in the assembly of bogies. The application requires entering two batch numbers of wheelsets.

The terminal application will require the following inputs (Fig. 8): production order operation feedback number (read from the chassis production order wizard that accompanies the entire chassis assembly), the chassis type number is displayed (material master record in SAP), number of wheelsets (preset according to the number of material components in the production order), tag number (read from the wheelset), the batch of wheelset (displayed and derived from tag number) and type of wheelset (master record of wheelset displayed from tag number is displayed). Subsequently, the application requests a scan of the second wheelset. By displaying the batch number on the terminal application, it is possible to visually check the customer batch number with the embossed number on the wheelset, which must be identical. After posting the wheelset to consumption on a production order, the assembly worker removes the tag from the wheelset, which can be used to identify the new wheelset. In the life cycle of the wheelset, the printing of paper labels is eliminated, and the tag can be used repeatedly until it is physically damaged.

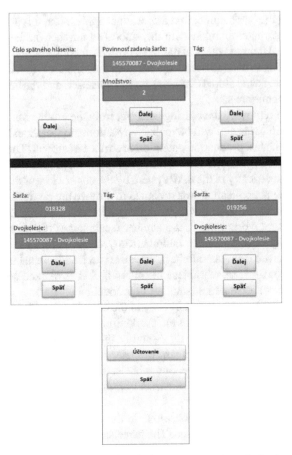

Fig. 8. Terminal application design – consumption of wheelsets

4   Conclusion

Due to the constant increase in the production of the researched company, and thus the increased demand for material handling within a large production area, the optimization of logistics processes, support of new technological equipment in the field of handling technology and identification equipment for marking parts and purchased materials for production. The whole logistics process is divided into sub-processes, and this presented paper deals with one of them - monitoring the life cycle of wheelsets. The process is integrated into the optimization of logistics processes of production and assembly of chassis, which has the ambition in the final solution of process monitoring without the support of paper documentation. The proposal to monitor the sub-process of the life of the wheelsets has approached this goal considerably. The paper background of the processing process occurs at the level of compiling wheel bearing plans, which will be addressed in the 3D company project launched in autumn 2020. It assumes that each production and assembly workplace will be equipped with monitors production instructions for operations performed at the workplace, displaying the necessary drawing documentation for the performed operation and monitoring performed operations directly at the workplace in real-time. The completion of this project is set for the horizon of 1 and 1.5 years, and the final solution should be put into productive operation in the middle of 2022. During this period, other sub-processes of logistics will be solved, in which a significant role is also involved—the information technology department. A new solution must be designed to identify the marking of chassis production from the production of the main assembly - the basic frame, through the technological frame of the chassis and to the final chassis, delivery of materials to assembly lines - kiting parts and their support in the SAP information system, purchasing materials in sets (purchase of brake elements), etc. The researched company is a modern, rapidly developing, dynamic design and development department with an advanced team of technologists, production workers, logisticians, and the information technology department.

References

1. Mandičák, T., Mésároš, P., Spišáková, M.: Impact of information and communication technology on sustainable supply chain and cost reducing of waste management in slovak construction. Sustainability **13**(14), 7966 (2021)
2. Drahotský, I., Řezníček, B.: Logistika- Procesy a jejich řízení, 1st edn. Computer Press, Brno (2003)
3. Basl, J.: Podnikové informační systémy. Grada Publishing, Praha (2002)
4. Lambert, M., Stock, J., Ellram, L.: Logistika. Computer Press, Praha (2000)
5. Řezníček, B.: Logistický Management, 1st edn. Pardubice (2000)
6. Čichovský, L.: Marketing zahraničního obchodu. Radix, Praha (1997)
7. Machková, H.: Mezinárodní Marketing, 2nd edn. Grada Publishing, Praha (2006)
8. Mandičák, T., Mésároš, P., Kanáliková, A., Špak, M.: Supply chain management and big data concept effects on economic sustainability of building design and project planning. Applied Sciences (2021).
9. Maassen, A., Schoenen, M., Fritck, D., Gabatsch, A.: SAP R/3 Kompletní průvodce, 1st edn. Computer Press a.s, Brno (2007)
10. Anderson, G.W.: Naučte sa SAP za 24 hodín. Computer Press a.s., Brno (2012)
11. Straka, M., Khouri, S., Rosova, A., Caganova, D., Čulkova, K.: Utilization of computer simulation for waste separation design as a logistics system. Int. J. Simul. Model. **17**(4), 583–596 (2018)
12. Kar, A.: SAP is an ocean and hence you need to pick one module and start working on it. SAP Community (2020). https://blogs.sap.com/2020/07/26/sap-is-an-ocean-and-hence-you-need-to-pick-one-module-and-start-working-on-it./

Sustainable Communications
and Computing Infrastructures

Hydrogen Production for Improved Transportation System as a Part of Smart Cities

Volodymyr Tymofiiv ⓘ, Samer Al-Rabeei(✉) ⓘ, Michal Hovanec ⓘ,
and Peter Korba ⓘ

Faculty of Aeronautics, Department of Aviation Engineering, Technical University of Kosice,
Rampová, 7041 21 Kosice, Slovakia
{Volodymyr.tymofiiv,Samer.al-rabeei,Michal.hovanec,
Peter.korba}@tuke.sk

Abstract. The main purpose of hydrogen production is to move closer to industrial technologies and the development of a transportation system that will help to improve the future. Industrial hydrogen production is an integral part of hydrogen energy, the first link in the hydrogen consumption life cycle. Hydrogen is practically not present on Earth in pure form and must be extracted from other compounds using various chemical methods. There are currently many ways of industrially producing hydrogen. The diversity of hydrogen production methods is one of the main advantages of hydrogen energy, as it increases energy security and reduces dependence on certain types of raw materials. Efficient hydrogen production will help successfully by integrating the hydrogen infrastructure of the European "Smart cities" model, which globally supports the overall improvement of the environment. The peak power of conventional nuclear reactors or other power plants can also be used. The rapidly growing demand for hydrogen from refineries and chemical plants is the develop-ment of low-cost technologies. There are already limited networks of hydrogen pipe-lines that allow production facilities to be located at a certain distance from users. One approach to reducing the volatility of wind and solar electricity is to produce hydrogen by electrolysis and supply it to the gas network.

Keywords: Hydrogen technology · Hydrogen production · Production facilities

1 Introduction

One of the most important treaties governing the activities of individual states, international organizations and environmental NGOs is the Paris Agreement, adopted under the UN Framework Convention on Climate Change in 2015 and signed in 2016. The Paris Agreement emphasizes the need to combat global climate change by adapting economies in changing conditions and by increasing the attention paid to this problem [1].

The point of this Arrangement, in working on the execution of the Show, including its goal, is to fortify the worldwide reaction to the danger of environmental change with regards to reasonable turn of events and destitution annihilation endeavors, including:

© ICST Institute for Computer Sciences, Social Informatics and Telecommunications Engineering 2022
Published by Springer Nature Switzerland AG 2022. All Rights Reserved
D. Perakovic and L. Knapcikova (Eds.): FABULOUS 2022, LNICST 445, pp. 221–233, 2022.
https://doi.org/10.1007/978-3-031-15101-9_16

(a) Holding the increment in the worldwide normal temperature to well underneath 2 °C above pre-modern levels and seeking after endeavors to restrict the temperature increment to 1.5 °C above pre-modern levels, perceiving that this would essentially lessen the dangers and effects of environmental change.

(b) Increasing the ability to adapt to the adverse impacts of climate change and foster climate resilience and low greenhouse gas emissions development, in a manner that does not threaten food production; and

(c) Making finance streams predictable with a pathway towards low ozone harming substance emissions and environment strong turn of events [2]

In addition to increasing the portion of sustainable power sources in the energy balance, the following three areas will assume a significant part in achieving climate goals - the development of electric batteries, carbon catch, storage and storage (CCUS) technologies and hydrogen energy. At the same time, CCUS is seen as an intermediary in the transition to new energy, as these technologies will require the creation of a large-scale infrastructure. At the same time, batteries and hydrogen are part of the vision of the future in Europe and other countries that have committed themselves to reducing CO_2 emissions. Hydrogen use is estimated to potentially reduce up to 51% of global carbon dioxide emissions [3].

Hydrogen, as a fuel that does not leave a carbon footprint during combustion, can be a solution to critical problems for new energy based on renewable energy sources [4].

1. It can be a solution to the problem of uneven production of renewable energy sources. Excess volumes of electricity in the system will be directed at the peak to the production of hydrogen by electrolysis techno-logy, which will become a guaranteed source of energy during the period of low production of renewable energy sources.

2. Unlike electric batteries, hydrogen is ready to ensure the reliability of long-distance transport operations, which is particularly important for air and sea transport.

3. Widespread use of hydrogen can solve energy transport problems. Instead of building long electricity networks, renewable energy can be directed to the production of hydrogen, which can then be transported to other parts of the world using the current natural gas transport infrastructure.

4. Many industries cannot be decarbonised with the help of electricity, and hydrogen in this case can serve as a medium to achieve that goal [5].

2 Theoretical Part

Hydrogen - a colorless, flammable, odorless and unscented vaporous substance that is the least difficult individual from the group of synthetic components. The hydrogen iota has a core comprising of a proton and has a positive electric charge. An electron conveying a unit of negative electric charge is additionally associated with this core.

In any case, it happens in immense amounts as a feature of the water in the seas, ice sheets, streams, lakes and air. It creates a larger number of mixtures than some other component of the Mendelian table of occasional components. As a component of incalculable carbon compounds, he is available in all creature and plant tissues and in oil [6].

Hydrogen molecules H_2 are very small, so they can pass through very fine, invisible to the pores in bodies. Hydrogen has the lowest density of all chemical elements. One liter of hydrogen H_2 under normal conditions weighs 0.09 g, (density is 0.09 kg.m-3). It is highly flammable. Together with oxygen, it forms an explosive mixture. It burns with a light blue flame with a high temperature of up to 3,100 C.

Hydrogen gas easily forms covalent compounds - so most of the hydrogen on Earth exists in molecular compounds such as water. Many of them, like methane, are organic. There are technologies that allow the extraction of hydrogen from methane and water, which can then be transported and used [7, 5].

The interest in hydrogen as a source carrier can be explained by its high calorific value −120 MJ/kg, which is at least four times higher than coal (~10–30 MJ/kg) or twice higher than natural gas (~50–55 MJ/kg). Because carbon atoms are not involved in the combustion process, hydrogen is a carbon-free energy carrier. In addition, it can be saved. Due to properties such as the ability to store hydrogen, its high calorific value and the absence of CO_2 emissions from combustion, hydrogen is attractive for use in various energy sectors.

All solid (wood), liquid (petrol, diesel,...) and gaseous fuels (methane, propane,...) long chains of carbon (C) and hydrogen (H) atoms make up the materials we use today. Methane is the smallest of them, having only one carbon atom and four hydrogen atoms (CH_4). We use oxygen (O_2) to break the bonds between atoms, releasing the energy trapped inside those bonds. Because carbon and hydrogen atoms mix with oxygen atoms during combustion, we invariably produce carbon dioxide (CO_2) and water vapor (H_2O).

$$CH_4 + 2O_2 \rightarrow CO_2 + 2H_2O \quad \Delta H = -890 \, kJ/mol \text{ (exothermic reaction)}$$

There are not many gases that do not produce carbon dioxide when burned. And one of these gases, which can be completely independent of carbon, is hydrogen. It consists of two hydrogen atoms and does not form any carbon dioxide when reacted with oxygen [9].

$$[[2H]]_2 + O_2 \rightarrow 2H_2O \quad \Delta H = -286 \, kJ/mol \text{ (exothermic reaction)}$$

It has many potential uses in many different areas of the economy. This can help decarbonise the production of energy consumed in transport, living space (especially heating) and industrial processes.

Not all industrial processes can be electrified and a carbon-neutral energy carrier is needed to fully decarbonise industrial production. Hydrogen is just one of the few substances that can be used for this purpose. Hydrogen and its derivatives are used in many industries, especially in the chemical and petroleum refining industries. Today, industry is the largest consumer of hydrogen. In all such examples, hydrogen can replace carbon processes.

Hydrogen is currently used in conjunction with oxygen in metal cutting, with a hydrogen-hydrogen flame having a temperature of up to about 3000 °C. It is also used as fuel for space shuttle rockets. In the chemical industry, this element is used for the production of important chemicals such as HCl, NH$_3$ (ammonia) or in the hardening of vegetable oils [10].

2.1 Differences in the Understanding of the Label

Hydrogen also can be produced using a different of sources and several different methods. The main sources for its production are divided into two groups: production from fossil fuels (natural gas, coal, heavy gasoline and other hydrocarbons) and production from renewable energy sources. Fossil fuels can be converted to production using various technological processes, generally classified as thermochemical, biochemical and photochemical conversion. Among these processes, the most common is steam reforming of methane and is currently used for most of the global hydrogen production [11].

Hydrogen can be classified depending on the source and method of production, and so far the main system of hydrogen classification is color classification (Table 1).

Brown and Black: Coal Gasification

The earliest method of producing hydrogen is to convert coal to gas. Gasification converts carbon monoxide, hydrogen, and carbon dioxide from organic carbonaceous compounds derived from fossil fuels. Gasification takes place at extremely high temperatures (more than 700 °C), with a controlled amount of oxygen or steam, and without combustion. Carbon monoxide is then converted to carbon dioxide and hydrogen by reacting with water.

Coal gasification is the reaction of carbon with water vapor or oxygen, resp. Both. Coal gasification principle: The basis is an endothermic reaction [12].

$$C(solid) + H_2O \rightarrow CO(gas) + H_2O$$

Gray color: steam reforming.

The majority of hydrogen nowadays comes from natural gas; it is carbon-bound and can be separated from it using a water-based process known as steam reforming. However, CO$_2$ is produced by the excess carbon synthesized in the prophesy. Gray hydrogen now accounts for the majority of production, emitting 9.3 kg of CO$_2$ per kilogram of hydrogen produced. When hydrogen is referred to be "gray," it signifies that it was created from fossil fuels without collecting greenhouse gases, and that the only difference between it and brown or black hydrogen is a minor quantity of emissions produced during the process.

The basis of the natural gas process of steam reforming is the reaction of methane with water: [13].

$$[[CH]]_4 + H_2O (\rightarrow \perp (1000\,°C))\ CO + [[3H]]_2\ \ \Delta H = 203\ kJ/mol\ (endothermic\ reaction)$$

$$CO + H_2O \rightarrow [[CO]]_2 + H_2\ \ \ \Delta H = -41\ kJ/mol\ (exothermic\ reaction)$$

Blue: steam reforming using CCUS / CCS.

Blue hydrogen is mostly made from natural gas via a method known as steam reforming, which involves combining natural gas with heated water to make steam. Hydrogen and carbon dioxide are produced, with the latter being recovered in industrial carbon capture, utilization, and storage (CCUS) systems. By transferring trapped CO_2 into underground cavities, such as recovered gas and oil deposits, or finding industrial uses for the trapped gas, CCUS programs aim to make blue hydro-gen production climate-neutral. However, because the technique does not actually prevent the generation of greenhouse gases, blue hydrogen is best described as "low CO_2 hydrogen" [14].

Turquoise color: pyrolysis of methane.

The method of obtaining natural-gas-derived hydrogen is currently in the experimental phase. The natural gas can decompose at too high temperatures to form hydrogen and solid-carbon due to a process named pyrolysis of methane. This hydrogen is called "turquoise" or "low carbon" hydrogen. Turquoise hydrogen has a low carbon footprint because carbon may be buried or employed in industrial processes like steelmaking or battery manufacturing to prevent it from escaping into the atmosphere.

Pyrolysis of methane (or cracking of methane) is a chemical process that breaks down methane or hydrocarbons in general into its elemental components: hydrogen and solid carbon. The reaction is endothermic [15].

$$[[CH]]_4 \rightarrow C\,(solid) + 2H_2 \quad \Delta H = 74,52 \text{ kJ/mol (endothermic reaction)}$$

Green color: electrolysis supplied by electricity from revivable energy sources.

Green hydrogen is produced from revivable electricity with the help of electrolysis. Electrolyzers split water into hydrogen and oxygen components using an electrochemical reaction that produces no carbon dioxide. Although hydrocarbons are currently the main feedstock used to produce hydrogen, the share of low-emission hydrogen is expected to increase in the long term and to dominate conventional technologies [16].

Water electrolysis is a physico-chemical process in which distilled water decomposes into oxygen and hydrogen by the action of a direct current. Due to the division of water molecules into parts, hydrogen and oxygen are formed in a ratio of 2: 1 [17].

$$H_2O + electricity \rightarrow H_2 + 0,5\ O_2$$

Pink color: electrolysis supplied by electricity from nuclear energy.

Pink is often used for hydrogen ginned by electrolysis using nuclear-energy. Nuclear energy is a very versatile technology and provides low-carbon electricity that can be used to produce pure hydrogen [18].

Table 1. Hydrogen classification

Color	Production source	Production technology
Gray	Natural gas	Most commonly through steam reforming from natural gas
Blue	Natural gas	Most commonly through steam reforming from natural gas along with the use of CCS technology
Turquoise	Natural gas	Pyrolysis of methane
Brown or black	Coal	Gasification
Green	Electricity from RES	Water electrolysis
Purple or pink	Electricity from nuclear power plants	Water electrolysis

3 Analytical Part. Global Use of Hydrogen Today and in the Future

At present, almost all hydrogen use is concentrated in industry. The four main uses of hydrogen currently are: oil refining (37 Mt/year), ammonia production (31 Mt/year), methanol production (13 Mt/year) and steel production by direct reduction of iron ore (5 Mt/year) (Fig. 1.). Almost of hydrogen comes from fossil fuels. [19] This current utilization of hydrogen is the premise of numerous parts of the worldwide economy and our regular routines. Their future development relies upon the improvement of interest for downstream items, in particular refined transport fuels, food fertilizers and building materials [20].

Interest for ammonia and methanol is expected to growing in the short to medium term, with the addition of new capacity providing relevant opportunity to expand the use of low-emission hydrogen routes. Efficiency gains can reduce the overall level of demand, but this will only partially offset the growth in demand. Regardless of whether it's petroleum gas with CCUS or electrolysis, the innovation is accessible to help the extra hydrogen request development anticipated for alkali and methanol will essentially assist with lessening outflows [21].

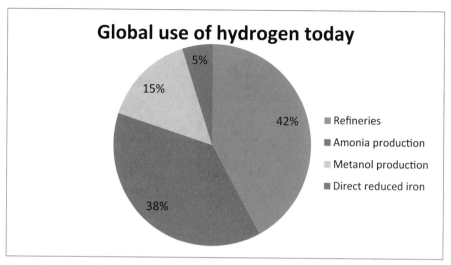

Fig. 1. Global use of hydrogen today. Source: IEA, Worldwide hydrogen interest by area in the Net Zero Situation, 2020–2030

In the long term, steel and high-temperature heat generation offers enormous potential for increased demand for low emission hydrogen. Currently, there are technological problems that are preventing widespread adoption of hydrogen in these areas, reducing costs and scaling up. In the long term, it should be technically possible to produce all primary steel with hydrogen, but this will require huge amounts of electricity with low carbon content (about 2500 TWh/year, or about 10% of the world's electricity production today) [22].

Hydrogen has likewise since a long time ago been known as a potential low-carbon transport fuel, yet it has been hard to fuse it into the vehicle fuel blend [23].

However, by 2030, hydrogen use in the various modes of transport is expected to be 8.55 Mt per year. In addition, ammonia is expected to be used as a fuel for ships, and by 2030 about 18 Mt of hydrogen will be needed to make it known (Fig. 2) [24].

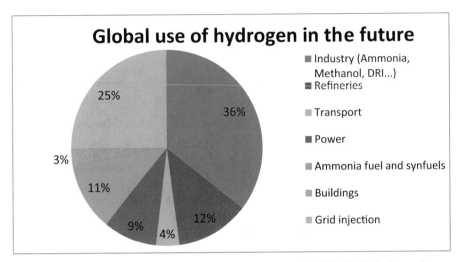

Fig. 2. Estimated global use of hydrogen in the future. Source: IEA, Worldwide hydrogen interest by area in the Net Zero Situation, 2020–2030

4 Practical Part- Comparison of Hydrogen Production Methods

Hydrogen demand in 2020 was ~90 Mt. Of this total hydrogen produced, 70 Mt was produced from fossil fuels and 19 Mt as a by-product in refineries and 0.5 Mt of hydrogen was produced using electrolysers. In the future, the share of "gray" hydrogen from fossil fuels, an increase in the share of low-emission "blue" hydrogen and a huge increase in "green" hydrogen are expected. In 2030, hydrogen production by electrolysis should reach 75–80 Mt and become the leading technology in the hydrogen production market. In general, the market for hydrogen production in 2030 should be around 210 Mt per year (Fig. 3) [25].

Costs

The cost of hydrogen gas is determined by the cost of raw materials and energy, as well as by the method of production. When hydrogen is produced from natural fuels, its costs depend linearly on the cost of the raw materials. In the electrolytic method of hydrogen production, its price depends on the cost of electricity by 70–90%, which means that the cost of hydrogen is affected by the parameters of the electrolyser and the price of electricity [26].

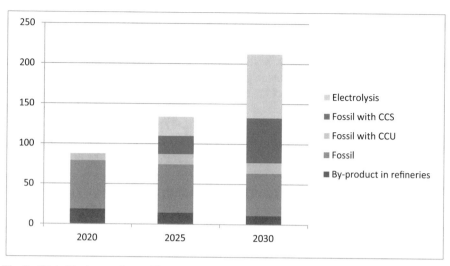

Fig. 3. Global hydrogen demand by production technology in the Net Zero Scenario, 2020–2030. Source: IEA, Hydrogen. Tracking report

Gray hydrogen is currently the cheapest option at around € 1 per kg, but in some regions it is as high as $ 3 per kg. For China and India, which import most of their gas, coal-based hydrogen is generally the cheapest option. If CCS technology is used to convert the cheapest gray hydrogen to blue, this will lead to a cost of around € 1.5 per kg (Table 2) [27].

Table 2. Cost of 1 kg of commercial hydrogen.

Hydrogen production process	Energy source	Efficiency, %	Cost, EUR / kg
Steam reforming	Natural gas	60–75	0,9–3.2
Steam reforming with CCUS	Natural gas	55–70	1,5–2,9
Gasification	Coal	60–80	1,2–2,2
Electrolysis	Renewables	35–45	3–7,5

Source: IEA

The most difficult aspect of hydrogen production, particularly from renewable sources, is supplying hydrogen at a lower cost. This means that the cost of hydro-gen must be less than € 4 per gallon of petrol equivalent, regardless of production technology. Research aims to increase the efficiency and longevity of hydrogen production technologies, as well as lower capital equipment, operation, and maintenance expenses, in order to lower the total price of hydrogen [28, 29].

Emissions

Greenhouse gas emissions from hydrogen production differ depending on the technology (Fig. 4). Hydrogen produced from fossil fuels isn't always clean exhibit the highest CO_2 emissions. Using natural gas or coal to generate electricity for electrolysis can result in a higher CO_2 intensity than gray or blue hydrogen due to conversion losses during power generation. If CCUS is used, hydrogen derived from natural gas with CCUS represents the lowest CO_2 intensity after hydrogen obtained from renewable or nuclear power, and the higher rate of capture of CCUS, the lower the CO_2 intensity of blue hydrogen [30].

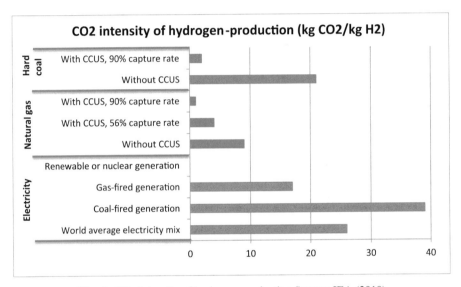

Fig. 4. CO_2 intensity of hydrogen production Source: IEA (2019)

Not only is it important to know how hydrogen is made, but also whether it is made on-site or off-site, leads to greater CO_2 emissions as CO_2 is released during the supply, storage and filling of hydrogen. When the same manufacturing technology is used, the off-plant hydrogen production process increases the CO_2 intensity as on-site cases. Different modes of hydrogen transport also result in different CO_2 emissions. The transport of compressed hydrogen is less carbon-intensive than the transport of liquefied hydrogen [31].

Possibilities of Using Hydrogen in Smart City

If we talk about the introduction of hydrogen into the SMART CITY model, then it is worth immediately noticing its several obvious advantages. When used with fuel cells, only water vapor is created instead of various greenhouse gases and microparticles. This feature of hydrogen has huge potential to prevent smog in car-crowded cities and to prevent huge CO_2 emissions from industry.

In addition, hydrogen is a universal energy carrier and a universal energy storage.

At the moment, 3 main sources of energy play the main role in cities: electricity, natural gas and petroleum products (gasoline and diesel). And just the same, hydrogen can combine these 3 energy sources or become a link connecting them. For example, it can be used to heat houses (instead of natural gas) and fill cars with it (instead of gasoline). That is, to influence those industries where there is not always the possibility of electrification. Also, in the event of a shortage of one of these sources, it will be possible to easily convert part of the electrical energy into hydrogen and increase the share of its use, for example, for heating [32, 33].

5 Conclusion

Hydrogen production advancements are in different transformative phases. A few advancements, for example, steam methane changing, are as of now business and can be utilized soon. Others, for example, sun oriented thermochemical water parting, photo electrochemical and organic, are in the beginning phases of research facility advancement and are viewed as possible pathways in the long haul.

The two main markets for hydrogen consumption today are ammonia and methanol production, but in the future hydrogen will be used for different purposes and in different sectors. Hydrogen demand in the oil refining industry is also expected to increase. Now 95% of the hydrogen produced is used by consumers for their own use and only 5% of it has been sold commercially on the market. The amount of free hydrogen on the market is likely to increase in the future.

In a conservative scenario of growing industrial hydrogen consumption, its share will increase from 70 million to 230 million tons per year by 2050. The share of commercial hydrogen will also increase, from 4 million to 140 million tons per year.

For example, to produce 140 million tonnes of hydrogen per year by 2050, HTGR power units with a total heat capacity of 400 GW should be built worldwide.

References

1. LNCS Homepage (2016). http://www.springer.com/lncs
2. United Nations, Framework Convention on Climate Change, Distr.: Limited 12 (2015). https://unfccc.int/resource/docs/2015/cop21/eng/l09r01.pdf
3. United Nations, Paris Agreement, Article 2, (2015). https://unfccc.int/files/essential_backgr ound/convention/application/pdf/english_paris_agreement.pdf
4. Rystad Energy Transition Report, Hydrogen Society, February (2021). http://petrodin.com/data/documents/2021-RYSTAD-Energy-Transition-Report.pdf
5. Tashie-Lewis, B.C., Nnabuife, S.G.: Hydrogen production, distribution, storage and power conversion in a hydrogen economy - a technology review. Chem. Eng. J. Adv. (2015). https://www.sciencedirect.com/science/article/pii/S2666821121000880. ISSN 2666-8211
6. Rissman, J., Bataille, C., Masanet, E., Aden, N., Morrow, W.R.: Technologies and policies to decarbonize global industry: review and assessment of mitigation drivers through 2070. Appl. Energy **266**, 114848 (2020). https://doi.org/10.1016/j.apenergy.2020.114848. ISSN 0306-2619
7. Universal Industrial Gases, Inc., Hydrogen (H_2) Applications and Uses, 15 September 2005

8. Ma, Y., Wang, X.R., Li, T., Zhang, J., Gao, J., Sun, Z.Y.: Hydrogen and ethanol: production, storage, and transportation. Int. J. Hydrogen Energy, **46**(54), 27330–27348 (2021). https://www.sciencedirect.com/science/article/pii/S0360319921021777. ISSN 0360-3199

9. Karuskevich, M., Ignatovich, S., Karuskevich, O., Maslak, T., Pejkowski, L., Kurdel, P.: Fatigue and overstress indicators for ultralight and light aircraft. Fatigue Fract. Eng. Mater. Struct.: FFEMS **44**(2), 595–598 (2021). ISSN 8756-758X

10. Scott, K.: Chapter 1: Introduction to electrolysis, electrolysers and hydrogen production. RSC Energy Environ Series, vol. 2020, no. 25, pp. 1–27 (2020)

11. Danish Energy Agency and Energinet, Technology Data – Renewable fuels (2017). http://www.ens.dk/teknologikatalog

12. Pareek, A., Dom, R., Gupta, J., Chandran, J., Adepu, V., Borse, P.H.: Insights into renewable hydrogen energy: recent advances and prospects. Mater. Sci. Energy Technol. (2020).https://www.sciencedirect.com/science/article/pii/S258929912030001X. ISSN 2589-2991

13. Marimuthu, S., Chinnathambi, D.: Computational analysis to enhance the compressible flow over an aerofoil surface. Aircr. Eng. Aerosp. Technol. **93**(5), 925–934 (2021)

14. Song, C., Liu, Q., Ji, N., Kansha, Y., Tsutsumi, A.: Optimization of steam methane reforming coupled with pressure swing adsorption hydrogen production process by heat integration. Appl. Energy (2015).https://www.sciencedirect.com/science/article/pii/S03062619150 06480. ISSN 0306-2619

15. Soltani, S.M., Lahiri, A., Bahzad, H., Clough, P., Gorbounov, M., Yan, Y.: Sorption-enhanced Steam Methane Reforming for Combined CO2 capture and hydrogen production: a state-of-the-art review. Carbon Capture Sci. Technol. (2021).https://www.sciencedirect.com/science/article/pii/S2772656821000038. ISSN 2772-6568

16. Schneider, S., Bajohr, S., Graf, F., Kolb, T.: State of the art of hydrogen production via pyrolysis of natural gas (2020)

17. Yuvaraj, A.L., Daniel, S.: A systematic study on electrolytic production of hydrogen gas by using graphite as electrode. Mater. Res. **17**, 83–87 (2014)

18. Bermudez, J.M., Hannula, I.: Hydrogen. Tracking report (2021). https://www.iea.org/reports/hydrogen

19. IEA Publications, The Future of Hydrogen, Japan (2019). https://www.capenergies.fr/wp-content/uploads/2019/07/the_future_of_hydrogen.pdf

20. Šváb, P., Korba, P., Hovanec, M., Ukáč, J., Hura, J., Al-Rabeei, S.: The Utilization of renewable energy sources in the construction and maintenance of transport infrastructure. In: Future Access Enablers for Ubiquitous and Intelligent Infrastructures: 5th EAI International Conference. Springer, Cham, pp. 362–373 (2021). https://link.springer.com/content/pdf/10.1007%2F978-3-030-78459-1.pdf. ISBN 978-3-030-78458-4

21. Acar, C., Dincer, I.: Comparative assessment of hydrogen production methods from renewable and non-renewable sources. Int. J. Hydrogen Energy **39** (2014). https://www.sciencedirect.com/science/article/pii/S0360319913025330. ISSN 0360-3199

22. Kumar, R., Joshi, S., Awasthi, S.: An intelligent system for audio emotion recognition. Int. J. Adv. Sci. Technol. (2019)

23. Bičáková, O., Straka, P.: Production of hydrogen from renewable resources and its effectiveness. Int. J. Hydrogen Energy **37**(16), 11563–11578 (2012)

24. Reigstad, G.A., Coussy, P., Straus, J., Bordin, C.: Hydrogen for Europe Final report of the pre-study. SINTEF Energy Research 22 08 2019 (2019).https://www.sintef.no/globalassets/sintef-energi/hydrogen-for-europe/hydrogen-for-europe-pre-study-report-version-4_medomslag-2019-08-23.pdf

25. Shibata, Y., Matsumoto, T., Kan, S.: Institute of energy economics, Japan, clean hydrogen: important aspects of production. International Cooperation, and Certification. Part 2, Tokyo/Wuppertal (2020). http://www.gjetc.org/wp-content/uploads/2020/07/GJETC_Hydrogen-Society-Study-II.pdf

26. Al-Rabeei, S.A.S., Korba, P., Hovanec, M., Šváb, P., Rácek, B., Spodniak, M.: Analysis of aviation pollution in the selected regions of the world. In: Perakovic, D., Knapcikova, L. (eds.) Future Access Enablers for Ubiquitous and Intelligent Infrastructures. Lecture Notes of the Institute for Computer Sciences, Social Informatics and Telecommunications Engineering, vol. 382, pp. 229–239. Springer, Cham (2021). https://doi.org/10.1007/978-3-030-78459-1_17

27. Hydrogen Council, McKinsey & Company, Hydrogen Insights Report (2021). https://hydrogencouncil.com/wp-content/uploads/2021/02/Hydrogen-Insights-2021-Report.pdf

28. Han, W., et al.: Simultaneous dark fermentative hydrogen and ethanol production from waste bread in a mixed packed tank reactor. J. Clean. Prod. **141**, 608–611 (2017)

29. Burhan, M., Shahzad, M.W., Choon, N.K.: Hydrogen at the Rooftop: compact CPV-hydrogen system to convert sunlight to hydrogen. Appl. Therm. Eng. (2017)

30. Balat, M.: Potential importance of hydrogen as a future solution to environmental and transportation problems. Sila Science & Energy Unlimited Company (2008)

31. Dincer, I., Rosen, M.A.: Sustainability aspects of hydrogen and fuel cell systems. Faculty of Engineering and Applied Science, University of Ontario Institute of Technology (2000)

32. Rohacs, J., Kale, U., Rohacs, D.: Radically new solutions for reducing the energy use by future aircraft and their operations. Energy **239**, 122420 (2022). https://doi.org/10.1016/j.energy.2021.122420. ISSN 0360–5442

33. Bossel, U., Eliasson, B.: Energy and the Hydrogen Economy, Oberrohrdorf, Switzerland (2003)

Improving the Quality of Services Provided by Air Transport Companies

Simona Pjurová$^{(\boxtimes)}$ (ID), Ingrid Sekelová (ID), Samer Al-Rabeei (ID), and Peter Korba (ID)

Technical University of Košice, Rampová 7, 041 21 Košice, Slovakia
{simona.pjurova,ingrid.sekelova,samer.al-rabeei,
peter.korba}@tuke.sk

Abstract. Increasing quality of service and experience of air transport by setting up a catering company that focuses on the food provided on business jets flights. The sector of business jet flights has a favourable perspective in the future as it is estimated to have the value of $ 21.76 billion by 2027. Every year, the quality of catering services in aviation is growing. The difference between the expectations of the passenger, i.e., the consumer, and what he receives as a result may be due to a lack of understanding of what the customer expects from the service. The purpose of the study was to analyse the current market status of private air carriers performing business flights and to assess their needs and their satisfaction with the existing air catering services. By means of a questionnaire, the business jet companies responded to a series of questions that were aimed at determining whether there is a need for a new-founded company concentrated on air catering. It was found out that the demand is higher than the offer, therefore a new-founded company could be successful at the market of business jet flight provided they comply with the needs of business jet companies that are now unfulfilled. This article proposes what a new-founded company should include in their business plan, and it establishes three possible scenarios for the company's future (pessimistic, realistic, optimistic).

Keywords: Quality of experience · Customer expectations · Onboard services · Flight catering

1 Introduction

Air transport is one of the most important ways of achieving economic growth and development. Among other, air transport integrates domestic markets with the global market, in other words, it interconnects the national, regional, and international levels. The aviation industry creates trade, promotes employment and tourism [1].

The International Civil Aviation Organization (ICAO) states on its website that commercial aircrafts make approximately 400 scheduled departures per hour. Passengers and cargo are transported by air carriers, which have a major impact on the social and economic development and sustainability of individual destinations [2].

© ICST Institute for Computer Sciences, Social Informatics and Telecommunications Engineering 2022
Published by Springer Nature Switzerland AG 2022. All Rights Reserved
D. Perakovic and L. Knapcikova (Eds.): FABULOUS 2022, LNICST 445, pp. 234–243, 2022.
https://doi.org/10.1007/978-3-031-15101-9_17

Airlines are constantly in competition, fighting for customers. Air catering and on-board services in most cases serve to distinguish one airline from another. We can include catering in the parts of the marketing strategy, which aim to attract new and keep old clients [3].

The difference between a business jet and other airlines is that on board of private flights, catering occurs almost on every flight and more solvent passengers are fond of the superior taste and quality of food or drink.

The aim of this article is to find out, through market analysis, whether private air carriers that provide business jet flights would welcome a new airline catering company and whether this new-founded company would be able to successfully enter the airline catering market.

2 Theoretical Part

Services provided on board aircraft, in particular air catering, play a key role in the perception of the travel experience from the passenger's point of view [4]. Nowadays, airline catering is certainly widely used as airline catering companies produce more than a billion meals per year [5]. There are several factors that can influence airline catering and one of those was also the penetration of low-cost airlines into the air transport market. They had a significant impact on traditional airlines [6] and consequently on airline catering.

2.1 Catering and Business Jet

Business travel can be defined as a trip made for the employee's work purpose, which is paid for by the employer, not by the employee. Business trips are related to business activities and the buyer is natural or legal person. In this flight category the main demands of the passengers are made upon fast and comfortable flight. Another demand is a high frequency of flights and the ability to change the flight plan in a short time. Business passengers represent a significantly higher profit for the airline than "leisure" passengers. The business passenger deals with the overall quality, experience in the process of checking in his flight, the services provided on board the aircraft, food and drinks, the comfort of the seats, entertainment, and adherence to the time schedule. Passengers in this class fly regularly and can therefore objectively evaluate and compare the services of different airlines [7].

Private jets are mostly privately owned by large corporations or high-net-worth individual. There is also the possibility on the market to order a one-off aircraft transport from companies that focus on such transport. This type of service is called "Air Taxi". Only a small number of people are transported in this type of transport. Arrival and departure are not scheduled and often the request to make such a flight comes in a short time. Passenger requirements are unique, and always met exactly according to the client's expectations, meaning what the client orders, he will receive. When eating, it is usually the case that the client requests a specific meal (for example from his favourite restaurant), which is then served on board the plane [8].

2.2 COVID-19 Pandemic and its Impact on Inflight Catering Market

Nowadays, the current topic is the infectious disease caused by the coronavirus SARS-CoV-2. The disease first appeared in December 2019. No one expected the world to slow down and have a monumental impact on both the people and the economy. The gastronomy industry and tourism suffered the biggest losses. With the measures against Covid-19 also came the closures of individual countries borders, so-called lockdown. Air traffic in Europe has fallen rapidly. According to the European Commission, only 40% of flights took place compared to the years before Covid-19 [9, 15].

However, a look at the past confirms that the aviation industry is a very unstable industry. It is not only airlines which are under constant pressure due to intense competition, increasing passenger numbers, and a constant need to monitor their costs, but they are also going through turbulences caused by government regulations and the health of individual countries' economies.

Air catering is always affected by current events in the world. For example, in 2002, the SARS-CoV epidemic broke out, affecting the serving of food on board. Airlines like Qatar Airways, Emirates, Singapore Airlines switched from metal cutlery to plastic, and staff who encountered food (even flight attendants who only heated and served food) had to use latex gloves [10].

SARS virus, like other viruses, is easily transmitted from person to person and the advantage of plastic cutlery is that it can be disposed after use. After the epidemic, several airlines returned to metal cutlery. In 2010, concerns were expressed about air carriers from Australia and New Zealand since plastic cutlery was used repeatedly on international flights, ten to thirty times. The companies objected that the cutlery is being sterilized and washed and justified that it permits them to save costs, protect the environment [11].

Unlike the SARS epidemic, the Covid-19 pandemic has hit the world and dealt a heavy blow to air traffic. The pandemic has prevented airlines from operating flights, many employees have lost their jobs and most airlines are now facing bankruptcy or seeking state aid.

Although these events may seem to slow progress in the aviation industry, the opposite is true. Quite several airlines continue to invest in new technologies and innovations and to implement quality management in their companies. Product quality is key for most airlines. Based on this information, it is possible that the aviation industry has shown much more effort, initiative, and enthusiasm for innovation than any other transport sector. As air transport is the primary mode of transport on long and cross-continental routes, it also has a direct impact on international tourism. Airlines are constantly striving to reduce ticket prices by reducing costs. In other words, airlines get rid of additional services such as meals and focus only on the main service, namely, to transfer a passenger from point A to point B for the lowest possible ticket price. The basis for gaining a competitive advantage is to control the prices and determine the lowest at the most optimal costs. Other incentives for customers are also used in a competitive environment. Many companies consider their customer satisfaction very important [12].

Despite the situation associated with the Covid-19 pandemic, the airline catering market has grown (see Fig. 1). The forecast estimates that the global aviation catering market will be $ 21.76 billion by 2027 [13].

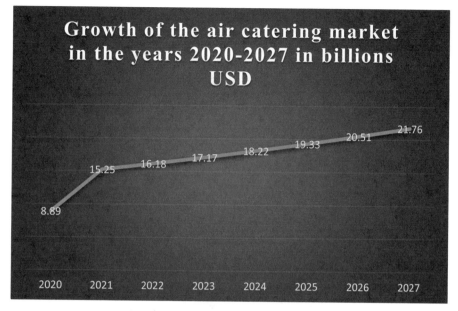

Fig. 1. Growth of the air catering market [13]

The restrictions of various countries that were imposed in order to prevent the spread of SARS-CoV-2 have caused a crisis not only in the aviation sector. Air transport must face significant constraints, which also affects the economic situation of airlines. Catering, which were provided on board of the aircraft, needed more changes. Prior to the pandemic, air food suppliers focused only on diseases that could be caused by food. Currently, however, the pandemic is responsible for increasing food safety control and increasing disinfection. These measures also lead to increased costs for airlines in boarding. The trend is an ordering system, where passenger orders food in advance, which he later consumes on board. The forecast predicts a large increase in catering services on board of the aircraft, mainly due to increased quality and focus on individual catering cultures. Diversification of different world tastes and meals (vegetarian, vegan) is considered to be very attractive for the passenger.

Figure 2 demonstrates the increase or decrease in the number of flights in 2020 compared to 2019 on the basis of different market segments. According to Fig. 2, we can see that COVID-19 had impact on all means of aviation transport, especially on low-cost and other scheduled flights. What we may find interesting is that the impact was not so significant in regard to Business Aviation flights. Flights in Business Aviation have a growing tendency as well as the other two types of flights which are represented in the figure, Business Aviation flight have a significant growth as they have a 40% increase in flights compared to 2019. This may be the result of the various restrictions which are posed by many countries. The common passengers of low-cost and commercial air carriers could have also suffered from the restrictions of COVID-19, and they may not have enough financial resources for traveling. This presupposition together with the number of restrictions and measures represent additional obstacles in travelling. On the other hand, a common passenger of business jet flights are typically more solvent people, who may not have suffered in terms of finances as greatly as the passengers of economy class.

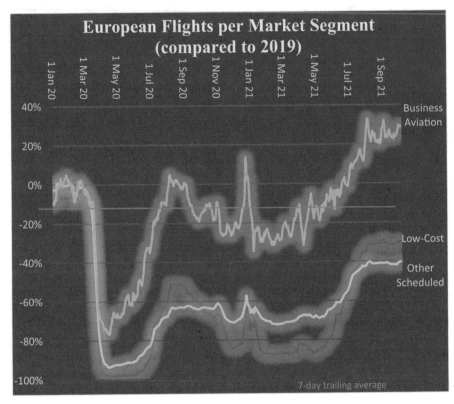

Fig. 2. European flights per market segment [14]

3 Methodology

The aim of this article is to show the current situation in the field of business jet transport, to find out the needs in catering of business jet companies and to propose a business plan of a company that would satisfy these needs.

Our focus was not limited only to Slovak Republic, in our research we also included Czech Republic, since the transport market of these two countries is to a certain extent interconnected. It also gives us the opportunity to approach more companies and to observe the results on a larger scale. A catering company that would be founded in Slovak Republic, would also very likely cooperate with business jet companies from Czech Republic and many other countries, since aviation transport is an international field.

In order to determine the needs in catering of business jet companies we performed qualitative research, which was in the form of a questionnaire that was made via Google Forms. The respondents received our questionnaire by an email. So as to maintain the objectivity of the research the responses were anonymous.

In our research we approached 10 business jet companies, namely ELITE JET s.r.o., Aeropartner a.s., Alpha Aviation, s.r.o., ABS Jets a.s., Time Air s.r.o., AIR PRESTIGE s.r.o., Silesia Air s.r.o., CTR Atmospherica Aviation a.s., Tatra JET s.r.o., Smartwings a.s. We received the responses of 8 companies, due to the anonymous nature of the questionnaire we cannot determine which 8 companies out of the 10 approached were the ones that responded to our questions. Among these companies we can find companies which have decades of experience, but also new companies that are were founded in the recent years.

These hypotheses whether they will be proved or disproved will reflect the current situation on the market of business jet catering and it will provide us with essential information of which aspects should the new catering company fulfil in order to be successful on the market of aviation transport. The hypotheses of our research were formulated as:

Hypothesis No. 1: Majority of the companies use catering services regularly on their flights.
Hypothesis No. 2: Majority of the companies use catering services provided by external supplier.
Hypothesis No. 3: Majority of the companies think that the catering market environment is not diverse enough.
Hypothesis No. 4: Majority of the companies are not completely satisfied with the level of catering services that are currently provided.
Hypothesis No. 5: Majority of the food provided on board is cold.

4 Results and Discussion

4.1 Results

The research questions are to prove or disprove the previously stated hypotheses about the current situation and the needs on the market of business jet catering in Slovak and Czech Republic. The analysis was done by descriptive statics. The questionnaire that was sent to the participants of the research contained the following research questions:

In Fig. 3 we can see results of the research. Concerning question 1 the results show that majority 88% of the companies use catering services regularly. This result proves our first hypothesis and demonstrates the quite high frequency of protentional future catering orders for the new company.

The second question proves the second hypothesis and results in an interesting finding that no company uses their own catering services, but all the approached companies use an external catering provider. This means that the market is full of possibilities, since the new company would function as an external provider, they could be successful because of the wide range of possible partner business jet companies.

Fig. 3. Results of the research

Most of the companies think that the market environment of business jet catering is diverse, but 25% say that they feel that there could be more catering companies, other 25% did not give their opinion about this issue. This disproves the third hypothesis. However, half of the respondents could possibly welcome a new catering provider this also manifest the number of opportunities for a new-founded company. The company could bring more diversity onto the market providing they would bring something new, e.g., local products, luxurious presentation, sophisticated menu, etc.

The captivating result in the question 4 is that 50% of the respondents said that they do not know whether they are satisfied or not with their catering services. The fourth proved hypothesis suggests that even though not all companies are dissatisfied, there is a place for improvement. Their current needs may be satisfied in a way, they are not especially content with it. This proves that the new-founded company could be successful provided it would comply with the needs and could truly satisfy them.

Last hypothesis is proved since most companies provide only cold food on board of their aircraft instead of previously cooked meals. The last answer shows which type of cuisine should the new-founded company focus on. The most probable reason for the preference of cold food, could be the limited space on the aircraft.

4.2 Discussion

Based on the obtained results we found out that there is higher demand than the offer on the market of catering for business jet companies. Even if companies performing such activities exist, their services are not of such quality that would completely satisfy all business jet carriers. We propose to establish a company that would provide food of superior quality. The company's effort should result in mutual trust or in other words above-standard relations with clients, suppliers.

After detailed analysis we came to the conclusion that a company that aims at finding success in Slovak and Czech Republic should work from Bratislava airport. It is a transport node which has a good connection with surrounding airports (Brno, Vienna). The new-founded company should also include in their portfolio restauration services, which could compensate possible loss caused by irregular orders of catering. The company should be able to react swiftly to the specific requirements of clients resulting from their eating habits, health issues, etc. In order to set apart from the competition, the company could focus their cuisine on simple fresh unrefined ingredients, which would come from local suppliers, for example with the Fair-trade trademark. For the company to become known to its potential clients, they should also invest to a large extent in the marketing and promotion of the company.

Three possible scenarios of the company's development were verified by calculations: pessimistic, realistic, and optimistic scenario. The pessimistic scenario of the company's development envisages a 10% occupancy of the restaurant. For example, the restaurant's total capacity would be 80 seats, here 10% represents eight people per hour. Let us say that the provision of catering services for air carriers would be once a week. The average expenditure per customer in the restaurant is set at € 20 and at air catering at € 300 / year. Revenues from the sale of own goods represent 15%. The determination of occupancy and sales of goods is based on data from a similar company in the same area of business. Due to the inaccuracy of the restaurant's occupancy estimates, an average of two unoccupied hours is expected during which the restaurant will be completely empty. The average opening hours of the restaurant is approximately 180 h per month (30 days) and the average occupancy in the 2021 marketing year is 11 520 people (8 months × 30 days). The volume of required raw materials makes up 30% of the expected revenues from own products. Legal person's income tax is calculated at a standard rate of 21%. After the first financial year in a pessimistic scenario, the company would have lost more than 117 731 €.

In the realistic scenario, 18% of the restaurant is occupied, which represents an average of 86.4 people per day, so the total annual attendance is 21 216 visitors. In this scenario, air catering would be provided twice a week. In the realistic scenario, the company would have a profit of approximately 185€ after their first year.

When calculating the optimistic scenario, we took into account 20% occupancy, the provision of air catering 4 times a week and the production of 33 packaged meals a day in the amount of 10 € / package. According to the optimistic scenario, the company would report a profit of approximately € 122 197 in the financial year 2021.

It would be advantageous for the company to set short-term and long-term goals. Short-term goals that should be completed within 5 years include, for example, the acquisition of a stable contract, at least 3% market share and the have contracts with at least 35% of private carriers within the Slovak Republic. The most important long-term goals over a 10-year period should be return on investment, optimization and cost reduction, and revenue maximization.

The founders of the company should not forget that there are risks with business. Adequate measures should be proposed for each potential risk, for example when input prices increase, the price of outputs should also change, if there is a lack of interest on the part of customers, it is necessary to use so-called aggressive marketing [16–19].

5 Conclusion

In conclusion, it can be stated that the area of providing catering in air transport is an extremely current issue. Based on the research we can see that there is a forecast that the market of business jet flight will continue to grow, therefore there will be also growth in the demand for air catering. The market environment was analysed based on a questionnaire, in which the degree of satisfaction with catering services in private airlines was determined. The questionnaire confirmed that there is an opportunity in the market in the field of aviation catering business. The proposal part demonstrates that the new-founded company could be successful, if the business plan is implemented well the probability of success of the company will be about 50%. The disadvantage is that the project cannot be tested on a smaller sample of customers which is the case with most business plans. Another disadvantage was represented by low wages of employees. The set wage level must increase by at least 20% per year to enable the employment of quality staff with adequate knowledge and a positive attitude towards customers. It is important to note that the company will start to return the invested capital several years after its opening. The company's turnover is not equal to the profit and a large share of funds is returned to business - to the reconstruction of premises, advertising and marketing costs, activities related to maintaining and developing the company in the market and developing a good reputation. In our future research we would like to focus on the customer's point of view, to establish their needs and their perspective on the catering provided in business jets. In addition to catering and other on-board services, we would like to continue to focus on intermodal cooperation, namely the integrated transport system. An integrated approach will allow to enjoy a "seamless" travel experience and replace different types of competition in their collaboration. In order to maintain a constant demand for air transport, it is necessary to constantly re-evaluate the efficiency of transport networks, i.e., their maximization.

References s

1. The World Bank. https://www.worldbank.org/en/topic/transport/brief/airtransport. Accessed 20 Nov 2021
2. International Civil Aviation Organisation: Future of Aviation. https://www.icao.int/Meetings/FutureOfAviation/Pages/default.aspx. Accessed 25 Nov 2021
3. Zahari, M.: In-flight meals, passengers' level of satisfaction and re-flying intention (2011). https://www.researchgate.net/publication/282636278_In-flight_Meals_Passengers'_Level_of_Satisfaction_and_Re-flying_Intention. Accessed 21 Nov 2021

4. King, T.: Inflight catering (2001). https://journals.sagepub.com/doi/10.1177/146735840100 300211. Accessed 26 Nov 2021
5. Pande, P.: Inside airline catering: from farm to plane (2020). https://simpleflying.com/airline-catering/. Accessed 23 Nov 2021
6. Statista. https://www.statista.com/statistics/934663/global-airline-catering-services-market-size/. Accessed 23 Nov 2021
7. Gilbert, D.: Retail marketing management. Harlow: Financ. Times Manag. 356 (1999). ISBN 978-0273-630-197
8. National Business Aviation Association. What is Business Aviation?. https://nbaa.org/bus iness-aviation/. Accessed 25 Nov 2021
9. Nariadenie Európskeho Parlamentu A Rady, ktorým sa mení nariadenie (EHS) č. 95/93 (2020)
10. Momberger K., Momberger, M.: Handling SARS (2021). http://www.mombergerairport.info/ the-newsletter/. Accessed 01 May 2021
11. Marcus, C.: Airline reuses plastic cutlery 30 times (2021). https://www.perthnow.com.au/ news/nsw/airline-reuses-plastic-cutlery-30-times-ng-6f2b5ccf6cc4b3fa87fb25dfabef5b99. Accessed 07 May 2021
12. Jones, P.: Flight Catering. Oxford: Elsevier, p. 319 (2004). ISBN 0-7506-6216-6
13. Mazareanu, E.: Global airline catering services market size 2020–2027 (2021). https:// www.statista.com/statistics/934663/global-airline-catering-services-market-size/#statistic Container. Accessed 25 Nov 2021
14. Eurocontrol.   https://www.eurocontrol.int/publication/eurocontrol-data-snapshot-19-eur opes-business-aviation-recovery-covid-19. Accessed 25 Nov 2021
15. Al-Rabeei, S.A.S., Korba, P., Hovanec, M., Šváb, P., Rácek, B., Spodniak, M.: Analysis of aviation pollution in the selected regions of the world. In: Perakovic, D., Knapcikova, L. (eds.) Future Access Enablers for Ubiquitous and Intelligent Infrastructures. Lecture Notes of the Institute for Computer Sciences, Social Informatics and Telecommunications Engineering, vol. 382, pp. 229–239. Springer, Cham (2021). https://doi.org/10.1007/978-3-030-78459-1_17
16. Cehlár, M., Lesniaková, A.: Podnikateľský plán a inovácie. Košice: Edičné stredisko/AMS, Fakulta BERG Technickej univerzity v Košiciach, p. 80 (2004). ISBN 80-8073-083-0
17. Seňová, A., Pavolová, H.: Podnikateľský plán a manažment inovácií v podnikaní. Košice: Edičné stredisko a redakcia AMS, Fakulta BERG Technickej univerzity v Košiciach, p. 99 (2007). ISBN 978-80-8073-888-4
18. Sundarakani, B., Razzak, H.A., Manikandan, S.: Creating a competitive advantage in the global flight catering supply chain: a case study using SCOR model (2018). https://www.res earchgate.net/publication/323668874_Creating_a_competitive_advantage_in_the_global_ flight_catering_supply_chain_a_case_study_using_SCOR_model. Accessed 02 Nov 2021
19. Grönroos, C.H.: Strategic Management and Marketing in the Service Sector. Krieger Publishing Company, Florida, p. 136 (1982). ISBN 978-9144-439-112

Development of Startups During the Covid-19 Pandemic

Jaroslav Hura, Samer Al-Rabeei$^{(\boxtimes)}$, Peter Korba , Michal Hovanec ,
Simona Pjurová , and Ingrid Sekelová

Faculty of Aeronautics, Department of Aviation Engineering, Technical University of Košice,
Rampová 7, 041 21 Košice, Slovakia

`Jaroslav.hura@student.tuke.sk`, {`Samer.al-rabeei`,`Peter.korba`,
`Michal.hovanec`,`Simona.pjurova`,`ingrid.sekelova`}`@tuke.sk`

Abstract. Currently, both domestic and global economies are facing a crisis associated with a new pandemic such as the coronavirus SARS CoV-2 (COVID-19). Economic leaders are addressing and looking for effective tools to deal with this crisis and start the economy as soon as possible, while mitigating the effects of the crisis as much as possible. In view of these facts, new startups in various sectors of the economy will play an important role in economic growth. At the same time, the world is facing another crisis - the oil crisis, which began with a price war between Russia and other oil-producing countries, followed by a decline in fuel demand due to reduced traffic. In this situation, in which the world economy finds itself, it is possible to assume that new technologies in the form of startups will be among the key ones in starting the economy. This article should highlight how startups can currently help the economy recover and what new risks the current crisis has brought to them. The start-up scene has long been characterized by a high degree of flexibility and the ability to adapt quickly to a new situation. The last year has been very challenging for many industries from a business perspective, e-commerce and the digital environment in general have often seen tens of percent growth. According to experts, startups, which operate in the mentioned segments, have also successfully dealt with the crisis.

Keywords: Startup · Startup subsectors · Global startup economy

1 Introduction

It is possible to meet the term Startup very often with the present, while there are several definitions and views of a startup. The European Private Equity and Venture Capital Association (EVCA) defines a startup as a company that is in the process of starting a business shortly after starting a business, but is not yet achieving it [1, 2].

P. Wells and L. Jeng, who work at Harvard Business School, consider a startup company that is moving from the stage of a business idea and preparing for the production, marketing and sale of the product itself. A business idea can be considered the very first stage of a company's life cycle. At this stage, the founders have not yet taken any steps

D. Perakovic and L. Knapcikova (Eds.): FABULOUS 2022, LNICST 445, pp. 244–254, 2022.
https://doi.org/10.1007/978-3-031-15101-9_18

to implement it. Later, when they start developing a product or analyzing the market, they move on to the so-called seed phase. Only then, at a time when they are starting a company, preparing production, marketing and simply preparing the entire business model, do they move to a stage where they can be described as start-ups. In Slovakia, often (especially in the media) the term startup still refers to a business idea or a company in the seed phase [1–3].

And Steve Blank states that the startup is looking for a repeatable and so-called scalable business model. This model is based on the potential to achieve significant revenue growth without significantly increasing costs. A simple example is a mobile application - whether you sell 100 applications or a million, your costs are practically the same, but sales (and profits) are significantly higher. The scalable business model is therefore a key prerequisite for achieving rapid growth [1, 4].

Startup in our conditions is practically not without international (or global) ambition - t. j. its goal should not only be Slovak, but e.g. also a Pan-European or global market [4, 5].

2   Theoretical Analysis

In the current situation associated with the pandemic of a new type of coronavirus SARS CoV-2, Startups are all the more important for economic growth because they create new jobs and introduce the latest technologies. Startups are also used by large technology companies, which they use to solve various tasks, and at the same time these companies represent the necessary investments for startups [6–8].

But every viable startup must provide such goods and services to its customers in order to stay in the market and continue to grow. Such a successful startup will start to create jobs, thus reducing the unemployment rate in the economy. The result of the pandemic of the new type of coronavirus SARS CoV-2 is the beginning of an economic crisis that has affected individual economies. The rapid rise in unemployment in major consumer markets will lead to an almost immediate reduction in consumer spending.

At present, a decrease of up to 50% is expected in some consumer categories. Ultimately, business expenses will be reduced in all categories at the discretion of each company. As a result, companies with high growth potential, start-ups and small and medium-sized enterprises, and thus the entire national economies of the world, will be quite affected [6, 9].

The global startup economy has produced 2.8 trillion dollars in economic value over the past two years, a 20% increase over the previous two-year period. This estimate comes from the 2019 Global Ecosystem Launch Report [6, 10].

According to an analysis carried out by startup genome (2020) (Table 1), it follows that:

In the field of "capital":

– 41% of startups worldwide are at risk of having cash to operate for only three months or less.
– Young start-ups only have cash for a few months, 29% were in this situation before the crisis, but the crisis put another 40% in this precarious situation.

- In the field of "jobs":
- Since the beginning of the crisis, 74% of start-ups have had to end their full-time employment.
- 39% of all startups had to lay off 20% or more of their employees and 26% had to lay off 60% or more of their employees.
- The largest share of companies in the reduction of the number of employees is North America (84%), followed by Europe (67%) and Asia (59%).

In the "market" area:

- Since the beginning of the crisis, 74% of startups have seen a drop in revenue. The main reason for the decline in revenues is the impact of the crisis on the industries that startups serve. Three of the four startups operate in sectors that have been severely affected by the COVID-19 crisis.
- It should be noted that every crisis creates opportunities. A small minority of companies are experiencing growth during this crisis. One in every 10 start-ups in the industry is experiencing growth.

In the field of "Operation and Management":

- Since December 2019, more than two-thirds of start-ups have reduced costs. However, some companies reduce costs very aggressively, with more than one in every 10 companies reducing costs by more than 60%.
- Nevertheless, technology startups are unique in that they can continue to operate with restrictive measures by national governments. Unlike technology startups, many traditional businesses, up to 96% of start-ups, said they continued to work during the crisis, even though they were severely constrained by restrictive measures.

Table 1. Reducing the cost of startups that they did in a given period of time.

	January 2020		February 2020		March 2020	
	The first half	The other half	The first half	The other half	The first half	The other half
Asia	4%	5%	6%	8%	18%	35%
Europe	5%	1%	5%	6%	19%	52%
North America	3%	1%	3%	8%	22%	44%

Source: Startup Genome 2020

In the field of "Policy":

- Approximately 60% of startups have already received or are expecting assistance from business support through national government policies.

– According to the founders and managers of start-ups, state aid would be most useful in the following order: 1. Subsidies to maintain the company's liquidity, 2. Investment support instruments, 3. Aid to protect employees and loans to maintain the company's liquidity [6, 11, 12].

Startups can start their journey from anywhere. This means that a startup can be based not only in a developed country. The higher the needs, the greater the opportunities for start-ups. Therefore, it is important to set up startups in underdeveloped countries, in conflict countries, or in countries that are new to business. The result will be not only the profits that startups will bring, but also the overall contribution of startups to the entire economy of the country.

Startups can be divided into two categories:

1. "Subsistence": Companies belonging to categories that will never become large companies. Entrepreneurs of these startups only do their job and at the same time ensure financial independence.
2. "Transformational": We expect these startups to have a significant impact on the economic growth of the economy. They plan to expand their business to other countries and so they plan to open branches in other countries around the world [12–14].

3   Methodology

Not only in a market economy, but the goal of every individual or business entity is to satisfy their needs and maximize the benefits of each of their input. The company's performance is a criterion of financial decision-making and ensures the survival and competitiveness of the company in the market. One way to define a company's performance is the company's ability to achieve the desired business results in the form of outputs that are consistent with the company's goals, expressed in measurable units. [9, 12].

According to the Startup Genome report for 2019, the global startup economy is growing steadily, generating $ 2.8 trillion between 2016 and 2018. This is an increase of 20.6% over the previous period. This value is at the level of the G7 economy.

Ten years ago, when oil sold for more than $ 100 a barrel, oil companies dominated the top ten, as can be seen in the table. Chinese oil giant PetroChine was the largest company in the world in 2008 with a market value of $ 728 billion. Five of the ten largest companies in the world were oil companies. Due to the revolution in electric vehicles, oil companies are unlikely to dominate the top 10 companies in the world.

Seven of the 10 largest companies in the world today are technology companies. Another interesting development is the growth of Chinese technology companies. Tencent (the equivalent of Chinese Facebook) and Alibaba (the equivalent of Chinese Amazon) are now the sixth and eighth largest companies in the world (Table 2). [6, 14, 15].

Table 2. Comparison of global companies in 2018 and 2008.

2018				2008			
No.	Company	Estalished	Market value (billions of USD)	No.	Company	Established	Marke value (billions of USD)
1	Apple	1976	890	1	PetroChina	1999	728
2	Google	1998	768	2	Exxon	1870	492
3	Microsoft	1975	680	3	General Electric	1892	358
4	Amazon	1994	592	4	China Mobile	1997	344
5	Facebook	2004	545	5	ICBC (China)	1984	336
6	Tencent (China)	1998	526	6	Gazprom (Russia)	1989	332
7	Berkshire	1955	496	7	Microsoft	1975	313
8	Alibaba (China)	1999	488	8	Royal Dutch Shell	1907	266
9	J&J	1886	380	9	Sinopec (China)	2000	257
10	JP Morgan	1871	375	10	AT&T	1885	238

Source: Startup Genome 2019

However, striving for the highest possible profit is associated with higher risk and financial instability. Such a traditional approach to measuring performance and its use in financial decision-making in the company has been replaced in recent years by additional so-called modern approaches to performance measurement that take into account several factors.

The definition of startup subsectors may be different, and these subsectors are not mutually exclusive, but on the contrary, some subsectors are interconnected as soon as possible, such as technologies such as software and artificial intelligence.

Division of startup subsectors [16, 17]:

Advertising Tech (Adtech) - includes various types of analysis and digital tools used in advertising and marketing. Extensive and complex systems are used to target, mediate or monitor advertising to target groups of any size and scope.

Advanced Manufacturing & Robotics - advanced manufacturing involves intelligent technology to improve traditional manufacturing products and/or processes. Robotics is the science and technology of robots, their design, manufacture and application.

Agriculture Tech (Agtech) & New Food - is the use of technology in agriculture, horticulture and water management to improve yield, efficiency and profitability through information monitoring and analysis of weather, pests, soil and air temperature.

Artificial Intelligence (AI), Big Data & Analytics - Artificial Intelligence, Data and Analytics refers to the field of technology dedicated to extracting meaning from large sets of raw data, often including simulations of intelligent behavior in computers.

Blockchain - is a decentralized method of data storage secured by cryptography. Cryptomens are one of many blockchain innovations. Companies that build their product/architecture on this decentralized and encrypted technology are defined as blockchain companies.

Cleantech - consists of sustainable solutions in the fields of energy, water, transport, agriculture and manufacturing, which include advanced materials, smart grids, water treatment, efficient energy storage and distributed energy systems.

Construction and Property Tech - They focus on improving the processes and methods of construction companies, offering increased productivity, cost savings, better safety, shorter delivery times and maximizing resources. Property tech helps organizations and individuals research, buy, sell, rent and manage real estate. Applications include property search, list of available properties, setting browsing dates, and finalizing leases and deals.

Consumer Electronics or Home Electronics (includes Wearables, Smart Devices) - consumer electronics or home electronics (including wearable devices, smart devices) includes electronic or digital devices designed for everyday use, including smart devices used for entertainment, communication and home office activities, such as and other wearable devices.

Cybersecurity - A set of technologies, processes, and practices designed to protect networks, computers, programs, and data from attack, damage, or unauthorized access.

Education Tech (Edtech) - deal with the development and application of tools (including software, hardware and processes) designed to redesign traditional products and services in education.

4   Research and Results

The current Covid-19 pandemic has caused major changes in the various sectors in which startups operate. The changes are mainly in the fact that in some sectors startups are in decline and, on the contrary, in some they show above-average growth. Figure 1 points to the development of startup sub-sectors according to the amount of investment and the impact of larger business transactions. The startup sub-sectors Advanced Manufacturing & Robotics, Blockchain, Agtech & New Food, AI & Big Data are the fastest growing in the world. And Fintech has also seen significant growth over the last 5 years. Similarly, Edtech and Gaming, which were in decline in 2019, have seen significant growth in recent years [16, 20, 21].

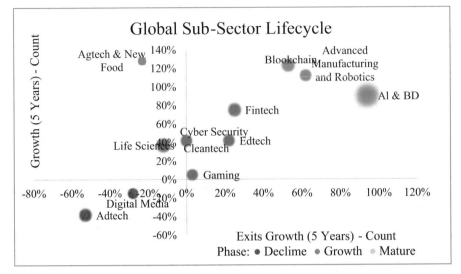

Fig. 1. Life cycle of selected startup subsectors according to the number of offers and deals. Source: https://startupgenome.com/ and authors.

On the other hand, Fig. 2 offers an alternative view of startup subsectors by measuring their growth based on the amount of investment and output value. This view largely reflects the growth of startup sub-sectors with higher investment values and their impact on output growth. It is interesting that the subsectors of startups AI & Big Data, or even Advanced Manufacturing & Robotics are experiencing a high level of growth, as shown by Fig. 1 but also Fig. 2 [16].

Based on the graphs, it can be seen that among the fastest growing subsectors of startups with financing agreements in the initial stage for more than five years are:

- Agtech & New Food (128%),
- Blockchain (121%),
- Advanced Manufacturing & Robotics (109%),
- AI & Big Data (98%).

And on the other hand, the declining subsectors include:

- Adtech (-35%),
- Digital Media (-21%)

Growth subsectors:

- Blockchain,
- Advanced Manufacturing & Robotics,
- AI & Big Data,
- Fintech.

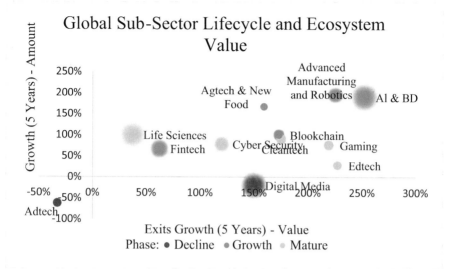

Fig. 2. Life cycle of selected startup subsectors and the value of the whole system according to the number of offers and deals. Source: https://startupgenome.com/ and authors.

The size of the five growing subsectors is growing at a significant pace, with an average growth of 107%. The Fintech sub-sector is a new participant in the group in this area due to higher investments than in other sub-sectors. AI & Big Data and Analytics are among the growth sub-sectors, accounting for up to 27% of all global startups. Agtech & New Food is the smallest subsector so far (Table 3) [16, 22, 23].

Table 3. Growth subsectors in the growth phase.

Subsector	Growth over a 5 - year period	Share in global startups
Agtech & New Food	− 14%	2%
Blookchain	52%	10%
Advanced Manufacturing and Robotics	61%	10%
AI & Big Data	93%	27%
Fintech	25%	10%

Source: https://startupgenome.com/ and authors

Start-up subsectors:

– Cybersecurity,
– Edtech,
– Cleantech,
– Life Sciences,

– Gaming.

Cybersecurity, Cleantech and Life Sciences are in the maturity phase. Edtech and Gaming are among the sub-sectors that have gone from declining to maturity. Taken together, these subsectors saw an increase of 33% and 3% in departures over the last five years (Table 4) [16, 24, 25].

Table 4. Startup subsectors in the maturity phase.

Subsector	Growth over a 5 - year period	Share in global startups
Cyber security	0%	8%
Edtech	22%	4%
Cleantech	0%	7%
Life sciences	– 11%	8%
Gaming	2%	5%

Source: https://startupgenome.com/ and authors

The subsectors in the downturn are:

– Adtech,
– Digital media.

Over the last five years, the Adtech and Digital Media subsectors have seen a decline compared to other startup subsectors. Gaming and Edtech are sub-sectors that have successfully re-entered the mature phase of the startup lifecycle in the treasure phase. This increase is probably caused by the COVID-19 pandemic period, which forced millions of people around the world to have fun at home and at the same time schools moved to the online space (Table 5).

Table 5. Startup subsectors in a phase of decline.

Podsektor	Rast za 5 - ročné obdobie	Podiel v globálnych startupov
Digital media	– 24%	4%
Adtech	– 51%	6%

Source: https://startupgenome.com/ and authors

5   Conclusion

The COVID-19 pandemic has shown that digitally oriented companies can do business from anywhere. At the same time, it can be said that startups - unicorns focused on IT technologies with a value in excess of billions of dollars, are not only in Silicon Valley as expected, but are worldwide. In 2021, two startups were born every day - unicorns. There are currently more than 2,000 companies in the world that can be considered startups - unicorns. As a 35 trillion dollar industries, technology currently has a major impact on cities and local communities, affecting all sectors. Startups are a fast and resilient engine of job growth, with the number of new jobs growing by an average of 10% year-on-year worldwide. And it is not only the established startups but also the younger generations of startups that create the same value as the older ones. More than a quarter of all companies worth $ 1 billion or more have achieved unicorn status this year. More and more international investment strategies are aimed at enabling startups to be set up, financed and expanded anywhere in the world, making local support even more important for supporting individual startup ecosystems. According to experts, the pandemic has helped many startups - especially those in the digital world - to accelerate their development, but also to identify other opportunities for business.

References

1. Šrenkel, Ľ.: What's the startup? (2015). https://www.podnikajte.sk/priprava-na-start/co-je-sta rtup
2. Al-Rabeei, S.A.S., Korba, P., Hovanec, M., Šváb, P., Rácek, B., Spodniak, M.: Analysis of aviation pollution in the selected regions of the world. In: Perakovic, D., Knapcikova, L. (eds.) Future Access Enablers for Ubiquitous and Intelligent Infrastructures. Lecture Notes of the Institute for Computer Sciences, Social Informatics and Telecommunications Engineering, vol. 382, pp. 229–239. Springer, Cham (2021). https://doi.org/10.1007/978-3-030-78459-1_17
3. BUSINESSMAP Ltd. Startup project management (2020). https://flow-e.com/startup-pro ject-management/
4. Corporate Finance Institute. What are Startup Valuation Methods? (2020) https://corporate financeinstitute.com/resources/knowledge/valuation/startup-valuation-methods/
5. Ondrišek, M.: Startups: what are they and how do they work? (2016). https://www.obcasn ecas.ukf.sk/2016/04/startupy-co-su-a-ako-funguju/
6. Startup genome. The Global Startup Ecosystem Report 2020 (GSER 2020) (2020). https:// startupgenome.com/
7. Digital Edenz. Why Startups are important for economic growth of a nation (2018). https:// digitaledenz.com/why-startups-are-important-for-economic-growth-of-a-nation/
8. Pinto, J.E.: Equity Asset Valuation, 2nd edn., p. 441. Wiley, Hoboken (2010). ISBN 9780470571439
9. Hoffeld, D.: 5 insights from behavioral economics that can help startups suc- ceed (2020). https://www.hoffeldgroup.com/5-insights-from-behavioral-economics-that- can-help-startups-succeed/
10. Herman, D.: Jumpstarting customer demand starts with government (2020). https://startupge nome.com/blog/jumpstarting-customer-demand-starts-with-government
11. Johnston, S.: Largest companies 2008 vs. 2018, a lot has changed (2018). https://milfordas set.com/insights/largest-companies-2008-vs-2018-lot-changed
12. KDB VERSATILE. Which Types of Economics Contribution Help New Start-ups? (2020). https://yourstory.com/mystory/economics-contribution-help-new-start-ups
13. Labun, J., Krchňák, M., Kurdel, P., Češkovič, M., Nekrasov, A., Gamcová, M.: Possibilities of increasing the low altitude measurement precision of airborne radio altimeters. Electronics 7(9), 191 (2018). ISSN 2079-9292

14. Little, W.: How to generate startup ideas (2020). https://www.startuprocket.com/articles/how-to-generate-startup-ideas
15. Moira, A.: How to manage a startup 6tips (2019). https://www.techrepublic.com/article/how-to-manage-a-startup-6-tips/
16. Startup genome. The Global Startup Ecosystem Report 2021 (2021) https://startupgenome.com/report/gser2021
17. Mggowan, E.: 10 real-world startup valuation methods (2018). https://www.startups.com/library/expert-advice/startup-valuation-methods
18. Nipapan Poonsatiansap CFP. How to Build a Successful Startup Business (2020). https://www.scb.co.th/en/personal-banking/stories/business-tips-for-successful-startup.html
19. Nasser Stéphane. 9 methods of startup valuation explained (2017). https://www.techinasia.com/talk/9-method-startup-valuation
20. Riani, A.: 5 decisions that will increase your chances of building a successful startup (2020). https://www.forbes.com/sites/abdoriani/2020/09/19/5-decisions-that-will-increase-your-chances-of-building-a-successful-startup/?sh=29d9e3af21a3
21. Richards, R.: How to value a startup company with no revenu (2019). https://masschallenge.org/article/how-to-value-a-startup-company-with-no-revenue
22. StartupDecisions.com.sg. Managing Startup Risks – An Entrepreneur's Guide (2019). https://www.startupdecisions.com.sg/startups/launch-and-growth/startup-risk-management/
23. Kale, U., Herrera, M., Nagy, A.: Examining pragmatic failure and other language-related risks in global aviation. Aircr. Eng. Aerosp. Technol. **93**(8), 1313–1322 (2021). https://doi.org/10.1108/AEAT-03-2021-0081
24. Schubarth, C.: Why do startups fail? Here are the top 20 reasons (2014). https://www.bizjournals.com/sanjose/news/2014/09/25/why-do-startups-fail-here-are-the-top-20-reasons.html?page=all. Accessed 15 Feb 2021
25. Vital, A.: Funders and founders. 24 startup ideas that investors are begging to fund (2015). https://www.businessinsider.com/24-startup-ideas-that-vcs-are-begging-to-fund-2015-4

Author Index

Printed in the United States
by Baker & Taylor Publisher Services